# No-Load Stocks

## Other McGraw-Hill Books by Charles B. Carlson

Buying Stocks Without a Broker

Free Lunch on Wall Street

# No-Load Stocks

How to Buy Your First Share and Every
Share Directly from the Company—
With No Broker's Fee

## Charles B. Carlson, CFA

Editor, *DRIP Investor*

**Revised and Expanded**

**McGraw-Hill**

New York   San Francisco   Washington, D.C.   Auckland   Bogotá
Caracas   Lisbon   London   Madrid   Mexico City   Milan
Montreal   New Delhi   San Juan   Singapore
Sydney   Tokyo   Toronto

**Library of Congress Cataloging-in-Publication Data**

Carlson, Charles B.
    No-load stocks : how to buy your first share and every share
directly from the company—with no broker's fee / Charles B.
Carlson.—Rev. and expanded.
        p.    cm.
    Includes bibliographical references and index.
    ISBN 0-07-011880-9
    1. Stocks.  2. Investments.  I. Title.
    HG4661.C328   1996
    332.63′22—dc21                                          96-36839
                                                                CIP

# McGraw-Hill

*A Division of The McGraw·Hill Companies*

    3 4 5 6 7 8 9 0   DOC/DOC   9 0 1 0 9 8 7

ISBN 0-07-011880-9 (PBK)

*The sponsoring editors for this book were David Conti and Allyson Arias, the
editing supervisor was Jane Palmieri, and the production supervisor was
Donald Schmidt. It was set in Palatino by Donald Feldman of McGraw-Hill's
Professional Book Group composition unit and Elberta Miklusak of Horizon
Management Services, Inc.*

*Printed and bound by R. R. Donnelley & Sons Company.*

McGraw-Hill books are available at special quantity discounts to use as
premiums and sales promotions, or for use in corporate training programs. For more information, please write to the Director of Special
Sales, McGraw-Hill, 11 West 19th Street, New York, NY 10011. Or contact your local bookstore.

This publication is designed to provide accurate and authoritative information in regard to the subject matter covered. It is sold with the under-
standing that the publisher is not engaged in rendering legal, accounting, or other professional service. If legal advice or other expert
assistance is required, the services of a competent professional person
should be sought.
            *—from a declaration of principles jointly adopted by a committee*
                *of the American Bar Association and a Committee of publishers*

   This book is printed on recycled, acid-free paper containing a
minimum of 50% recycled, de-inked fiber.

*To Amber, Anthony, Christina, Christopher,
Joshua, Meghan, and Sarah;
to their tired parents, grandparents, and
great-grandparents;
and, of course, to Auntie Dee*

# Contents

## 5. Why More No-Load Stocks Are on the Way                83

# Author's Note

This book is a comprehensive guide to what I call no-load stocks. These are stocks that you never need to purchase through a broker. Your *first* share and *every share* can be bought *directly* from the company.

While I have tried to give accurate and up-to-date information concerning no-load stock programs, readers should understand that companies frequently change aspects of these programs. It's likely that certain features of programs discussed in the book have changed since the book's publication. An entire program may have been suspended or even eliminated. Fortunately, it's more likely that new no-load stock programs have been implemented since these pages left the printer. Because of frequent plan changes, it is always best to read the company's plan prospectus, which provides all the details of the program, before investing.

Because of my work in this area, I maintain a list of no-load stocks that is updated continuously. As a service to readers, this updated list of all no-load stocks and their telephone numbers is available free of charge by writing NorthStar Financial, Inc., 7412 Calumet Avenue, Suite 200, Hammond, Indiana 46324-2692. Use the code words "No-Load Stocks" when making requests. Please include a business-size, self-addressed stamped envelope.

# Preface

No-load mutual funds have become the investment of choice for millions of small investors—for good reason. Mutual-fund investing is *easy*. No brokers. No commissions. No hassles. No big minimum investments. Just request an application via a toll-free number, fill it out, return it with your check, and that's all there is to it. What could be easier? Certainly not stock investing!

Well, the fact is that there are a growing number of stocks in which you can buy your *first* share and *every share* directly, without a broker and often without commissions, just as with a no-load mutual fund. Better still, these no-load stocks™, as I call them, possess other attractive features usually associated with mutual-fund investing:

- Automatic cash investments via electronic funds transfers from an investor's savings or checking account
- IRA investing, with the company providing the custodial services
- The ability to sell stock, in some cases over the phone, for little or no commission

Despite the many benefits of no-load stocks, it's possible that you may never have known that such stocks exist. That's not surprising. The companies operating no-load stock plans aren't permitted, under mandate from the Securities and Exchange Commission, to advertise the programs aggressively. And stockbrokers, who are often the only source of investment information for individual investors, aren't likely to extol the virtues of no-load stocks, for obvious reasons. Thus, the reason for this book: to make individual investors aware that there is an increasingly viable investment alternative to no-load mutual funds, one combining the best elements of both stocks and mutual funds.

Many Wall Street purists regard no-load stocks as an investment having only limited appeal for a limited segment of the investing public. I disagree. The last decade has seen an explosion in the number of do-it-yourself investors who feel comfortable making their own investment decisions and want to invest directly, without a broker. I know these investors would love to invest directly in individual stocks if such direct-purchase programs were widely available. Furthermore, my position as editor of *DRIP Investor* and *No-Load Stock Insider* investment newsletters keeps me in touch with literally thousands of individual investors, and rarely a week goes by without one of my subscribers inquiring as to what companies permit direct investment for initial purchases.

Need more evidence that investors want no-load stocks? Exxon, one of the more prominent no-load stocks, implemented its program in March 1992. In the first month of the program, the company received 50,000 phone calls and opened 25,000 new accounts. Those are big numbers, especially when you take into account that Exxon had to remain relatively closemouthed about the program to avoid the wrath of the SEC. Who knows how many individuals would have invested directly with Exxon had they known about the program?

Despite the view of naysayers—many of whom are "gatekeepers" who make a living providing investors with access to the markets— that no-load stocks are nothing more than a passing oddity, several forces are at work which should push the number of no-load stocks sharply higher in the months and years ahead. But investors don't have to wait to get started investing in no-load stocks. Indeed, many quality companies offer the programs today. To find out which ones, read on.

I think you'll be glad you did.

*Charles B. Carlson*

# Acknowledgments

I would like to thank the readers of *DRIP Investor* and *No-Load Stock Insider* investment newsletters for their comments concerning no-load stocks. Their interest in the subject was one of the driving forces that caused me to write this book. I would also like to thank Jim Volpe of First Chicago Trust Corporation of New York and Robert Smith of Houston Industries for their unique insights.

Special thanks go to my editor at McGraw-Hill, David Conti, for his suggestions, criticisms, and, most of all, patience.

I would be remiss if I didn't thank the entire staff of NorthStar Financial, Inc., especially Avis Beitz and Elberta Miklusak, for assistance on this project. Judy Allison and Juliann Kessey also deserve special mention for their research efforts.

Finally, I'd like to thank two good friends of mine, Jeff Kallay and his wife Jean, for their continuing support and counsel.

# Introduction

In a perfect world, investors would be able to do the following:

- Go to a McDonald's and buy two Big Macs, two orders of fries, two Cokes, and two shares of McDonald's stock.
- Shop at Wal-Mart Stores for bug spray, suntan lotion, and lightbulbs and pick up five shares of Wal-Mart stock at the checkout counter.
- Buy a new Jeep Grand Cherokee, as well as 15 shares of Chrysler stock, from your local Chrysler/Jeep dealership. (Better still, the dealer gives you the 15 shares as its way of saying "Thanks.")
- Purchase a Reese's peanut butter cup and return the coupon inside for a 3 percent discount on purchases of Hershey Foods stock directly from the company.
- Fill out the application form on the back of the Kellogg's Cocoa Krispies box and return it along with your money to buy 10 shares of Kellogg stock for the kindergarten capitalist in your family.

In short, a perfect world for investors would be one in which you could invest directly with the company of your choice.

No broker.

No commissions.

Just you and the company.

Unfortunately, as most of you know, stock investing isn't nearly that easy. In fact, buying stock is like attending your high school prom—you can't get in until you pass the chaperone, who makes sure you pay your admission fee and agree to abide by the house rules. Of course, in the case of the stock market, the chaperone is the broker, who charges what amounts to an admission fee every time you buy or sell stock. However, many of us didn't believe we needed a chaperone at the prom, and I'm sure many of us feel the same way about investing in the stock market. We can do it ourselves, thank you.

On the other hand, investing in no-load mutual funds is pretty close to a perfect world for investors. You invest directly, with no sales fee, and usually in amounts that don't break your piggy bank.

To be sure, mutual funds have their downsides relative to individual stocks, such as "hidden" costs in the way of annual management expenses, redemption penalties, and 12b-1 marketing fees, not to mention the potential for unwanted tax liabilities as a result of capital-gains distributions. Furthermore, the performance of most mutual funds, to put it kindly, has been mediocre.

What if an investment existed that combined the best elements of no-load mutual funds with the best elements of individual stock investing? In other words, what if there were no-load *stocks*?

Well, guess what—no-load stocks do exist, and they're the subject of this book.

What exactly is a no-load stock? As you'll read in Chapters 1 and 2, no-load stock programs permit investors to buy their first share, and every subsequent share, directly from the company, without a broker.

Shares are purchased in much the same way as shares are purchased in a no-load mutual fund:

- Investors call the company, usually via a toll-free number, to request an application form and a plan prospectus.

- The company mails the materials directly to the investor.

- Once the investor receives the materials and completes the application, he or she makes the initial investment directly by returning the application and a check to the company.

- Once the initial investment has been made, investors are free to make subsequent purchases directly with the company.

In addition to direct investing, no-load stocks share other attributes with no-load mutual funds, such as monthly automatic cash investments and IRA investing. Best of all, investors pay little or no fees when investing in no-load stocks.

Of course, just because an investor is able to buy stock directly from a company doesn't make the stock a worthwhile investment. The overriding factor to consider with any investment is its quality and long-term total-return prospects. For guidance when investing in no-load stocks, Chapter 3 provides a number of strategies to help you incorporate no-load stocks into your investment program.

By now, I'm sure some of you are saying that, while no-load stocks are interesting, they still don't match the attraction of no-load mutual funds. Certainly, no-load mutual funds merit their place in nearly any investment program. However, I believe that individual stock ownership, perhaps via no-load stocks, is an excellent way to round out a diversified investment portfolio. Furthermore, I maintain that while the mutual-fund industry has done a masterful job of portraying all the benefits of mutual-fund investing, there are several downsides to mutual-fund investing—negatives which are lessened or eliminated when investing in no-load stocks. These mutual-fund "myths" and how no-load stocks stack up against no-load mutual funds in terms of cost and performance are explored in Chapter 4.

I wish this book had twice or three times as many pages as it does. That would mean that hundreds of no-load stocks exist today. Unfortunately, that's not the case. However, while the number of no-load stocks is small compared with the thousands of stocks on the various exchanges, the increase in no-load stock programs in the last 2 years has been impressive. An improved regulatory environment is fueling growth in the number of no-load stock plans. The ability of corporations to derive several benefits from offering these plans is another driving force behind the implementation of no-load stock programs. Thus, the number of no-load stock programs should grow sharply over the next several years. I examine the reasons that more no-load stocks are on the way in Chapter 5.

The book includes a complete review of all no-load stock programs in Chapter 6. Addresses, telephone numbers, stock symbols, program details, business profiles, and performance ratings are provided for all no-load stocks.

Many of you may see similarities between no-load stocks and dividend reinvestment plans (DRIPs), programs which I discuss in depth in my first book, *Buying Stocks Without a Broker* (McGraw-Hill). However, it's important to understand that no-load stocks are not merely extensions of companies' DRIP plans, but much more. No-load stocks represent a whole new way of investing in stocks, a way which provides choices and options heretofore not available to the small stock investor.

History tells us that most revolutions start slowly, building momentum over time until a critical mass of support is reached. At that point, change begins to occur, not incrementally, but exponentially. Revolutions in the financial markets are no different. Just look at no-load mutual funds. In the early years, the flow of money into mutual funds was a trickle rather than a flood. However, over time, as the merits of mutual-fund investing became more widely recognized, huge amounts of money began to pour into these once "obscure" investments. Today, there's no mistaking the revolutionary impact mutual funds have had on the investment landscape.

Could no-load stocks be the next revolution on Wall Street? Let's hope so.

# 1
# What's a No-Load Stock?

What does McDonald's, the restaurant giant, have in common with Fidelity mutual funds? Or Exxon, a leading oil company, with T. Rowe Price mutual funds? Or Procter & Gamble, the consumer-products company, with Vanguard funds? Or Ameritech, one of the regional Bell telephone companies, with Janus funds?

On the surface, it appears that these companies have nothing in common with no-load mutual funds, especially when it comes to making purchases in these two types of investments. No-load mutual funds allow you to deal directly with the fund family, without using a broker or paying a commission. On the other hand, stocks such as McDonald's, Exxon, Procter & Gamble, and Ameritech require you to use a broker to make your purchases, right?

Well, you might be surprised to learn that McDonald's, Exxon, Procter & Gamble, and Ameritech are just four of the growing number of publicly traded companies in which investors may buy their first share and every share of stock *directly from the firm*—without using a broker. McDonald's, Exxon, Procter & Gamble, and Ameritech are what I call *no-load stocks*.

## What's a No-Load Stock?

No-load stocks share many of the features that are usually associated with no-load mutual funds.

## Direct Investing—With No Brokers

The most obvious common trait of no-load mutual funds and no-load stocks is that both are purchased without using a broker. In both cases, investors deal directly, via the mail.

The process for buying no-load stocks is the same as for buying no-load mutual funds:

- *Call for information.* Investors must first contact the company to obtain an application form and a plan prospectus. The plan prospectus describes in great detail all the aspects of the no-load stock program—what the minimum is for the initial investment, when the funds will be invested, how investors may sell shares through the company, and any other features the plan offers. In most cases, companies handle inquiries via toll-free telephone numbers, similar to the toll-free numbers provided by no-load mutual funds.

**INVESTOR SERVICES PLAN**

# TEXACO INC.
## NEW ACCOUNT APPLICATION FORM

**IMPORTANT:** Return this application together with your check in the enclosed envelope.

**ACCOUNT REGISTRATION**
(Follow format provided on Reverse Side)
Please check appropriate box:  SINGLE: ☐  JOINT: ☐  CUSTODIAL: ☐  TRUST: ☐

CITIZENSHIP:  U.S.: ☐  FOREIGN: ☐

Make check payable to:
**TEXACO INC.**
Indicate Amount of Investment Enclosed

($250 Minimum- $120,000 Per Year)

NAME (1)

NAME (2) (If applicable)

NAME (3) (If applicable)

SOCIAL SECURITY/TAXPAYER I.D.#  (For a Custodial Account please provide minor's Social Security #)
(For a Trust Account please provide Taxpayer I.D. #)

STREET ADDRESS (P.O. BOX)

CITY                STATE            ZIP CODE

DAYTIME PHONE #

CUSTODIAL ACCOUNTS ONLY: (State in which minor resides)

**DIVIDEND REINVESTMENT**
Participants may either reinvest 100% of dividends, or receive a dividend check.
Please specify your choice below.

☐ 100% Dividend Reinvestment
☐ I wish to receive a Quarterly Dividend check.

**In order that we may serve you better, please fill out the optional information below.**
Please indicate if you have the following organizational or investing affiliations:  Texaco Employee: ☐   NAIC Member: ☐
Texaco Credit Card Holder: ☐   Other: _____
Do you subscribe to any of the following newsletters for individual investors?:  Profitable Investing: ☐   Donaghue's Money Letter: ☐
DRIP Investor: ☐   Better Investing: ☐   Other: _____

**ACKNOWLEDGEMENTS AND AUTHORIZATIONS**
I acknowledge receipt of the prospectus describing the details of the Investor Services Plan (the "Plan") and hereby request that the above account be enrolled in the Plan. Enclosed is a check or money order for the amount indicated above to be applied toward the purchase of shares for the above account. I understand that the account's participation is subject to the Terms and Conditions of the Plan as set forth in the prospectus that accompanied this application form, and that enrollment may be discontinued at any time by written notice to Texaco Inc., Investor Services Plan, 2000 Westchester Ave., White Plains, New York 10650.

I hereby appoint Texaco Inc. as agent for applying dividends as payment for any such shares purchased for the above account under the Plan.

Under penalties of perjury, I certify that the Social Security/Taxpayer I.D.# indicated above is true and correct and that I am not subject to back-up withholding per the Internal Revenue Code. Please note that if a Social Security/Taxpayer I.D. # is not provided, back-up withholding tax will be withheld from dividend payments.

Signed: _____   Date: _____

Revised 3/95

**Figure 1-1.**  Texaco's application form for its direct-purchase plan.

---

**GENERAL GUIDELINES FOR STOCK REGISTRATION**

---

The manner in which stock may be registered is governed by various state laws. The following are intended as general guidelines indicating some of the more common forms of stock registration. Some examples are shown below. If you have any questions regarding a specific form of registration, we suggest that you consult with an attorney.

**SINGLE ACCOUNT:**

Individual's Name    Mary H. Wilson
NAME (1)

**CUSTODIAL ACCOUNT:**
(Registration of stock for a minor)

Custodian's Name    Mary H. Wilson as custodian
NAME (1)
Minor's Name    for John Wilson, Jr.
NAME (2)
Note: The address may be the custodian's or the minor's. All correspondence will be sent to address provided.

**JOINT ACCOUNT:**

John Wilson and Mary Wilson Jt Ten
NAME (1)
Social Security Number of first person listed
SOCIAL SECURITY #
Note: Unless otherwise specified, all joint accounts will be registered as Joint Tenants with Right of Survivorship (abbreviated "JT TEN") and not as Tenants in Common.

**TRUST ACCOUNT:**

Trustee Name(s)
NAME (1)
Trust Name (Not required)
NAME (2)
Date of Trust
NAME (3)

---

**ANY QUESTIONS
ABOUT THE INVESTOR SERVICES PLAN?**

Please feel free to call us on our
TOLL FREE number 1-800-283-9785
Monday-Thursday 9:00-12:00 & 1:00-3:00 EST
Friday 9:00-12:00 & 1:00-2:00 EST

**Are you interested in learning more about personal investing or joining an investment club?**
Texaco supports the objectives of the National Association of Investors Corporation (NAIC), a non-profit organization dedicated to the education of individual investors. For information about investing and investment clubs, write to:
**National Association of Investors Corporation
711 West Thirteen Mile Road
Madison Heights, MI 48071**

Please make sure this address
appears in window when mailing

Texaco Inc - Investor Services Plan
P O Box 10818
Newark NJ 07193-0818

**Figure 1-1.** (Continued.)

An easy way to get the prospectus and enrollment information for a growing number of no-load stock plans is by calling the Direct Stock Purchase Plan Clearinghouse hotline—(800) 774-4117. The clearinghouse, a joint venture between NorthStar Financial, Inc. and Shareholder Communications Corp., provides one-stop shopping to receive the necessary materials to get started investing in many no-load stock plans. The 24-hour hotline is a free call for investors. The costs of operating the clearinghouse are shouldered by participating companies.

- *Fill out the application form.* Once you've received the material in the mail, read the prospectus and fill out the application form. Texaco's application form is shown in Figure 1-1.

- *Cut a check.* To make your initial investment, make out a check to the company or its transfer agent. Instructions will be given on the application form. Make sure that your initial investment falls within the parameters for the minimum and maximum investment.

- *Mail it to the company.* Put your check and application form in an envelope and return it to the company. In some cases, the company will include a return envelope in the application material.

And that's it.

In most cases, your initial investment will automatically enroll you in the company's dividend reinvestment plan and/or stock purchase plan. With these programs, you can have your dividends reinvested as well as make additional cash investments to purchase more shares.

## Low Investment Minimums

A big reason mutual funds are so popular with small investors is that they don't require huge investments to get started. Most mutual funds have minimums of $1000 to $2000 and usually lower the minimum for investments in an individual retirement account. Some mutual funds have minimums as low as $100. A few mutual funds even waive the minimum investment if you agree to invest $100 or more a month. Investing in such small increments is appealing to investors with limited pocketbooks. Fortunately, no-load stocks have taken their cue from the mutual-fund industry and have made their minimum initial investments quite affordable. Indeed, in the case of Wisconsin Energy, a leading electric utility, the minimum initial investment is just $50. Procter & Gamble requires a minimum initial investment of just $250. What's nice about such low minimums is that an investor can diversify among several no-load stocks with very little money. In fact, Chapter 3 will show you how to build a "mini" portfolio of four quality no-load stocks with an initial investment of $450.

Not only do no-load stocks make it easy to get started by having low investment minimums for the initial purchase; they make it even easier to continue accumulating stock over the long term. For example, in the case of Viad, once you have made your initial purchase and have enrolled in the stock purchase plan, subsequent investments may be made for as little as $10 at a time. In general, investment minimums for subsequent purchases in no-load stock programs are $10 to $100— much lower than the minimums in most no-load mutual funds. The beauty of such low minimum requirements is that you can add to all your no-load stock holdings with a relatively small investment each month. In Chapter 3, I'll show you how to make monthly contributions to four no-load stocks for a total of just $275.

If you have deeper pockets, no-load stocks are still an attractive investment option. Like mutual funds, which permit huge investments, most no-load stocks have maximum investment amounts that will be adequate for nearly every investor. For example, Exxon permits annual investments of up to $100,000. Several no-load stock programs have annual investment maximums of $50,000 or more. And remember—other than in a no-load mutual fund, where else can you invest such large sums of money and pay little or no commissions?

## Regular Statements and Record-Keeping Assistance

Another way no-load stocks and mutual funds are similar is in the regular statements each sends to their investors. Figure 1-2 shows a statement from Exxon. Companies with no-load stock programs send a statement to investors after every investment. The statement shows the number of shares purchased; the purchase price; the total number of shares held in the account; and, in some cases, the total value of the shares. Companies also provide a year-end statement to assist you at

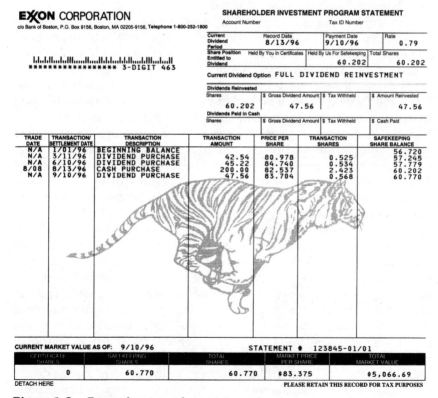

**EXXON** CORPORATION

c/o Bank of Boston, P.O. Box 9156, Boston, MA 02205-9156, Telephone 1-800-252-1800

**SHAREHOLDER INVESTMENT PROGRAM STATEMENT**

Account Number                    Tax ID Number

| Current Dividend Period | Record Date 8/13/96 | Payment Date 9/10/96 | Rate 0.79 |
|---|---|---|---|
| Share Position Entitled to Dividend | Held By You In Certificates | Held By Us For Safekeeping 60.202 | Total Shares 60.202 |

Current Dividend Option  FULL DIVIDEND REINVESTMENT

Dividends Reinvested

| Shares | $ Gross Dividend Amount | $ Tax Withheld | $ Amount Reinvested |
|---|---|---|---|
| 60.202 | 47.56 | | 47.56 |

Dividends Paid in Cash

| Shares | $ Gross Dividend Amount | $ Tax Withheld | $ Cash Paid |
|---|---|---|---|

| TRADE DATE | TRANSACTION/ SETTLEMENT DATE | TRANSACTION DESCRIPTION | TRANSACTION AMOUNT | PRICE PER SHARE | TRANSACTION SHARES | SAFEKEEPING SHARE BALANCE |
|---|---|---|---|---|---|---|
| N/A | 1/01/96 | BEGINNING BALANCE | | | | 56.720 |
| N/A | 3/11/96 | DIVIDEND PURCHASE | 42.54 | 80.978 | 0.525 | 57.245 |
| N/A | 6/10/96 | DIVIDEND PURCHASE | 45.22 | 84.740 | 0.534 | 57.779 |
| 8/08 | 8/13/96 | CASH PURCHASE | 200.00 | 82.537 | 2.423 | 60.202 |
| N/A | 9/10/96 | DIVIDEND PURCHASE | 47.56 | 83.704 | 0.568 | 60.770 |

CURRENT MARKET VALUE AS OF: 9/10/96                STATEMENT #  123845-01/01

| CERTIFICATE SHARES | SAFEKEEPING SHARES | TOTAL SHARES | MARKET PRICE PER SHARE | TOTAL MARKET VALUE |
|---|---|---|---|---|
| 0 | 60.770 | 60.770 | $83.375 | $5,066.69 |

DETACH HERE                                  PLEASE RETAIN THIS RECORD FOR TAX PURPOSES

**Figure 1-2.**  Exxon direct-purchase statement.

tax time. My experience has been that statements from firms offering no-load stocks are easier to decipher than typical brokerage statements. Another benefit is that companies and their transfer agents provide an excellent source for assistance in piecing together historical trading information. This information is especially important when determining a stock's cost basis for tax purposes.

## Direct Ownership

When you buy shares directly from a no-load mutual fund, you are the registered owner of the fund shares. That's not always the case when investors buy stock. Indeed, although this may surprise you, most stock investors are not the registered shareholders of the companies in which they invest. In fact, it's possible, indeed likely, that your company has no record of you as a shareholder. How can that be?

The fact is that, unbeknownst to many investors, their shares are held in "street" name—in other words, in the name of the brokerage firm that purchased the shares for you.

There are two ways to own stock—in street name or as a registered shareholder on the books of the corporation. The identity of street-name investors is withheld from the company. All correspondence between the investor and the company goes through the brokerage firm.

The reason many investors end up with street-name accounts is that this is the method of ownership that brokers push. To be sure, holding shares in street name has certain advantages, primarily ones of convenience. The amount of paperwork is reduced, since brokerage houses act as custodian of your funds, providing regular consolidated statements that help in record keeping and tax preparation. In street-name accounts, investors don't have to worry about storing certificates. Street-name ownership also makes selling easier because the shares are immediately available to the brokerage firm to sell.

The benefits of street-name ownership, however, carry a price. What you gain in convenience with a street-name account, you lose in control and flexibility. For example, want to sell your shares? If the stock is held in street name, the odds are that you'll sell through the broker that bought your shares. Thus, street-name ownership greatly reduces your ability to shop for the cheapest commissions; you are, in effect, locked in to paying the commissions of the brokerage firm where your shares are held. Sure, you can always reregister the shares in your own name, take ownership of the stock certificates, and sell the shares through any broker you'd like. However, many brokers charge dearly to register shares in the investor's name, and the reregistration process can drag on forever.

In addition to locking up an investor's assets, brokers like street-name accounts because they can earn fees from lending street-name shares to short sellers (investors who sell borrowed shares) and other investors. It's perfectly legal for a brokerage firm to lend your shares if you have a margin account, just as it's perfectly legal for a bank to loan your money. And, as with the bank which receives interest on loans made with your money, brokerage firms earn fees on your shares that they lend to investors.

Another cost of having stock registered in street name is that it precludes you from enrolling in company-sponsored dividend reinvestment and stock purchase plans (DRIPs). In nearly every case, companies with DRIPs require participants to be registered shareholders. Investors who want to buy stock directly from a company cannot do so if their stock is held in street name.

Missing out on special shareholder perks and discounts is another potential cost of having stock registered in street name. Many companies provide special discounts, freebies, and giveaways to their shareholders. For example, Wrigley, Wm., Jr., the chewing-gum company, traditionally sends each shareholder 20 packs of gum every year around Christmas. Brown-Forman, the spirits and consumer-products company, has made available in the past to shareholders 50 percent discounts on Lenox china and Hartmann luggage. In many instances, the perks are available only to registered shareholders, not street-name holders. [For further information on shareholder perks and freebies, let me plug my book *Free Lunch on Wall Street: Perks, Freebies, and Giveaways,* published by McGraw-Hill and available by calling (219) 852-3220.]

Fortunately, when you buy no-load stocks, you automatically become a registered shareholder with the company, the same as if you bought mutual-fund shares directly from the fund company. As a registered shareholder, you have control over the shares. If you want to take possession of stock certificates in order to sell through a broker of your choice, notify the company and certificates will be sent immediately.

## Safekeeping Services

When you purchase shares in a mutual fund, you are not sent share certificates. Rather, your holdings are recorded in book-entry form. No-load stock programs have adopted a similar system of recording ownership. Shares purchased in no-load stock programs are registered in book-entry form. There are no physical certificates. However, if a shareholder wants to take possession of the stock certificate, all he or she has to do is notify the company or its transfer agent, and a certificate will be created and sent to the investor. Such safekeeping services are attractive because they relieve investors of having to store stock certificates. Any of you who have gone through the hassle of getting a replacement certificate because your certificate was lost, stolen, or damaged know the value of having the shares held by the company in book-entry form.

## Fractional Shares

When you invest, say, $1000 in a no-load mutual fund, all your money is invested, regardless of the net asset value of the mutual fund. In other words, a $1000 investment in a mutual fund with a net asset value of $23.50 will buy 42.553 shares, and the mutual fund will carry the investor on its books with an investment of 42.553 shares, fractional shares and all.

It's a different story when you buy individual stocks. Let's say you want to invest $1000 in McDonald's, and the stock is trading at $53.25 per share. Even though your $1000 is worth 18.779 shares of McDonald's, no broker is going to sell you fractional shares. What this forces investors to do is invest not on their own terms, but on those offered by the broker. Want to invest a full $1000 per month in a stock, regardless of the price? You can't if you go through a broker. You'll have to invest amounts that buy whole shares.

I know some of you are probably thinking I'm making a mountain out of a molehill, but I disagree. The mutual-fund industry understands that small investors don't necessarily think in terms of how many shares they can buy each month in a stock or mutual fund; they think in terms of the number of dollars they can squeeze out of their monthly budgets to invest. The mutual-fund industry accommodates small investors by giving them an opportunity to invest their entire budgeted investment each and every month, regardless of whether the investment buys whole shares or fractional shares; the brokerage community does not.

Fortunately, no-load stocks have parted ways with traditional stock investing by allowing an investor's entire investment to go toward whole and fractional shares. Try getting a Charles Schwab or Merrill Lynch broker to do that for you. And no-load stocks will also allow you to purchase fractional shares with subsequent monthly purchases once you've enrolled in their stock purchase programs.

## Frequent Purchases

Mutual funds will accept money from investors at any time. Of course, so will brokers, but they'll also take their cut each time. One drawback of no-load stocks is that the opportunities to purchase stock each month are limited. Most no-load stocks invest money only once a month. However, that situation is changing. No-load stocks are realizing that investors want the flexibility to make more frequent purchases, especially if a stock drops in price. Thus, several no-load stock programs have instituted policies for more frequent purchases. Exxon and McDonald's, for example, will buy shares once a week for investors in the stock purchase program. McDonald's will even buy shares daily, if practical. Look for more no-load stocks to institute weekly, and perhaps even daily, purchases over the next few years.

## Frequent Sells

Selling a mutual fund is easy—it requires just a phone call in many instances. And in most cases, no fees are charged for selling mutual-fund shares. Selling stock through a no-load stock program, unfortunately, is not as easy. In most cases, the companies require a sell notice in writing, and it may take 5 to 10 business days to sell the shares and additional time to remit the funds to the investor. In addition, most no-load stocks charge fees to sell shares for investors, although these fees are still smaller than traditional brokerage commissions. Fortunately, the situation is improving. A growing number of no-load stocks offer telephone redemption. For example, Amoco permits investors to sell stock through its no-load stock program with just a phone call. A number of no-load stocks will allow you to submit sell instructions via fax. As no-load stock programs become more mainstream and companies become more comfortable with adding enhancements to them, look for improvements in the speed and cost of selling shares through the programs.

## Dividend Reinvestment

Mutual funds give investors the option of receiving cash dividends and capital distributions or having them reinvested in the fund. As a rule, mutual funds don't charge investors to reinvest dividends. Having dividends reinvested in additional shares is an excellent way to build your investment over time. No-load stocks also give investors the option of having their dividends reinvested, and most of the firms charge no fees for providing this service.

## IRA Investing

Most no-load mutual funds permit investors to place their mutual-fund investments in an individual retirement account (IRA), and the fund acts as the custodian for the account. Because of this feature, mutual funds offer one of the easiest ways to save for retirement. Unfortunately, including individual stocks in an IRA is not as simple in many cases. In order to do so, you must have a custodian for the account. Brokerage firms are the usual custodians for IRAs that hold individual stocks. The problem with this arrangement is that investors incur large commissions any time they buy or sell stock in the IRA. Fortunately, a number of no-load stocks provide an option for investors to include their investments in an IRA, and the company or its agent provides custodial features. No-load stocks which offer an IRA option include Ameritech, Barnett Banks, Exxon, Mobil, and Morton International.

The IRA feature is one of the newer enhancements among no-load stocks, but it is one that is expected to grow over time, for a variety of reasons. First, having an IRA in a no-load stock program provides an avenue for a company to gain a piece of the trillion-dollar retirement investing market. As the population continues to age, this investment segment will continue to grow in importance. A company that wants to snare retirement money for its own equity base will be more competitive if it offers an IRA program to investors. Also, a secondary benefit of the IRA option is the nature of the relationship between investor and corporation. As discussed in Chapter 5, companies like a stable shareholder base, one focused on long-term investing. Such a base means that the stock will be less vulnerable to the erratic trading that sometimes occurs in stocks controlled by institutional investors, who are more short-term oriented than individual investors. IRA investing implies investing for the long haul. An IRA program brings more long-term investors to the shareholder base, a development that many companies view as positive.

Another reason IRAs will be more commonplace in no-load stock programs is that individual investors want them. First Trust Corp., a Denver-based firm which provides custodial services for retirement plans, conducted a survey examining three IRA programs. The study found that, while investors choose a particular direct-purchase program because of expected financial returns, they also want greater investment choices and flexibility. IRAs offer an additional choice for investors, and the study showed that, all things being equal, firms offering IRAs in their direct-purchase plans were perceived as more attractive by individual investors than companies that didn't offer IRAs.

If there is a drawback to IRAs offered by no-load stocks, it's the fees. There is a trend in the mutual-fund business to eliminate fees on IRAs, although some mutual funds require that investors have at least $10,000 in an IRA before the fee is eliminated. On the other hand, the IRA fees in no-load stocks—usually $20 to $55 per year—although not onerous, could add up over time. However, as IRA programs grow in popularity and the firms have a larger number of accounts in them, economies of scale could help to lower the annual fees. Also, I wouldn't be surprised to see firms lower or eliminate the annual administrative fees once an investor's IRA exceeds some minimum amount, as is the case with mutual funds.

## Automatic Investment Programs

Most mutual funds offer automatic investment programs. These services allow a mutual fund to withdraw electronically a predetermined amount of money each month from an investor's savings or checking account to make regular investments in the mutual fund. Investors like such programs because they simplify the investment process, save time, reduce postage costs, and ensure that investors will invest regularly in their mutual funds.

For example, let's say you own the Fidelity Magellan fund. Fidelity will set up a system whereby the firm withdraws a minimum of $100 per month from your checking account to purchase fund shares. The beauty of this arrangement is twofold. First, you don't have to worry about forgetting to invest each month in your fund, nor do you have to pay the postage to send your payment to Fidelity. In addition, automatic investment services provide an excellent way to *dollar-cost average* in the fund. Your $100 investment will buy fewer fund shares when the fund is expensive and more shares when the fund is cheap. While dollar-cost averaging doesn't ensure a profit, it does ensure that the average cost of your investments will always be less than the average selling price of the stock or mutual fund at the time your purchases were made.

Dollar-cost averaging in stocks can be a valuable tool for disciplined investors, but it can also be expensive. Buying increments of stock every month, especially with amounts as small as $50 or $100, will expose you to huge commission charges. In fact, depending on your broker, your $50 monthly investments could be all but chewed up by an equal amount in commission costs.

Fortunately, several no-load stock programs offer automatic investment programs for investors. Barnett Banks offers monthly automatic cash investments for just a $25 minimum. DQE, an electric utility in the western part of Pennsylvania, has an automatic investment option for a minimum of $10. Exxon offers monthly automatic investments with a minimum of $50. Automatic investment services have been one of the fastest-growing enhancements to no-load stocks and should be more prevalent in the future.

## The Evolution of No-Load Stocks

### NYSE's Monthly Investment Plan

The roots of no-load stocks stem back as far as the 1950s and the New York Stock Exchange's Monthly Investment Plan. It may seem hard to believe, but at one time the New York Stock Exchange not only encouraged small investors to own stock, but also made it incredibly easy to do so. The Monthly Investment Plan, sponsored by New York Stock Exchange member firms, provided a simple and economical way for individuals to invest as little as $40 every 3 months to buy shares in some 1200 NYSE stocks, common and preferred. An investor could sign up for the program at any member firm. All trades went through the brokerage firm, which received a small fee. The commission, according to a 1961 brochure, was a flat 6 percent of the investment when the amount invested was $100 or less. For the minimum $40 investment, the charge was $2.26. For investments of over $100, the 6 percent commission gradually decreased until, with an investment of $1000—the monthly maximum investment permitted in the plan—the commission was $14.85, or 1.5 percent of the amount invested. Investors could make simultaneous payments into a number of stocks with a single check. Another feature of the program permitted participants to have their dividends reinvested for additional shares. Participants were also able to sell their shares through the plan for a small fee. There were no contracts or start-up fees, nor did participants have to agree to contribute every month or every quarter. It was easy to enroll. Investors could either contact a brokerage firm or use an enrollment form which was included in the introductory brochure (Figure 1-3).

Despite what sounds like a perfect program for small investors, the Monthly Investment Plan died out over time. Although the individual with whom I spoke at the New York Stock Exchange couldn't remember why, my guess is that member firms got tired of taking such small orders for small fees and stopped supporting the plan.

### DRIPs

The next step in the evolution of no-load stocks was the development of corporate dividend reinvestment plans (DRIPs). DRIPs have been around for more than two decades—AT&T offered one of the first prominent DRIP plans in 1973—and are going strong today. The programs, sponsored by some 900 publicly traded corporations, allow investors to buy stock directly from the companies. Shares are pur-

**Figure 1-3.** *(Courtesy New York Stock Exchange Archives)*

On MIP transactions the commission is a straight 6% when the amount invested is $100 or less. Over $100 the charge is progressively less than 6%, as shown in the following table, with a minimum of $6 for each transaction. The same charges apply to sales. Of course, the more you invest at one time, the lower the rate of commission. For example, here are some typical transactions:

| PAYMENT | AMOUNT INVESTED AT ODD-LOT PRICES | COMMISSION* AMT. % | |
|---------|-----------------------------------|------------|-----|
| $   40  | $  37.74  | $  2.26 | 6.0 |
| 60      | 56.60     | 3.40    | 6.0 |
| 80      | 75.47     | 4.53    | 6.0 |
| 100     | 94.34     | 5.66    | 6.0 |
| 200     | 194.00    | 6.00    | 3.1 |
| 300     | 293.14    | 6.86    | 2.3 |
| 500     | 490.10    | 9.90    | 2.0 |
| 1000    | 985.15    | 14.85   | 1.5 |

*In some cases the commission may be less. For instance, on an investment of $980, in a stock selling at $140, the minimum commission would be $10.50, because where the amount of money involved is $100 or more, the minimum charge shall not exceed $1.50 per share.

There are no opening or starting fees, no dues, assessments or custody fees.

After the broker's commission is deducted from your payment, the exact number of shares your dollars will buy is figured to four decimal places. It's like buying $5 worth of gasoline. For example, $50 will buy 2.6206 shares of a stock selling for $18 a share, and 0.2621 of a share of a $180 stock.

**Figure 1-3.**  *(Continued.)*

If you wish, you may have several MIP's, making payments either simultaneously or at alternating dates. Let's suppose you want to make one monthly payment for two stocks, a chemical and a utility. A payment of $100, after deducting commissions, would buy $47.17 of each stock.

Or perhaps you might want three quarterly Plans, with a payment due each month. You could buy, let's say, an oil stock in January, April, July and October; a steel stock in February, May, August and November; and a food stock in March, June, September and December.

You can receive your full shares whenever you request them, or when you terminate your Monthly Investment Plan. There is no charge for delivery on termination of the Plan, or when you request 50 shares or more. If your request is for less than 50 shares, *and you do not terminate the Plan,* there will be a C.O.D. handling charge of $1 plus mailing costs. When you take delivery of shares, your name will be registered on the company's books as a stockholder, so your dividends on those shares can no longer be reinvested automatically in your MIP account.

After each of your purchases, you will be mailed a confirmation showing the amount of money received, number of shares bought, price, commission paid and total shares held for your account at that time—together with a reminder of your next scheduled payment. Since you do your investing by mail under this convenient Plan, there's no need to visit your broker's office to make payments.

**Figure 1-3.**   *(Continued.)*

# The 50 STOCKS most popular with investors using the MONTHLY INVESTMENT PLAN

| Symbol | In Order of Popularity as of November 24, 1961 | Year Consecutive Annual Dividend Payments Began | Latest 12 Months Cash Dividends (Incl. Extras) | Price Per Share 12/1/61 | Yield** |
|---|---|---|---|---|---|
| GM | General Motors Corp.<br>Cars, trucks, appliances | 1915 | $2.00 | $55 | 3.6% |
| IBM | Int'l Business Machines Corp.<br>Sells, leases bus. machines | 1916 | 2.20a | 579 | 0.4* |
| T | American Tel. & Tel. Co.<br>Bell telephone system | 1881 | 3.45 | 133⅛ | 2.6* |
| GE | General Electric Co.<br>Electrical equip., jet engines | 1899 | 2.00 | 80⅝ | 2.5 |
| MMM | Minnesota Mining & Mfg. Co.<br>Adhesives, abrasives | 1916 | 0.63 | 73½ | 0.9* |
| DOW | Dow Chemical Co.<br>Industrial chemicals | 1911 | 1.45 | 75⅜ | 1.9* |
| TY | Tri-Continental Corp.<br>Closed-end investment co. | 1945 | 1.47 | 51¾ | 2.8 |
| J | Standard Oil Co. (N.J.)<br>Petroleum products | 1899 | 2.25 | 48½ | 4.6 |
| GEN | General Telephone & El. Corp.<br>Tel. hldg. co., electronics | 1936 | 0.76 | 25⅜ | 3.0 |
| PFE | Pfizer (Chas.) & Co.<br>Drugs, chemicals | 1901 | 0.80 | 50 | 1.6 |
| SY | Sperry Rand Corp.<br>Electronic controls, bus. mach. | 1934 | 0.19a | 22¾ | D |
| RCA | Radio Corp. of America<br>Electronics, TV, radio brdcast. | 1940 | 1.00a | 52⅜ | 1.9* |
| SA | Safeway Stores, Inc.<br>Chain grocery stores | 1927 | 1.50 | 62⅛ | 2.4* |
| P | Phillips Petroleum Co.<br>Petroleum products | 1934 | 1.70 | 59 | 2.9 |
| EK | Eastman Kodak Co.<br>Photo equip., synthetic fibers | 1902 | 2.25 | 108¾ | 2.1 |
| SD | Standard Oil Co. of Calif.<br>Petroleum products | 1912 | 2.00 | 55 | 3.6 |
| MTC | Monsanto Chemical Co.<br>Chem., synthetic fibers | 1925 | 0.98a | 52⅝ | 1.9* |
| S | Sears, Roebuck & Co.<br>Mail order, retail stores | 1935 | 1.40 | 84½ | 1.7* |
| GO | Gulf Oil Corp.<br>Petroleum products | 1936 | 1.02a | 40¾ | 2.5* |
| LEM | Lehman Corp.<br>Closed-end investment co. | 1930 | 0.53e | 34⅜ | 1.5 |
| CG | Columbia Gas System, Inc.<br>Natural gas pipelines | 1943 | 1.10 | 28⅝ | 3.8 |
| ACY | American Cyanamid Co.<br>Pharmaceuticals, chemicals | 1934 | 1.60 | 45 | 3.6 |
| UK | Union Carbide Corp.<br>Chem., plastics, metal alloys | 1918 | 3.60 | 128¾ | 2.8 |
| AL | Aluminium Ltd.<br>Aluminum | 1939 | 0.70t | 27 | 2.6 |
| IT | Int'l Tel. & Tel. Corp.<br>Electronic & communic. equip. | 1951 | 1.00 | 58⅛ | 1.7 |

**Yield based on dividends paid in latest 12 months (including extras) and December 1 price.
a—Adjusted for stock dividends and splits.
e—Excludes dividends paid from security profits

12

**Figure 1-3.** *(Continued.)*

Under the Monthly Investment
Plan there are some 1200 stocks
on the New York Stock Exchange
from which to choose.
Here's the latest list of the
50 most popular with MIP buyers.

| Symbol | In Order of Popularity as of November 24, 1961 | Year Consecutive Annual Dividend Payments Began | Latest 12 Months Cash Dividends (Incl. Extras) | Price Per Share 12/1/61 | Yield** |
|---|---|---|---|---|---|
| DD | duPont de Nemours (E. I.) & Co. Nylon, chemicals | 1904 | $6.75 | $239½ | 2.8% |
| WX | Westinghouse Electric Corp. Elec. equip., atomic energy | 1935 | 1.20 | 39¾ | 3.0 |
| RLM | Reynolds Metals Co. Aluminum producer | 1942 | 0.50 | 37¼ | 1.3 |
| MRK | Merck & Co., Inc. Medicinal chem. drugs | 1935 | 1.60 | 89½ | 1.8 |
| GD | General Dynamics Corp. Aircraft, missiles, submarines | 1936 | 0.50 | 27 | D |
| MAD | Madison Fund, Inc. Closed-end investment co. | 1939 | 0.60e | 29⅞ | 2.0 |
| OLM | Olin Mathieson Chemical Corp. Chemicals, drugs, metals | 1926 | 1.00 | 39¾ | 2.5 |
| LIT | Litton Industries, Inc. Electronic equip., bus. mach. | — | — | 155¼ | — |
| BS | Bethlehem Steel Corp. Steel, shipbuilding | 1939 | 2.40 | 41⅛ | 5.8 |
| BC | Brunswick Corporation Bowling equip., pleasure boats | 1937 | 0.40a | 53⅜ | 0.7* |
| ELG | El Paso Natural Gas Co. Natural gas pipelines | 1936 | 1.30 | 25⅞ | 5.0 |
| AC | American Can Co. Cans & containers | 1923 | 2.00 | 48⅛ | 4.2 |
| PCG | Pacific Gas & Electric Co. Operating public utility | 1919 | 2.75 | 105¾ | 2.6* |
| UGC | United Gas Corp. Natural gas system | 1944 | 1.50 | 41 | 3.7 |
| X | U. S. Steel Corp. Basic & finished steel, cement | 1940 | 3.00 | 79 | 3.8 |
| TXN | Texas Instruments, Inc. Electronic devices | — | — | 109½ | — |
| TX | Texaco Inc. Petroleum products | 1903 | 1.49a | 54¼ | 2.7* |
| AMF | American Machine & Foundry Co. Recreational eq. indust. mach. | 1927 | 0.85a | 37⅛ | 2.3* |
| AA | Aluminum Co. of America Aluminum | 1939 | 1.20 | 57⅜ | 2.1 |
| AV | Avco Corporation Aircraft parts electronics | 1957 | 0.58 | 25¼ | 2.3* |
| WIN | Winn-Dixie Stores Inc. Chain grocery stores | 1943 | 0.77 | 39½ | 1.9* |
| LLT | Long Island Lighting Co. Operating public utility | 1950 | 1.48 | 57½ | 2.6* |
| M | Montgomery Ward & Co., Inc. Mail order, retail stores | 1936 | 1.00 | 31⅜ | 3.2 |
| GT | Goodyear Tire & Rubber Co. Tires, rubber, chem. prods. | 1937 | 0.88a | 44¾ | 2.0* |
| NP | Northern Pacific Ry. Co. Railroad | 1943 | 2.20 | 43 | 5.1 |

*—Dividend rate increased since December 2, 1960.
D—Dividend rate decreased since December 2, 1960.
t—Subject to tax withheld by a state, territory or foreign government.
Sources: Wall Street Journal; Standard & Poor's Dividend Record.

13

**Figure 1-3.** *(Continued.)*

# How to fill in your MIP Purchase Order—

1 Remove the purchase order from the back cover of this book (opposite pages). Fill in name of the Member Firm with whom you wish to open your account in the space above the word "Gentlemen". Date the order. A separate purchase order is needed for each stock you decide to buy. If you want more than one Plan, additional purchase order forms are available from your Member Firm office.

2 Fill in dollar amount of payments you plan to make—$40 minimum—and cross out either Monthly or Quarterly, whichever doesn't apply.

3 Fill in name of company LISTED ON THE NEW YORK STOCK EXCHANGE whose stock you want to buy. You may make your selection from some 1200 such stocks.

4 Indicate amount of payment accompanying purchase order. You may start your Plan with any amount from $40 to $1000. Many investors start their plans with an initial payment larger than the amount planned for later regular purchases, thus getting their accounts off to a good start.

5 Print your full legal name, not initials, your address, occupation, and citizenship. A married woman should use her given and maiden names in addition to her married name, and give her husband's occupation.

6 Sign the application.

7 Attach your check or money order, make payable to your Member Firm. This payment must accompany the purchase order. Instructions for subsequent payments will be sent to you with your confirmations of purchases. NEVER MAIL CASH!

8 To be eligible to have an MIP account, you must be at least 21 years of age. In addition, you must be a U.S. citizen, or a resident alien filing a U.S. income tax return, or a resident of Canada.

9 Before you mail the purchase order to your Member Firm, be sure: • All spaces are filled in and all questions answered • You have used your legal signature in signing the purchase order • You have enclosed a check or money order made payable to your Member Firm.

**Figure 1-3.** *(Continued.)*

CUT ALONG THIS DOTTED LINE

## MONTHLY INVESTMENT PLAN
of
Members New York Stock Exchange

### PURCHASE ORDER

................19......

(Name of Member Firm to be filled in)

Gentlemen:

IT IS MY PRESENT INTENTION TO INVEST WITH $.............. monthly

PAYMENTS IN .................... quarterly
(fill in name of stock) LISTED ON THE

NEW YORK STOCK EXCHANGE, COMMENCING WITH AN INITIAL PAYMENT OF
$.................., FOR WHICH MY CHECK OR MONEY ORDER IS ATTACHED.

Each remittance for my account ($40 minimum), less your commission, will be applied by you, as my broker, to the purchase of full shares of the stock named above and/or a fractional interest in such a share. Purchases will be made at the first odd-lot price established after the day the payment is credited to my account. See Terms and Conditions #2, #3 and #4.

Cash dividends, and proceeds from the sale of rights or special distributions are to be automatically reinvested in my account, unless you are otherwise notified by me in writing with respect to future cash dividends and proceeds.

I reserve the right to cancel this order at any time, without penalty or charge, by written notice to you. You also may cancel this order at any time by written notice to me. Purchases made before the receipt of a cancellation notice will not be affected by such notice.

THE TERMS AND CONDITIONS SET FORTH ON THE
REVERSE SIDE ARE PART OF THIS PURCHASE ORDER.

Mr.
Mrs.
Miss ........................  ........................
(Print Full Legal Name)  (Legal Signature)

........................  ........................
(Street Address)  (Business or Occupation)

........................  ........................  ........................
(City, Zone and State)  (Citizenship)  (Social Security No.)

FOR OFFICE USE ONLY

(Member Firm Identifying  (Name of Member Firm)  (Authorized Initials for
Number—Not Over 4 Digits)  Opening a New Account)

chased in two ways: with dividends that the firm reinvests in additional shares and with optional cash payments permitted in most plans.

The DRIP concept was similar to that of its predecessor, the NYSE Monthly Investment Plan, with one big difference. DRIPs represented a way for investors to deal directly with companies to purchase stock—a revolutionary development within the context of how financial markets work. Prior to DRIPs, the only avenue to invest in stocks was through the brokerage community. Even the NYSE's Monthly Investment Plan, with all its attractions, required a broker to make the transaction. DRIPs were different. Now investors could deal directly with companies, without an intermediary, to buy stock.

DRIPs have taken direct investing to a new level, but there is a catch. In order to enroll in most DRIPs, investors must be registered shareholders of at least one share. Unfortunately, getting that first share can present all sorts of problems. Many brokers won't even handle a one-share purchase, and those that do charge dearly for it. Thus, in order to take advantage of all that DRIPs have to offer, you still have to use a broker to buy the first share.

### The First No-Load Stocks

It wasn't until the early 1980s that companies decided to take their DRIPs the final step and allow even initial purchases to be made directly. Pioneers of this no-load stock concept were Citicorp, Control Data, and W. R. Grace. One impetus for the programs was a perceived need by the firms to broaden their shareholder bases to include individual investors. As discussed in Chapter 5, companies benefit in a variety of ways from offering DRIPs and no-load stock programs. Diversifying the shareholder base is one way to limit corporate control by institutional investors while bringing on board more small investors, who tend to be more loyal and long-term oriented.

Over time, more companies adopted no-load stock programs, adding various features along the way. Perhaps the programs most responsible for the continued evolution of no-load stocks were those introduced by Exxon and Texaco. Both companies expanded the types of services offered in a no-load stock program. The fact that both firms were popular names with investors, as well as components of the widely followed Dow Jones Industrial Average, helped spur interest in no-load stocks among investors as well as corporations.

### Do-It-Yourself Investor

The evolution of no-load stocks has been greatly impacted by the growth of the do-it-yourself investor. I don't think there's any question that individuals are more sophisticated now about stocks and investing than they've been in the history of the stock market. One reason is the explosion of inexpensive and available information. Financial magazines, newspapers, newsletters, and television and radio shows have helped to demystify the financial markets for millions of investors. And with computers and inexpensive software and databases, even individuals with modest means have the ability to store, analyze, and manipulate huge amounts of data to improve investment decision making. The end result is a more informed investor who wants to call his or her own investment shots while saving money in the process.

In the era of fixed commissions, there was little incentive to educate yourself concerning investments. You were going to pay the same high brokerage rates regardless of whether you or your broker selected your investments. The SEC changed everything when it eliminated fixed commissions on "May Day"—May 1, 1975. May Day gave birth to a new player on the financial scene: the discount broker. Investors were now faced with the option of either using a full-service broker— and paying top dollar in commissions for his or her expertise and resources—or using a discount broker and saving a bundle on commissions. Practically overnight, the value of becoming a self-reliant investor jumped dramatically. Consequently, over time, more and more investors began educating themselves on stocks and investing in general. The growth of the do-it-yourself investor produced a bonanza for the discount brokerage community. Indeed, Charles Schwab, the leading discount broker, saw its total revenues increase roughly 476 percent from 1986 to 1995. Over that same time frame, Merrill Lynch, the top full-service broker, saw revenues grow by only 124 percent.

## No-Load Mutual Funds

Charles Schwab doesn't work for free, however, which means do-it-yourself investors still pay a fee to gain access to the market. Wouldn't it be great to buy investments and pay no fee? Enter no-load mutual funds.

The Investment Company Institute, a mutual-fund trade group, credits the Scudder fund family with starting the first no-load mutual fund way back in the 1920s. However, it wasn't until more than five decades later that no-load funds truly came into prominence. Just as discount brokers benefited from the growth of the do-it-yourself investor in the 1980s, no-load mutual funds benefited from investors' desire to shave or even eliminate transaction costs.

Was it the professional money management available with mutual funds that spurred demand? The ability to diversify with limited funds? Certainly these two factors contributed to the growth of mutual-fund investing. Still, it's difficult to discount the importance of convenience and commission-free investing in the growth of no-load mutual funds. Little wonder that Exxon and other pioneers in no-load stocks incorporated features from the no-load fund industry into their no-load stock programs. Clearly, no-load mutual funds had a huge role in shaping today's no-load stock programs and cultivating demand for direct investment of stocks.

## Who Needs a Middleman?

When you strip everything away, stockbrokers are middlemen who bring buyers and sellers together. What's been happening to middlemen in today's business world?

- Wal-Mart Stores, the retailing giant, no longer deals with middlemen. The firm goes directly to suppliers to purchase products, saving the distributor's 3 to 5 percent cut.

- Factory outlets, mail-order catalogs, "category-killing" retailers, and warehouse clubs are making middlemen an endangered species in a variety of consumer markets.

- It's estimated that one in five homes is sold each year by the owners, without the help of a real-estate broker.

- Individuals can now buy such financial products as insurance and treasury securities without using a broker.

- On-line services, such as CompuServe and America Online, as well as the Internet, allow individuals to buy anything from clothes to airplane tickets—all without going through a middleman.

Why the death of the middleman? Information and communication are much cheaper today than they were even a decade ago. It's not surprising that the elimination of the middleman has made its way into the financial markets. A broker's biggest weapons—contacts and knowledge—are less proprietary. Stockbrokers are some of the best-paid middlemen in the business world—the nation's retail and institutional stockbrokers had incomes of more than $78,000 and $147,000, respectively, in 1995, according to the Securities Industry Association. Steep fees provide extra incentive for the buyer and seller to find a way to do without brokerage services. No-load mutual funds are perhaps the most obvious example of the trend toward the elimination of the middleman in the financial markets. No-load stocks are the next logical step.

## Investing in No-Load Stocks

Now that you know what no-load stocks are and how they've evolved over time, you're no doubt wondering:

- *What companies offer no-load stock programs?*   To learn more about specific no-load stock programs, see the comprehensive reviews of all no-load stocks in Chapter 6.

- *How does an investor incorporate no-load stocks into an investment program?*   Investment strategies using no-load stocks are discussed in Chapter 3.

# 2

# Emerging Trends in the No-Load Stock World

The last 2 years have been extremely dynamic for no-load stocks, both in the number of no-load stocks started as well as in the types of plans implemented by corporations. This chapter examines emerging trends that will have major impacts on no-load stock plans going forward.

## Fees, Fees, Fees

When I first began writing about no-load stocks several years ago, most of the plans charged no fees, thus making them true no-load investments. However, over the last 2 years a variety of fees have been creeping into more and more plans. The fees come primarily in three forms:

- *One-time enrollment fees.*   These fees are usually on the order of $5 or $10 but can reach as high as $20.

- *Annual account administrative fees.*   These fees are usually $3 to $5 per year, although a few plans charge annual administrative fees of $15.

- *Per transaction fees.*   These fees often range from $1 to $10 per investment plus 5 to 10 cents per share purchased.

Why are companies charging fees? One reason is that the fees help defray the costs of operating the plans. Remember that every investor who enrolls in a no-load stock plan becomes an investor that the company must service. Shareholder-servicing fees, which cover such items as corporate annual and quarterly reports, proxy statements, and plan statements, can be as high as $12 to $18 per year. Companies are using fees as a way to offset the increased costs of new shareholders as a result of the plans.

Firms also use fees to help "qualify" investors. Companies don't want small investors who buy a few shares and are never heard from again. By charging fees, companies hope to eliminate all but committed investors.

As you would guess, the emergence of fees has not been a welcomed event as far as investors are concerned. Below are excerpts from letters I received following the announcement of McDonald's no-load stock plan—a plan which has a variety of fees:

> I, for one, think it stinks....I will soon close my McDonald's account. I hope this isn't a trend to weed out us smaller investors.

> Have you seen the new prospectus that McDonald's has out—what they call "MCDirect?" It is terrible! The fees are so high they are really discouraging the young investors!

> I am rather disappointed by McDonald's new "MCDirect Shares" program. I particularly dislike the $5 plus commission fee for an investment made by check. While I have been purchasing shares of McDonald's at $50 per month by check for several years, I am unwilling to commit to making automatic investments of $100 per month via ACH debit.

> I'm sure you will hear the howls from many other investors over the new fees that McDonald's is imposing on its program. As far as I'm concerned, McDonald's is no longer a suitable choice because of the $5 fee on purchases.

Certainly these investors were not pleased with the fees in McDonald's no-load stock plan. However, I think it is important that investors keep an open mind toward fees. For example, let's look at McDonald's plan to see just how onerous the fees really are. First, the company charges an annual administrative fee of $3. Second, the firm charges a one-time enrollment fee of $5. Third, the firm charges a fee of $5 plus 10 cents per share for each purchase via check (the total fee is capped at $10). However, if investors purchase additional shares via automatic debit from their bank account, the transaction fee falls to $1 plus 10 cents per share (total fee capped at $6). So, if you invest $100 every month in McDonald's via automatic debit, your monthly commission will be approximately $1.20. If you invest with a check, your commission charge jumps to $5.20.

How does that compare with buying McDonald's via a broker? It would not be unusual to pay a minimum brokerage fee of $20 to $35 to purchase $100 worth of stock. And for big purchases of McDonald's stock, the plan's fees seem extremely minute. McDonald's allows annual investments of $250,000. If you have deep pockets and make a one-time purchase of McDonald's stock of $25,000, your total commission would be just $10.

I'm a shareholder of McDonald's, so I'm feeling the "bite" of its new fee arrangement. But is the McDonald's plan truly that "fee happy"? I don't think so.

I know that there are plenty of you reading this who disagree with me. You're probably saying, "Sure, the fees are small if you are a big investor. But no-load stocks are geared to smaller investors, and paying $5 for a $100 investment (a 5 percent commission) is a lot." My point is that the plan still provides an attractive alternative to buying stock via the broker. One comment I received from an investor provides an important perspective that should not be lost amidst McDonald's fees. The individual mentioned to me that while he was not exactly pleased with the new McDonald's plan, he would be happy to see Walt Disney—which does not have a direct stock purchase plan—offer a similar plan to investors. And that's my point—better to have a plan that may be imperfect than to have no plan at all. Many companies increasingly believe it is necessary to adopt fees in order to justify offering these plans. For all its imperfections, the McDonald's plan is still one more option that investors can consider.

Now I'm not arguing that fees don't matter. What I'm saying is that at least I would like to have more than one option (i.e., the broker) when buying stock. McDonald's, via its no-load stock plan, is giving me an alternative. I can choose to stay with the broker, take advantage of McDonald's plan, or buy some other no-load stock where the fees are less onerous or nonexistent.

Bottom line: Don't discard a no-load stock plan merely because the firm charges various fees. Weigh the fees against other criteria—the investment quality of the stock, the impact of fees given your investing habits, more attractive alternative no-load stock plans, and so on.

## New Services

Chapter 1 explained a number of services—monthly automatic investment services, IRA options, telephone redemptions, frequent purchases and sells—that are common in no-load stock plans. Fortunately, a number of newer no-load stock plans are adding to these services with some innovative features that should make the plans even more attractive.

For example, Ameritech, a regional Bell company, has an interesting "borrowing" provision in its no-load stock plan. Ameritech's plan participants with $2000 or more of stock can receive a loan against those shares amounting to half the value of the stock. In addition, participants in the plan holding stock worth $4000 or more may receive a line of credit of up to 75 percent of the value of their holdings. The "loan program" provides a way to take advantage of the value of your plan holdings without having to liquidate the shares. Your holdings in the plan will still be eligible for dividend reinvestment, and participants may still make additional cash investments.

Another interesting wrinkle to a no-load stock plan is being offered by U S West. This regional Bell company restructured its stock into two separately traded "target" stocks—U S West Communications Group and U S West Media Group—that track the performance of separate operations of the company. U S West Communications comprises the firm's regulated local telephone operations. U S West Media Group comprises cable television, wireless information services, and directory publishing operations. U S West Communications pays a dividend on its stock; U S West Media Group does not. Both stocks offer no-load stock programs whereby investors may make their initial purchases with a minimum initial investment of just $300 per company. The interesting wrinkle in these no-load stock plans is that holders of U S West Communications can have their dividends reinvested to purchase additional shares of either U S West Communications or U S West Media Group. Given corporate America's penchant for spinning off companies, it would not be surprising to see this feature adopted by more companies over time.

Another new feature that makes it easier for investors to get started is the waiving of the minimum initial investment for investors who agree to invest a lesser amount every month via automatic investment services. For example, Wal-Mart Stores has a minimum initial investment of $250. However, Wal-Mart will waive the minimum if an investor agrees to invest a minimum of just $25 each month via automatic debit from his or her bank account. McDonald's and Ameritech also offer this feature. Both companies have minimum initial investments of $1000. However, they will waive the minimum if an individual agrees to invest a minimum of $100 per month via automatic debit.

As more no-load stock plans are implemented, the pressure will be on companies to differentiate their plans in order to have them stand out among the crowd. Thus, don't be surprised to see such innovations as limit purchase orders, stop-loss orders, cash management accounts, and other features available in no-load stock plans in the next few years.

## Changing of the Guard

The typical no-load stock plan has been implemented traditionally by utilities, banks, and other large, dividend-paying companies.

However, one of the trends emerging in the no-load stock industry is the increase in "atypical" firms offering plans. For example, a number of small companies traded on Nasdaq or the American Stock Exchange are now offering plans. Eastern Co., a maker of locks and security products with annual sales of less than $70 million, offers a no-load stock plan. ABT Building Products, a Nasdaq-traded manufacturer of specialty building products and hardly a household name, offers a no-load stock plan. ABT Building Products is especially unique in that the firm does not pay a dividend—a major departure from the traditional company offering a no-load stock plan. Other firms with no-load stock plans that don't pay dividends include AirTouch Communications and U S West Media Group. The fact that non-dividend-paying companies are now offering no-load stock plans opens the door for literally any publicly traded company to offer a plan—an exciting development for investors who like to focus investments on smaller, growth-oriented companies.

## International Investing

Investing in international mutual funds has been extremely popular in recent years. The benefits of international investing, such as enhanced diversification, have been trumpeted by the mutual-fund industry with great success. One reason mutual funds have become the vehicle of choice for investing overseas is that direct stock investment in foreign countries is still a bit cumbersome. The advent of American Depositary Receipts (ADRs)—securities that trade on the U.S. exchanges and represent ownership in shares of a foreign company—has lowered the barriers of investing in foreign-based companies.

ADRs are issued by U.S. banks against the actual shares of foreign companies held in trust by a correspondent institution overseas. Often, ADRs are not issued on a share-for-share basis. Instead, one ADR may be the equivalent of 5 or 10 ordinary shares of the company.

ADRs have become popular in recent years. One reason is convenience. Investors can buy and sell ADRs just like ordinary shares, eliminating the need for currency translations. Commissions to purchase ADRs are smaller than what would be charged if the securities were purchased on foreign markets.

Although ADRs offer plenty of pluses for investors, there are some things to consider before investing. Currency fluctuations will impact ADRs. When local currencies strengthen versus the dollar, the return on the ADR is boosted. Thus, if you own shares in a foreign company whose stock market is rising and whose national currency is strengthening against the dollar, you're getting a double-powered boost to your portfolio. Conversely, if the dollar is strengthening against the nation's currency of your ADR, returns will suffer.

Until recently, there were no ADRs that offered no-load stock plans. However, that situation has changed. Morgan Guaranty Trust Company, a major provider of services for ADR companies, has started its Shareholder Services Program (SSP). The program allows investors to make initial stock purchases in a number of foreign companies whose ADRs are administered by Morgan Guaranty. Each ADR's no-load stock plan has the same terms. The minimum initial investment is $250. Subsequent investments may be as low as $50 up to $100,000 per year. Fees in the plan include a $15 annual account administrative fee and a per transaction fee of $5 plus 12 cents per share. Purchases are made as often as once a week. Investors can sell their shares directly through the plan with a phone call, and sales are made daily. The following is a list of ADRs participating in the program (each of these companies is reviewed in Chapter 6):

Aegon (Netherlands)

Amway Japan (Japan)

Banco Santander (Spain)

British Airways (United Kingdom)

British Telecommunications (United Kingdom)

Cadbury Schweppes (United Kingdom)

CSR (Australia)

Dassault Systemes (France)

Empresa Nacional de Electricidad (Spain)

Fiat (Italy)

Grand Metropolitan (United Kingdom)

Imperial Chemical Industries (United Kingdom)

National Westminster Bank (United Kingdom)

Nippon Telegraph and Telephone (Japan)

Norsk Hydro (Norway)

Novo-Nordisk (Denmark)

Pacific Dunlop (Australia)

Rank Group (United Kingdom)

Reuters Holdings (United Kingdom)

Sony (Japan)

TDK (Japan)

Telefonos de Mexico S.A. de C.V. Series L (Mexico)

Unilever (Netherlands)

With the continuing development of global economies and the furtherance of free trade with foreign partners via various trade agreements, it makes sense that overseas firms would want to make their shares more readily available to U.S. investors via no-load stock plans. Thus, ADRs offering no-load stock plans could be one of the fastest-growing segments of the no-load stock world over the next 2 years.

Interestingly, many U.S. companies are making it easier for foreign investors to invest directly via their no-load stock plans. Many of these companies have extensive overseas operations and/or plans to expand overseas and thus are courting foreign investors for much the same reasons they want U.S. individual investors. The following companies are among those U.S. firms which permit foreign investors to participate in their no-load stock plans:

AFLAC, Inc.

Ameritech Corp.

Amoco Corp.

Atlantic Energy, Inc.

Atmos Energy Corp.

Barnett Banks, Inc.

Bob Evans Farms, Inc.

CMS Energy Corp.

COMSAT Corp.

Duke Realty Investments, Inc.

Energen Corp.

Exxon Corp.

First USA, Inc.

Hawaiian Electric Industries, Inc.

Home Properties of NY, Inc.

Houston Industries, Inc.

Integon Corp.

Kerr-McGee Corp.

McDonald's Corp.

Morton International, Inc.

NorAm Energy Corp.

Oklahoma Gas & Electric Co.

Oneok, Inc.

Pinnacle West Capital Corp.

Portland General Corp.

Tyson Foods, Inc.

U S West Communications Group

U S West Media Group

Urban Shopping Centers, Inc.

UtiliCorp United, Inc.

WICOR, Inc.

Wisconsin Energy Corp.

WPS Resources Corp.

My guess is that most future no-load stock programs will be available, not only to investors in all 50 states, but also to foreign investors.

## No-Load Stocks in Cyberspace

The advent of the information highway, paved with the likes of CompuServe and America Online, as well as the Internet with its World Wide Web, has made calling a broker obsolete for many investors. Indeed, many services exist today that allow investors to buy stocks and mutual funds via the computer. True, all these electronic-trading services are connected to mutual funds or brokerage firms, which ultimately conduct the transaction. However, the technology is certainly in place to eliminate the brokerage firm, allowing investors to connect directly with companies to buy and sell shares.

Actually, such a system already has been tested. Spring Street Brewing broke new ground in 1995 when it arranged an initial public offering (IPO) for its stock on the Internet. The company posted news of its stock offering on an electronic bulletin board. Interested investors could communicate with Spring Street via the electronic board and receive the full IPO prospectus. The firm raised some $1.5 million from its innovative IPO.

Andrew D. Klein, the chief executive of Spring Street Brewing, says he has taken calls and received letters from numerous companies interested in exploiting the Internet to sell stock directly to investors. "There are an enormous number of small companies that are very excited about the opportunity to use the power of the Internet to reach out to public investors willing and interested to buy development-stage, venture-capital-type equity," Klein said in an article in *Securities Industry Daily*. Klein said that the Internet could also be used by bigger companies. "On IBM's home page, a buyer and seller could meet each other, and then have a trade without having any broker involved." Indeed, at the time of this writing, Klein was in the process of developing an Internet-based system for underwriting and trading stocks.

When I read about Spring Street Brewing, I couldn't help but get excited about the possible marriage of the no-load stock concept with computer technology. Buying stocks directly from companies via the Internet, receiving account statements electronically, logging into your no-load stock account at a particular company via your home computer—all this, and much more, will likely be available soon.

Already companies have taken a number of small steps to get the word out about their no-load stock plans via the Internet. Mobil, for example, has its no-load stock prospectus and enrollment form on the company's web site (http://www.mobil.com). The firm said that in the first 4 months, investors pulled down nearly 1000 "electronic" enrollment forms. While that number may not seem like a lot, it's a start. In fact, it would not be surprising to see that number grow exponentially over time as more investors use the Internet. From Mobil's standpoint, the on-line world offers an extremely cost-effective way (no mailing or printing costs for enrollment materials) to interact with prospective investors. Another on-line service that's worth exploring for no-load stock information is offered by NetStock Direct Corp. (http://www.netstockdirect.com). Finally, my firm's web site (http://www.DRIPInvestor.com) has information on no-load stocks, including an on-line version of the Direct Stock Purchase Plan Clearinghouse. As mentioned in Chapter 1, the clearinghouse provides one-stop shopping for information on a growing number of no-load stock plans. Investors can request prospectuses and enrollment information on many no-load stocks either by calling the clearinghouse's 24-hour toll-free hotline—(800) 774-4117—or by accessing the web site and making requests on-line. In either case, there is no charge to investors for using the clearinghouse. The costs of the clearinghouse are shouldered by participating companies.

## Beyond No-Load Stocks

While the focus of this book is on buying stock directly from companies, the essence of no-load stocks—direct investing—does not have to stop at just stocks. Why can't investors buy bonds directly? Or pre-ferred stock? Or convertibles? Or tax-preferenced investments? This section looks beyond no-load stocks to offer some ideas on how to expand the no-load concept to other investments.

### Follow the Mutual-Fund Lead

For ideas on how to expand the no-load stock concept, the mutual-fund industry, as usual, is an excellent source. No-load stocks have copied a number of the most attractive attributes of no-load mutual funds—IRAs, automatic investment programs, and telephone sales. Why not copy other aspects of the no-load mutual-fund industry?

**Corporate Bonds.**   Billions of dollars are invested in no-load bond funds. Investors buy these funds in the same way as no-load stock funds—directly from the fund group, without a broker and without commissions. If a company can sell its stock directly to individual investors, why can't the firm sell bonds directly as well? The demand from investors certainly seems to be there. A Harris poll of individual investors found that 71 percent of respondents would be "very or somewhat interested" in buying corporate bonds directly from corpo-rations. Another indication of demand for direct purchase of fixed-income investments is the success of the Treasury Direct plan offered by the U.S. Treasury and Bureau of the Public Debt. Individuals who want to buy Treasury bills, bonds, and notes can do so without using a broker by buying Treasury securities directly from Federal Reserve banks and the Bureau of the Public Debt. (For further information about this program, write the Federal Reserve Bank of Richmond, Public Service Department, P.O. Box 27471, Richmond, VA 23261.) If investors' appetite for buying Treasury securities directly is great, it's not a stretch to think that similar demand exists for buying corporate bonds directly.

Firms have danced around the notion of direct bond investing for individual investors. Houston Industries permits participants in its no-load stock plan to reinvest bond interest to purchase additional com-mon shares. However, no firm to my knowledge has yet to sell its cor-porate debt directly. Mechanically, it doesn't seem like it should be that difficult to sell bonds directly. Utilities, with their customer stock pur-chase plans, seem well suited to peddling debt through a customer bond purchase program. Since investors buy utilities primarily for income, selling bonds directly to customers makes sense.

My guess is that no firm wants to be the "pioneer" in offering a no-load bond plan, since legal fees to get a new plan through the SEC could be substantial. Nevertheless, all it takes is one firm—one firm which sees the value in offering a no-load bond program and whose top management is willing to make the sacrifices in time and money to get a program approved. Once one company demonstrates that such a program is possible and, indeed, successful, pressure is placed on other firms, especially those in the same industry, to follow suit.

**Preferred Stock.**   The Vanguard fund family offers a no-load mutual fund that invests primarily in preferred stock. The fund has assets of nearly $300 million. Might some of the same investors in the Vanguard Preferred Stock fund want to invest directly in company preferred stocks?

As was the case with bonds, companies currently dance around the notion of issuing preferred stock directly. Several firms, including Minnesota Power & Light, allow participants in their plans to reinvest dividends on preferred stock to purchase additional common shares. The next step would be for, say, a utility to sell preferred stock directly to customers.

**Convertible Bonds.**   A convertible bond is a debt obligation which allows the owner to tender the bond to the corporation and convert it into a given number of shares of stock. Companies like convertibles, since the bonds carry lower yields than straight corporate bonds. Investors like them because they pay decent yields while providing the ability to convert into common stock. An indication of their appeal is that a number of mutual-fund groups have funds devoted exclusively to convertible securities. Since demand exists for these funds, it stands to reason that there would be demand to purchase convertibles directly from companies.

**Tax-Preferenced Investments.**   Tax-exempt mutual funds, which invest in such tax-preferenced investments as municipal bonds, garner billions of dollars a year. Clearly, investors, especially those in the top tax brackets, like to shield their income from taxes. I'm sure investors in the top tax brackets wouldn't mind saving commissions by buying tax-preferenced investments directly from the issuer.

Municipal bonds are sold by states, counties, cities, and other political bodies. "Munis," as they are often called, come primarily in two flavors—general obligations, which are backed by the full faith and credit of the issuer and repaid from taxes received by the issuing body, and revenue obligations, which are sold to finance a particular project and are repaid from income earned on the project. A third type of municipal bond is an industrial development bond. These are bonds sold to build plants that are then leased to privately owned corporations. Industrial bonds help attract new businesses to a community.

What makes buying municipal bonds directly from the issuing agents so interesting is that, as with utilities and their customer stock purchase plans, municipalities maintain strong ties to their service users. Thus, it's relatively easy for a municipality to publicize a bond offering to its local market. What's in it for the municipality to sell bonds directly? The municipality pockets the fees it otherwise would pay a bond syndicate. Also, by owning bonds, local residents may take more of an interest and be more supportive of the project.

**Government Securities.**   Mutual funds that invest in everything from student loans to FHA mortgages are favorites of investors. I've already discussed how an individual can put together his or her own mutual fund of Treasury securities by buying directly from the Federal Reserve banks. What if other government and quasi-government arms offered direct purchase of their investments? What if you could buy a Ginnie Mae bond directly from the Government National Mortgage Association? Or a Sallie Mae bond from the Student Loan Mortgage Association? It's not as strange as it sounds. Since many government agencies have their own electronic bulletin boards into which individuals can tap via a modem, finding out information about a pending offering—and even placing an order—would be rather simple.

## Conclusion

This chapter is an attempt to bring investors up to date on the latest developments in the no-load stock world. Clearly, no-load stock plans have evolved into much more than merely vehicles to buy the first shares of stock in a particular company. New investor services, not to mention new ways for investors to interact with companies, will shape the no-load stock plans of tomorrow. To be sure, investors will likely foot at least part of the bill for these services. However, when weighing the pros and cons of no-load stock plans, don't forget to consider first and foremost the investment quality of the underlying stock. After all, what ultimately matters most is not whether a company charges fees, has a "loan program" in its plan, or allows investors to buy shares on-line. Rather, how well the stock performs over time will have the most impact on your portfolio and should always be the overriding factor when choosing the no-load stock programs of today and tomorrow.

# 3

# Investment Strategies Using No-Load Stocks

Investors use literally hundreds of different investment strategies with varying degrees of success. There are those investors who buy stocks only when the P-E ratio (the stock's price per share divided by 12-month earnings per share) is below the market average. There are investors who buy only stocks which yield at least 4 percent and have paid higher dividends annually for at least a decade. Some investors buy only stocks that trade below book value. And still other investors buy shares in companies whose earnings have risen in each of the last five quarters and whose price performance is strong relative to its competitors.

## What Makes a Strategy Profitable?

What's the best investment strategy? There really is no one answer to that question, and that's what makes stock investing so interesting and challenging. Any investor, from the novice to the expert, can achieve excellent results using widely different investment approaches.

I would argue, however, that while no single way of investing ensures success, profitable investment strategies, whether investing in mutual funds, stocks, or no-load stocks, often have a number of common elements.

### Focus on the Long Term

Over the years, I have seen thousands of investors' portfolios. Those investors who have achieved the most success have focused on long-term performance. What's long term? Ask three investors, and you'll get three different answers. Some investors believe "long term" is until lunchtime; others believe it's a lifetime. I'm somewhere in between. Long-term investing to me is investing with a time horizon of at least 5 years and more likely 10 to 15 years.

Why do I think long-term investing is so important? A 1991 study by two college professors, P. R. Chandy and William Reichenstein, shows that the biggest risk associated with stock investing is not being in the market at the wrong time, but being out of the market at the right time. The professors looked at monthly market returns from 1926 through 1987. What they found was that if the 50 best monthly returns were eliminated, the S&P 500's 62-year positive return disappears. In other words, if you had chosen the absolutely wrong 50 months to be out of the market but were invested in the market the remaining 93.3 percent of the time, your return would have been nil. The study went on to find that if an investor missed the 26 best monthly stock returns, his or her return would have been roughly equivalent to the return on Treasury bills over the same time frame.

T. Rowe Price, the mutual-fund company, conducted a study examining stock purchases at the exact worst time each year from 1969 to 1989. In the study, $2000 was invested each year in the S&P 500 index at the annual peak, and dividends were reinvested quarterly. The study found that even if an individual invested at the market's high point each year, his or her account value at the end of the 20-year period would have been more than four times his or her cumulative investment during that time.

Ibbotson Associates, a Chicago-based research firm, found that investors who held stocks for 5 years would have lost money in only seven of sixty-plus 5-year periods since 1926, and four of those seven periods encompassed the 1929 crash. And in every 15-year period dating back to 1926, the S&P 500 index produced a positive return.

True, a few investors are quite successful at timing the market and trading stocks. However, those investors, judging from the reams of studies conducted, are the rare exception. (See Figure 3-1 for a look at 25 years of stock market history.)

Another reason a long-term approach is preferable is that it holds down trading costs. Frequent trading generates commissions, which eat away at a portfolio. Frequent trading also creates potential tax liabilities. Every time an investment held outside of a retirement account is sold, a potential tax liability is created. Currently, gains on stocks held for less than a year are taxed as ordinary income. For investors in the highest tax bracket, that means Uncle Sam takes nearly 40 percent of the profit. Gains on investments held for more than a year are taxed

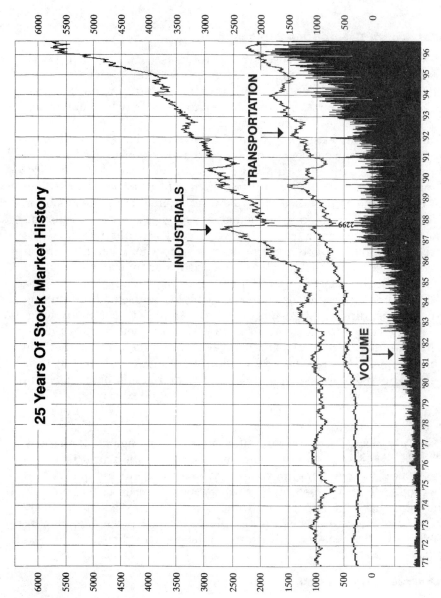

**Figure 3-1.** Twenty-five years of stock market history.

at only 28 percent, which provides an incentive to invest with a time horizon of at least one year. And investors who never sell stock defer taxes indefinitely.

## Maintain a Disciplined Approach

Another common trait of successful investors is a disciplined approach to investing. The director of the T. Rowe Price study previously cited stated, "For those with a long-term investment horizon and the discipline to stay the course, the commitment to invest may be more important than the timing of the investment."

Disciplined investing has a number of facets. First, a disciplined investment approach means adherence to an investment strategy over time. Too often, investors adopt the "investment strategy of the week" approach to their portfolios. This week, they focus on value investing; next week, momentum investing; the week after, high-dividend stocks. Unfortunately, investors who change approaches frequently often do so at exactly the wrong time. When value stocks are out of favor, that's the time to invest if you're a long-term investor, not when they are on every broker's buy list. Sticking to a particular investment strategy provides some ballast to a portfolio during volatile market periods.

Disciplined investing also means staying the course and not shifting gears depending on short-term developments. I've seen many long-term investors become short-term traders when their holdings registered a quick 25 percent gain. Conversely, I've seen traders become long-term investors when a position went against them but they refused to take a loss. If you are a long-term investor, be a long-term investor. If you determine that you want to trade stocks, be a trader. Know what you are going to do with your investments before you invest, and stick to your strategy.

Finally, disciplined investing often means going against the crowd. The stock market is perhaps the only market in the world in which merchandise becomes more sought after the more expensive it becomes. "Buy low, sell high" is everyone's favorite cliché, but few investors have the nerve to buck the crowd and buy when stocks are out of favor. However, being a disciplined investor means stepping up to buy or sell when the herd is going in the opposite direction.

## Diversify—To a Point

Successful investors realize the importance of diversification. However, proper diversification doesn't necessarily mean that you have to own 40 stocks, 10 mutual funds, bonds, real estate, precious metals, coins, baseball cards, and an ostrich farm. In fact, investors may often be too diversified across investments.

Surprisingly, research has shown that a stock portfolio of roughly 15 to 20 issues can provide adequate diversification, especially if this portfolio is combined with other investments, such as corporate bonds, Treasury securities, and foreign investments. More on diversification across investments as well as diversification across time periods is discussed later in the chapter.

## Limit Transaction Costs

A hard fact of investing, but one overlooked by many investors, is that transaction costs erode the value of your investments. If you pay a broker $100 in commissions, that's $100 that will never return a dime to you this year or any year. If you pay a mutual fund 2 percent on your $25,000 holding, that $500 will never make you any money. Herein lies the real impact of transaction costs: Not only do you lose the use of the money in the year you pay for the transaction, but in every year after. Paying $500 in mutual-fund fees in year 1 is bad enough. But the loss isn't just $500—it's $500 plus lost interest in years 2, 3, 4, and so on. What's $500 in 20 years at 8 percent interest per year? $2330. And that's just one year's commission. Pay $500 each year for 20 years at 8 percent, and your total loss is $24,711.

Another way of looking at fees is in terms of annual portfolio performance. For example, let's say your stock portfolio climbs 15 percent before commissions, and your buddy's is up only 13 percent. It seems your portfolio did better, right? But if your trading costs amounted to 3 percent of the value of your portfolio, and your friend's trading costs were less than 1 percent, your friend actually did better for the year.

Low costs are one of the major drivers behind the success of the Vanguard family of mutual funds. Vanguard is the second-largest fund family in the country, with $225 billion under management. Vanguard's mutual funds have achieved impressive performances for the most part. One reason is that Vanguard traditionally has among the lowest fees in the business. This difference is especially significant when comparing the performance of Vanguard's money-market and fixed-income funds against the competition. Vanguard has learned the secret that, if you keep costs down, your investments don't have to work as hard to produce good results.

I'm sure some of you are saying that fees don't matter—it's performance that counts. That's usually the rationale given by investors who've enjoyed 15 to 20 percent annual portfolio gains over the last decade and don't mind paying 1 or 2 percent a year in fees. One prob-

lem with the bull markets of the 1980s and 1990s is that they desensi-
tized investors to the impact of fees. "Who cares about a 2 percent load
fee when I'm earning 20 percent on my money?" "How much can that
3 percent wrap fee or that 2 percent commission charge hurt me when
my portfolio is rising 18 percent per year?" The problem is that the
returns of the last decade have been extremely atypical. It may surprise some of you, but the average annual return on stocks since 1926
is less than 11 percent. And that's before inflation. When you take into
account inflation plus annual trading fees, the return shrinks dramatically. What if the next decade sees below-average market returns? That
1 or 2 percent annual fee could be the difference between a winning
and losing portfolio.

Moral of the story: Successful investors understand the impact of
transaction costs on a portfolio and take that into account when devis-
ing an investment strategy. Smart investors limit trading activity,
watch commissions and fund fees, and invest directly whenever possible. Remember, a portfolio's risk and return are inseparable. The only
way to increase expected returns without taking on more risk is by
lowering transaction costs. Read that statement again. *The only way to
increase expected returns without increasing risk is to cut transaction costs.*

## Investing in No-Load Stocks

If you look again at the four keys to investment success—invest for the
long term, maintain a disciplined approach, diversify, and control
trading costs—it's no wonder that no-load mutual funds have become
so popular. Indeed, no-load funds, via automatic investment services
and low investment minimums, provide an easy way to invest regularly
for long-term gains; funds provide diversification; and no-load funds
provide a relatively low-cost investment alternative. However, for
each of the reasons that mutual funds make sense for investors, no-
load stocks work as well or better.

### Long-Term Investing in No-Load
### Stocks

No-load stocks provide excellent vehicles for long-term investing.
First, investment minimums are quite low in most no-load stocks—
usually $100 to $500 to get started and $100 or less for additional
investments. Thus, it's easy to maintain an investment program over
time, even if your financial situation changes because of a new baby,
college tuition, or even a job layoff.

Second, and perhaps more importantly, investing for the long term means investing in no-load stocks with good potential over the next 5, 10, 20, or even 30 years. Fortunately, a number of no-load stocks are what I consider to be excellent long-term investments. These companies, which include such blue chips as Exxon, McDonald's, and Procter & Gamble, have the strong market positions, healthy finances, and favorable sales and earnings growth prospects that should produce solid capital gains over the long term. For guidance as to the best no-load stocks for long-term investing, refer to the performance ratings which appear with each no-load stock review in Chapter 6.

A final reason which makes long-term investing in no-load stocks easy is that several programs have set up mechanisms to promote long-term investing. One of these mechanisms is the automatic investment service which is offered by several no-load stocks. This system makes monthly investing a "no-brainer," because money is withdrawn automatically from your checking or savings account. Another mechanism is the emergence of IRA options in certain no-load stock programs. IRAs represent the essence of long-term investing, and no-load stocks offering an IRA feature provide an excellent avenue to maintain a long-term investment program.

## Disciplined Investing with No-Load Stocks

One of the keys of disciplined investing is establishing an investment program that is free from the dangerous emotions that can kill portfolio performance. Admittedly, freeing the investment process from emotions is easier said than done, especially when it comes to making rational, disciplined decisions during extremely volatile market periods. One strategy that strips the investment process of emotion is dollar-cost averaging, which was discussed briefly in Chapter 1.

In a nutshell, dollar-cost averaging entails the investment of a fixed amount of money on a regular basis, either every month or perhaps every quarter. For example, let's say you own shares of the Fidelity Magellan fund. Dollar-cost averaging says that you invest the same amount of money every month, perhaps $200. When Fidelity Magellan's net asset value is, say, $79, your $200 investment buys 2.53 fund shares. When the fund's net asset value is, say, $60, your $200 buys 3.33 shares. Herein lies the beauty of dollar-cost averaging. By making the same $200 investment, you buy more shares in the fund when Fidelity Magellan is down and fewer shares when it is up in price.

No-load stocks are excellent vehicles for dollar-cost averaging for much the same reasons as mutual funds are. First, no-load stocks will invest all your money into both whole and fractional shares. That is, all your monthly $200 investment will go toward stock. Being able to invest dollar amounts makes it easier to establish a dollar-cost averaging program. Second, because there are little or no fees when buying no-load stocks, making monthly purchases doesn't cost a fortune in commissions, as it would when buying stocks through a broker. Finally, the automatic investment service provided by several no-load stocks makes it easier to maintain a dollar-cost averaging strategy, since your investments don't depend on your remembering to send a check each month to the company.

Variations of dollar-cost averaging based on the stock's current price, the 52-week price range, dividend yield, or P-E ratio have been developed in an attempt to give more leverage to the strategy. For example, let's say your valuation model indicates that the stock or fund is undervalued. Instead of making your customary $200 investment, you decide to invest $250. Conversely, perhaps your valuation model indicates that the stock is overvalued by 20 percent. You may decide to lower your monthly investment to $150.

Intuitively, modified dollar-cost averaging is appealing, as you leverage your investments on the downside while limiting investments on the upside. However, the problem with such a program is that you are injecting timing into the equation on the basis of your perceptions of value—the very thing that you were trying to avoid with dollar-cost averaging. Perhaps your valuation model is flawed. You may be buying ever-decreasing dollar amounts of a stock in a company that becomes a huge star. Under straight dollar-cost averaging, you would still be protecting yourself from buying too many shares at the top, but at least you'd be buying larger dollar amounts. The other problem with modified dollar-cost averaging based on valuation models is that you are buying greater dollar amounts as the stock drops than you would under basic dollar-cost averaging. While this strategy will pay off when the stock turns around, it is especially disastrous if the stock continues to fall. Still, if you are daring and want to leverage a dollar-cost averaging strategy by applying certain valuation models, you can still do so using no-load stocks.

## Value Averaging

Another form of dollar-cost averaging which can be employed using no-load stocks is value averaging. Value averaging says that, instead of making the same investment each month in a stock or mutual fund, you vary the amount invested so that the value of the portfolio increases by a fixed sum or percentage each interval.

For example, let's say that, instead of investing $500 each month, you want the value of your investment to rise by $500 each month. In month 1, the value of your investment rose $200. Under value averaging, you would add $300 to the investment to achieve your plan of having the investment increase $500 each month. Now, let's say that the investment rose $600 in a given month. Since you want the investment to rise only $500 under value averaging, you would sell $100 worth of the investment. Conversely, let's say the value of the investment dropped $200 in a given month. Since you want the value of the investment to rise $500 each month, you would have to contribute $700 for that month—$200 to offset the loss plus $500 to increase the value of the portfolio.

An easy way to compare value averaging with basic dollar-cost averaging is to think in the following terms:

- With dollar-cost averaging, you know how much you'll invest, but you don't know what the value will be at the end of your investment horizon.

- With value averaging, you know how much your portfolio will be worth at the end of your investment horizon, but you don't know how much it will cost out of your pocket.

When examined in these terms, it's easy to see that value averaging is a more aggressive strategy than dollar-cost averaging. The total amount you invest is not constrained, as it is under dollar-cost averaging. Another negative of value averaging compared with dollar-cost averaging is that the strategy could create more transaction costs, since you may have to sell shares to stay within your parameters. The selling also creates tax consequences. Finally, value averaging requires more monitoring than a basic dollar-cost averaging program.

Still, studies have shown that returns from value averaging compare favorably with dollar-cost averaging. Michael Edleson, who popularized value averaging with his book *Value Averaging: The Safe and Easy Strategy for Higher Investment Returns* (International Publishing), ran 50 computer simulations over a variety of 5-year market periods. More than 90 percent of the time, value averaging outperformed dollar-cost averaging.

Which method is appropriate, especially for investors in no-load stocks? I think it depends to a large extent on how much time you want to spend monitoring your portfolio, how aggressive you want to be (remember that value averaging is more aggressive, since there is no cap on how much you invest to maintain the system), and how much you can afford to invest. If you invest $25 or $50 in a particular no-load stock each month, it's easier to dollar-cost average. However, if you invest $1000 or more a month, value averaging may be more attractive to you.

### Diversify with No-Load Stocks

Diversification in a portfolio is critical to controlling risk while maximizing returns. Most investors think of diversification only in terms of the number of stocks held in a portfolio. However, diversification has more than one face.

I've already talked about two forms of diversification and how they apply to investing in no-load stocks. Long-term investing is really a form of time diversification. The potential risk, as measured in volatility, of stock returns in any given year is relatively high. However, volatility of portfolio returns is considerably less over a longer holding period. The reason is simple: Time can make up for a multitude of portfolio sins. The longer you hold a portfolio, the better your chances that poor performance in a given year is offset by strong gains in subsequent years.

Another way of looking at diversification across time is in the following example: A 75-year-old and a 30-year-old each owns an index mutual fund. An index mutual fund tracks the performance of a popular stock market index, such as the Standard & Poor's 500. Even though both investors have the exact same investment, the 75-year-old faces much greater risk owning the index fund, since the 75-year-old doesn't have much time to make up for a bad year. On the other hand, the 30-year-old who plans to buy and hold the fund for the long term faces much less risk owning the index fund, since chances are that a poor return in one year will be offset by gains in the future. In a nutshell, time diversification works because rates of return across time are not correlated; what the market does this year or next has no bearing on its performance 5 or 10 years from now.

Another form of time diversification that I've already discussed is dollar-cost averaging, or any other investment strategy that requires steady buying over an extended period of time. When investors dollar-cost average, they are spreading their purchases out over time. This diversification of investment ensures that an investor doesn't invest all his or her money at the absolute peak of the market.

A third form of diversification is across securities, which is best described in the familiar maxim "Don't put all your eggs in one basket."

In academic terms, portfolios are affected by two types of risk: *systematic* and *unsystematic*. Systematic risk, also called market risk, is the volatility that affects all securities. Systematic risk cannot be eliminated by diversification. However, unsystematic risk, or firm-specific risk, can. Examples of unsystematic risk include lengthy labor strikes, the death of the CEO, lawsuits, and any other risk which specifically affects a firm's investment potential. This form of risk can be reduced or even eliminated through proper diversification.

The concept of correlation, which is important in time diversification, is also critical in diversification across securities. For example, let's say that an investor has a portfolio consisting solely of 25 electric utilities (by the way, I've seen portfolios like this). Is such a portfolio diversified merely because it holds 25 different companies? Of course not, since the return on each electric utility in the portfolio will likely be closely correlated with every other one. Conversely, a portfolio of 25 stocks spanning a variety of industries could have very little or even no unsystematic risk.

This simple example brings up an important point. Too often, investors associate diversification with holding many stocks—50, 100, 200, or more stocks, just like the mutual funds own.

One reason investors are under the misconception that proper portfolio diversification requires many stocks is that such a view of the investment world is pushed strongly by the mutual-fund industry. A main selling point of mutual funds is the ability for investors to spread a modest investment across hundreds of stocks in a single portfolio. But before you accept what mutual funds tell you about diversification, it's important to look at the facts. Academic studies have shown that in order to have adequate, albeit imperfect, portfolio diversification, investors need to own roughly 15 to 20 stocks in a portfolio. Of course, these stocks must not have a high degree of correlation. After 20 stocks, unsystematic risk in a portfolio is reduced very little by adding additional stocks to the mix.

So why do some mutual funds hold 100 or even 1000 stocks? Because they have to in order to invest their funds. In the case of Fidelity Magellan, the fund's assets of $55 billion are spread over more than 400 stocks, which means that the average investment per stock is a whopping $137 million. If Magellan held only 50 stocks, the average investment per company would be a staggering $1 billion. The bottom line is that Magellan doesn't own over 400 stocks because owning that many enhances portfolio diversification; it owns over 400 stocks because it cannot afford to have any larger sums of money in any one stock. It's hard enough for Magellan to get in or out of a stock without affecting its price when the fund owns $137 million of the stock; it would be impossible if Magellan owned $1 billion of the stock.

Admittedly, the Magellan fund is an extreme example of why mutual funds own a lot of stocks. Still, many mutual funds may have little choice but to own a lot of stocks, and it has nothing to do with proper portfolio diversification.

Perhaps a more telling point is reflected in the diversification approach by billionaire Warren Buffett, arguably the greatest investor of our time. Buffett runs Berkshire Hathaway, a publicly traded company which is basically an investment vehicle for Buffett. How many holdings does Buffett have in his multibillion-dollar investment portfolio? Fewer than 20.

Which brings me to diversification across assets and no-load stocks. I'm sure some of you are saying that the limited number of no-load stocks makes it difficult to achieve proper portfolio diversification. I agree that a portfolio consisting solely of no-load stocks may have limitations in terms of proper diversification. However, that isn't enough to disqualify no-load stocks from consideration. In fact, I think that a selected portfolio of no-load stocks will afford a reasonable level of diversification. Furthermore, when held with bonds, mutual funds, and other investments, no-load stocks can enhance a portfolio's diversification.

## Low-Cost Investing with No-Load Stocks

The fourth key to a successful investment strategy is limiting transaction costs. We've already touched upon the importance of keeping transaction costs low, but it bears repeating. Brokerage commissions, load fees, redemption fees, and wrap fees all come right out of your pocket. You may never actually see these fees. Chances are, you don't even know when you pay them, since—at least in the case of mutual funds—you rarely write a check to cover the fees. They're just taken from your account each year. Nevertheless, their impact on portfolio performance is very real.

Fortunately, no-load stocks offer an excellent way to hold down transaction costs. Indeed, like no-load mutual funds, many no-load stocks do not charge a sales fee on initial and subsequent investments. But no-load stocks go one step further than mutual funds in that annual management or administrative fees are rarely associated with such stocks. It's not uncommon for some no-load mutual funds to charge 1 to 2 percent annually to manage and administer your fund. While those percentages may seem small, over time their impact can be huge.

Let's say that you have $50,000 in a no-load stock portfolio, and another $50,000 in a typical equity mutual fund. And let's say that your no-load stock portfolio and your mutual fund, over a 20-year period, both post an average annual return—before "carrying costs"—

of 11 percent (that's almost the average annual return for stocks since 1926). How much would you have in each portfolio at the end of 20 years? In your no-load stock portfolio, you'd have a little over $403,000.

What about the mutual fund? When you factor in the fund's 1.5 percent annual "carrying cost," the fund's value increases to only $298,000—roughly $105,000 less than the no-load stock portfolio.

So the next time someone asks why you invest in stocks rather than mutual funds, tell him or her you've got your reasons.

About 100,000 of them.

### Focus on Quality

You probably noticed that not one of my four keys to investment success mentioned picking "value" stocks or stocks showing rising earnings momentum. While these and other strategies can be successful, investment philosophies are really a matter of personal preference and investing style. The following is a brief discussion of my approach to investing.

I regard my stock investments as long term—*extremely* long term. Indeed, I look at stock investing with 10- to 15-year time horizons at a minimum. Thus, my portfolio focuses on quality companies that meet the following criteria.

**Longevity.** If I'm investing for 15 years in a company, I need that company to be around for that long. One way for a company to ensure survival is by maintaining a rock-solid balance sheet, with minimal long-term debt and ample cash flow.

**Strong Track Records.** "Past performance is no guarantee of future success," as the mutual-fund sales literature often states. Such is the case with stock performance. A company that has done well in the past may miss industry changes which hurt market share and profits. Nevertheless, I think that, in certain industries, a company's track record is important in evaluating future prospects. How has the company weathered recessions in the past? What competitive moves has the company made to guard market share? What has been its earnings-growth history? Does the firm usually raise its dividend every year? If a firm has a history of making the right decisions, your chances increase that its positive performance will continue into the future.

**Stability/Growth Prospects of the Industry.** If you have read my first book, *Buying Stocks Without a Broker* (McGraw-Hill), you know I'm not a huge fan of most cyclical companies. Sure, there are times when cyclical stocks capture Wall Street's attention and skyrocket. However, since I'm not trying to trade stocks, I prefer to invest in companies which operate in industries that are stable and have discernible long-term growth prospects.

**Defensible Market Positions.** I prefer companies that have defensible market positions because of strong brand names, proprietary products, or competitive advantages, such as being a low-cost producer.

Of course, by following these criteria, I've missed my share of stocks which fell outside these parameters but did extremely well. However, I believe a focus on quality will serve the average investor quite well over the long term. Fortunately, as shown in the reviews in Chapter 6, a number of no-load stocks meet my criteria for investing. That's why my own portfolio includes such no-load stocks as Exxon, McDonald's, Procter & Gamble, and Regions Financial.

## Model Portfolios Using No-Load Stocks

There are a number of ways to incorporate no-load stocks into an investment portfolio. This section examines a variety of ways to be your own mutual-fund manager by building a portfolio using no-load stocks.

### "Starter" Portfolios for the Financially Challenged

Let's face it, for many of us money is so tight that investing in anything except the essentials is almost a laughable concept. Oh sure, if you're real careful with your money, you might end up with an extra $75 or $100 each month. But what can you do with that piddling amount, other than put it in the bank?

How about no-load stocks?

With just $100, you can invest in a couple of quality no-load stocks, and with a little bit more, you can build positions in several issues. The following are "starter" portfolios based on their minimum initial investments.

### $100 Portfolio

Johnson Controls, Inc.

Wisconsin Energy Corp.

*Comments:* Is this portfolio properly diversified? Of course not. Is this an example of putting all your eggs in one basket? Perhaps. But it's a start, and it's tough to overstate the importance of getting started in any investment program. So many times individuals with limited funds never get into the game, since they feel they never have enough to start. That's not the case with no-load stocks. It is better to start with just two companies, build up your holdings, and diversify as your funds grow than never start at all. Furthermore, with just your $100 investment, you're buying into two pretty good companies. Wisconsin Energy is one of the top utilities in the country. Johnson Controls has strong positions in a variety of industries, including temperature control systems for buildings. If you want to maintain a regular investment program in these two issues, it'll cost you just $75 a month.

## $450 Portfolio

Johnson Controls, Inc.

McDonald's Corp.

Procter & Gamble Co.

Wisconsin Energy Corp.

*Comments:* If you have a few more dollars to invest, you can add two more quality no-load stocks to the portfolio. Since a number of no-load stocks have $100 minimums, you have a variety from which to choose. One of my favorites in this price range is McDonald's. McDonald's is the leading restaurant operation in the world. The firm's track record of growth is impressive. McDonald's direct stock purchase plan has a minimum initial investment of $1000. However, the firm will waive the $1000 minimum if an investor agrees to automatic monthly investments of at least $100. Thus, you need only $100 to get started in McDonald's. Procter & Gamble's minimum initial investment is $250. Procter & Gamble has a stable of quality brand names. Both McDonald's and Procter & Gamble have good market positions and favorable long-term growth prospects. The total amount you need to make minimum monthly investments in these four companies is $275.

## $700 Portfolio

Exxon Corp.

Johnson Controls, Inc.

McDonald's Corp.

Procter & Gamble Co.

Wisconsin Energy Corp.

*Comments:* With an additional $250 initial investment, you could add Exxon to your portfolio. Exxon is one of the top no-load stocks in the market. The issue combines worthwhile growth potential with an attractive yield. Exxon also offers a number of appealing options in its no-load stock program, such as an IRA and automatic investment services. How much would you need to invest in all these companies on a monthly basis? Just $325.

## $1200 Portfolio

AirTouch Communications, Inc.

Exxon Corp.

Johnson Controls, Inc.

McDonald's Corp.

Procter & Gamble Co.

Wisconsin Energy Corp.

*Comments:* For investors with slightly deeper pockets, you can add AirTouch Communications, a leading cellular telephone company. The firm has a solid position in a rapidly growing industry. A monthly investment program in all these stocks would cost $425.

## $2050 Portfolio

AirTouch Communications, Inc.

Ameritech Corp.

Exxon Corp.

Home Depot, Inc.

Johnson Controls, Inc.

McDonald's Corp.

Procter & Gamble Co.

Regions Financial Corp.

Wisconsin Energy Corp.

*Comments:* The additions to this portfolio are Ameritech, one of the regional Bell companies resulting from the breakup of AT&T; Regions Financial, a leading regional bank; and Home Depot, one of the leading retailers in the world. Ameritech's program works in the same way as McDonald's plan in that Ameritech will waive the $1000 minimum initial investment if investors agree to invest automatically a minimum of $100 each month. A communications stock provides a nice complement to the rest of the portfolio. Regions Financial has an outstanding record of earnings and dividend growth and gives the portfolio exposure to the financial-services sector. Home Depot has superb long-term growth prospects and is an excellent holding for any investor. What is the minimum amount needed to invest in these nine companies each month? $575.

What I hope these "starter" portfolios show is that it doesn't take $5000 or more to start investing in stocks. With as little as $100, you can begin investing in good, sound stocks. And with a little over $2000, you can create a surprisingly diversified portfolio of nine companies as well as add to the portfolio each month with reasonable amounts of money.

## Blue-Chip Portfolio

Investors who buy only "name" stocks should find no shortage among the list of no-load stocks. The following stocks represent well-known companies that have established dominant positions in their worldwide, national, or regional markets:

AFLAC, Inc.

Ameritech Corp.

Amoco Corp.

Barnett Banks, Inc.

Exxon Corp.

Home Depot, Inc.

McDonald's Corp.

Morton International, Inc.

Procter & Gamble Co.

Regions Financial Corp.

Reuters Holdings PLC

Wal-Mart Stores, Inc.

*Comments:* This portfolio contains names familiar to most investors. Amoco and Exxon are highly regarded oil issues. Procter & Gamble's stable of top brand names is well known to investors and consumers alike. Ameritech is one of the largest telephone companies in the country and provides a way to play the development of the information highway. Barnett Banks and Regions Financial dominate their regional banking markets. AFLAC and Reuters Holdings are leaders in the insurance and information-services industries, respectively. Home Depot and Wal-Mart are leaders in their respective retailing markets. Morton International provides exposure to the salt, specialty chemicals, and automotive airbag markets. This portfolio would be a nice start for an investor who is building a portfolio of 15 to 20 good blue-chip issues. Minimum initial investment: $4175.

## Retirement Portfolio

Given their long-term appeal, no-load stocks make an excellent investment for a long-term, tax-preferenced account such as an IRA. Unfortunately, putting no-load stocks in an IRA is not as easy as it appears.

The key for including no-load stocks in an IRA is to find a custodian to oversee the account. Brokerage firms, except in rare instances, won't provide custodial services for investors who want to hold no-load stocks in a self-directed IRA. The reason is that, in order to participate in a no-load stock program, the shares must be registered in the name of the investor, not in street name. However, brokers will provide custodial services only for accounts in which securities are held in street name. Chances are, if you approach a broker about providing custodial services for an IRA with no-load stocks, he or she will try to convince you to have the stock reregistered in street name. Keep in mind, however, that you'll be unable to participate in a company's no-load stock program if the shares are held in street name.

Also be aware that the broker may try to sell you on his or her firm's "dividend reinvestment plan." A number of brokerage firms have developed what amounts to a synthetic dividend reinvestment plan. These programs allow investors to have their dividends reinvested for little or no fee. The brokerage firms also allow these stocks to be included in IRAs on which they provide custodial services.

When investigating these brokerage-sponsored DRIP plans, it is important to realize that they are different from company-sponsored no-load stock and dividend reinvestment plans. First, in order to participate in the broker's plan, the shares must be held in street name, which automatically eliminates you from participating in the company's no-load stock and dividend reinvestment plans. Furthermore, the ability to buy additional shares directly from the company for little or no commissions is lost. If you want to buy additional shares, you'll pay the brokerage firm's full commission rates of perhaps $30 or more per investment. When a broker tells you that his or her firm offers a plan similar to your no-load stock program and that you can include these investments in an IRA, the plan may not be as attractive as it sounds.

One possible option for a custodian is your bank. Try your local bank's trust department to see if it would be willing to provide custodial services for an IRA holding no-load stocks.

Another option is to contact one of the companies that specializes in providing custodial services. One firm that provides custodial services for IRAs with no-load stocks is First Trust. Contact the firm—at (800) 525-2124—for information and a fee schedule.

Once you've secured a custodial agent, you could include any no-load stock in a retirement portfolio. No-load stocks especially appropriate for a retirement account are Ameritech, Amoco, Exxon, and Regions Financial.

One last way to include no-load stocks in a retirement account is by investing in those firms which offer an IRA option as part of their no-load stock programs:

Ameritech Corp.

Atmos Energy Corp.

Barnett Banks, Inc.

Centerior Energy Corp.

Connecticut Energy Corp.

Connecticut Water Service, Inc.

Exxon Corp.

McDonald's Corp.

Mobil Corp.

Morton International, Inc.

Oklahoma Gas & Electric Co.

Oneok, Inc.

Philadelphia Suburban Corp.

Portland General Corp.

UtiliCorp United, Inc.

## Problems with No-Load Stock Investing

Up to this point, I've addressed mostly the positives of investing in no-load stocks and ways to incorporate no-load stocks into a well-rounded portfolio. However, I would be remiss if I didn't point out some of the shortcomings of no-load stocks as well as provide ways to deal with potential problems.

## Diversification Concerns

One problem that has already been discussed is the limited diversification of a portfolio invested exclusively in no-load stocks. Even though the number of no-load stocks is growing, and there are a variety of ways to build "mini" portfolios from no-load stocks, the fact is that the number of no-load stocks, when compared with the thousands of stocks listed on the exchanges, is rather small. But I think it's important to realize that, for reasons discussed in Chapter 5, the number of no-load stocks will increase dramatically over the next few years. With a larger pool of no-load stocks from which to choose, diversification opportunities will improve.

Also, just because you may not have the funds to invest in 20 or 30 no-load stocks doesn't mean that you cannot incorporate a few into a portfolio consisting of bonds, stocks, and mutual funds in order to enhance diversification. One of the questions I receive all the time is, "Should I invest in stocks or mutual funds?" Quite frankly, I've never figured out how stocks and mutual funds became an either/or issue. I personally own both stocks and mutual funds and am pleased to say that both can exist profitability in a portfolio. While I believe that individual stocks have a number of advantages over mutual funds (these advantages are discussed in depth in Chapter 4), I'm not so provincial that I ignore the benefits of mutual funds. That's why I have both in my investment portfolio. The point I'm trying to make is that, even if you own a number of stocks and mutual funds already, you still may be able to take advantage of all that a no-load stock gives you while enhancing the diversification of your existing portfolio.

Bottom line: No-load stocks can go a long way toward enhancing diversification of an existing portfolio, especially for investors with limited investment capital.

## Speed of Execution on the Buy and Sell Sides

One of the major benefits of investing via a broker is speed of execution. You can buy or sell stock almost instantaneously if you are willing to transact at prevailing market prices. Such execution speed gives you ample control over the price at which you buy or sell stock.

Unfortunately, transaction speed is slowed when investing in no-load stocks. Remember the process for investing in no-load stocks: Call the company for information, wait for the application to arrive, fill out the application, cut a check, and return the forms to the company. This process can take 3 weeks or more from the time you make the phone call to the time your funds are invested by the company. In that time, the stock price could have fluctuated significantly. There's a chance that the stock could have moved higher and out of what you perceive to be a good buying range. The flip side is that the stock could have fallen into an even more desirable buying range. These potential fluctuations also occur with monthly investments. Many no-load stocks buy shares once a month, which means there could be a time lag between when your funds are received and when they're invested.

Because of these lags, no-load stocks are not trading vehicles. However, over the long term, such price fluctuations should wash out and not have a major effect on a portfolio.

The time lags on the buy side also apply to the sell side. Let's say you want to sell your shares. Most no-load stocks will permit you to sell the stock directly through the plans. The advantage of selling through the company is that commissions are usually much cheaper than if you sold through the broker. The downside to selling through the company is that it may take 5 to 10 business days before your transaction is made and additional days for the funds to be remitted to you. This time lag leaves the door open for price fluctuations prior to the execution of your sell order. However, there's always the possibility that the stock will rise and your sale is executed at a higher price than you expected. Again, such fluctuations probably wash out over the long term, but they can make a big difference on a short-term basis.

What are some ways to deal with the time lags when buying and selling no-load stocks? One strategy is to send your money to the company as close as possible to the investment date (investment dates are listed in the plan's prospectus). In this way, your money is not sitting around for weeks without earning interest (companies don't pay interest on funds awaiting investment in their stock purchase plans). Also, you can have a better idea of the price range at which you'll be buying shares if you wait until close to the investment date.

Another way to improve the buy process is by taking advantage of the company's automatic investment services, if such services are available. These services ensure that you won't miss an investment date and help get your funds to the company at the proper time.

A way to deal with the time lag on the sell side is to put yourself in the position to sell stock quickly if need be. All no-load stock plans will issue certificates to investors upon request. Let's say that, over time, you've built up a holding in a particular company of 500 shares. There's nothing stopping you from contacting the company and requesting that it send you certificates representing, say, 200 shares of stock. With certificates in hand, you now have the ability to go to any broker and immediately sell your holdings. Keep in mind that to get quicker transaction speed, you'll probably pay considerably more in commissions. Still, for investors who want greater flexibility, taking possession of certificates representing a portion of your holdings in the plan is definitely a way to speed up the process when you want to sell.

As mentioned in Chapter 1, a number of no-load stocks have been addressing the time-lag issue by improving the buy and sell processes. For example, Exxon and Home Depot make investments on a weekly basis rather than monthly. Wal-Mart and McDonald's will buy shares on a daily basis when practical. McDonald's is also among the growing number of no-load stocks that has taken measures to improve things on the sell side. McDonald's allows its no-load stock investors to sell stock with just a phone call. Look for more no-load stocks to implement procedures which streamline the buy and sell processes.

### Record-Keeping Headaches

One criticism I often hear about direct-purchase plans is that they're a nightmare when it comes to keeping records. These record-keeping headaches usually occur when shares are sold and a cost basis needs to be determined for tax purposes.

Certainly, any investment in which there's frequent buying of small—sometimes fractional—amounts of stock presents challenges for investors. But these challenges aren't necessarily intrinsic to no-load stocks. The challenges exist when using a dollar-cost averaging program or, for that matter, any program that makes regular investments to buy whole and fractional shares. If you buy mutual-fund shares every month, you're faced with the same challenges in determining your cost basis as buying shares in a no-load stock every month.

Fortunately, companies provide an excellent source of information to ease the record-keeping hassle. First, companies send statements after each investment. Second, at the end of the year, companies provide a 1099 form to show the amount of dividends that you received or had reinvested. (Remember: Dividends that are reinvested still count as income for tax purposes.) These statements are similar to the statements you receive from your broker or mutual fund.

Now, let's say you want to sell shares in a no-load stock. It's critical that you have records indicating the price at which you bought the shares. This determines your cost basis, which will determine whether the sell transaction generates a gain or loss. If you've kept good records, you can use the specific-shares method, which means you can pick which shares you are selling and use the appropriate purchase price. If you don't have good records, you'll have to use the first-in, first-out method, which means the cost basis is the purchase price of the first shares purchased. This method will likely lead to bigger taxes, since it's more likely that the first shares purchased have the largest gains. Determining a cost basis with no-load stocks, especially if your investments were buying fractional shares, is extremely difficult without proper records. Companies and their transfer agents may be able to help you piece together your buying history. However, it's always best to keep and record information that the company provides in the regular statements. If this is done, record-keeping headaches are limited.

## Conclusion

This chapter has covered a lot of ground in terms of investing in no-load stocks and pitfalls to avoid. Remember that merely because a company has a no-load stock program doesn't make it a good investment. Investors need to do their homework when considering any investment, including no-load stocks.

# 4

# No-Load Stocks versus No-Load Mutual Funds

To say that mutual funds have become the investment of choice of investors is an understatement. Indeed, money in mutual funds now totals over $3 trillion. Perhaps an even more telling statistic reflecting investors' insatiable appetite for funds is the fact that there are now more mutual funds than stocks listed on the New York and American Stock Exchanges.

A big reason for the growth in mutual funds was the development of the no-load concept. Not only did no-load mutual funds eliminate the sales fee, but they also changed the way investors interact with funds. Load funds are sold by brokers; no-load funds are sold directly, without an intermediary. Making it possible for small investors to deal directly with mutual funds via the mail was a key factor in their popularity.

## Mutual-Fund Myths

The mutual-fund industry has done a masterful job of selling no-load funds as the only investment that makes sense for small investors. However, what the fund industry doesn't tell you is that mutual funds have their own imperfections which need to be considered by investors. Indeed, the attraction of no-load mutual funds—often at the expense of ownership of individual stocks—may not be all it's cracked up to be. This chapter explores common myths surrounding mutual-fund investing and examines aspects of mutual-fund investing relative to investing in no-load stocks.

## Myth 1: Mutual Funds Are Safe Investments

Contrary to what many investors believe, mutual funds, including money-market mutual funds, are not federally insured investments. Even mutual funds sold by banks are not federally insured, although a study by the American Association of Retired Persons showed that less than 20 percent of those surveyed understood that mutual funds bought at a bank are not federally insured. And if you use the word *safe* to mean that mutual funds are immune to sharp downturns, you're wrong as well. Just ask holders of the Steadman Technology and Growth fund, who saw their investments decline 77 percent for the 10-year period through 1995. Or the holders of the Monitrend Gold fund, who saw the value of their holdings drop nearly 63 percent in the 5-year period through 1995. Or the American Heritage fund, which posted a nearly 31 percent decline in 1995. Remember that mutual funds are only as safe as the securities in which they are invested.

**From a No-Load Stock (NLS) Perspective.** *Are mutual funds safer than no-load stocks? I won't attempt to argue that diversification doesn't matter in limiting downside risk, and diversification is easier to achieve with no-load mutual funds than with no-load stocks. Still, investors who choose no-load mutual funds over a portfolio of no-load stocks or stocks in general may be surprised to see just how unsafe these funds are during declining markets.*

## Myth 2: I Can Expect Above-Average Performance from My Mutual-Fund Investment

You can expect above-average performance, but you probably won't get it. In any given year, it's not unusual for at least two-thirds of all mutual funds to underperform the market as measured by the Standard & Poor's (S&P) 500. For the 10-year period ending 1995, only funds specializing in international, science and technology, and health-care equities outperformed the S&P 500. General equity funds in that period posted an average annual gain, including reinvested dividends, of 12.83 percent versus the return on the S&P 500 for the 10-year period of 14.86 percent.

Several factors account for the lackluster performance of most funds. First, many academics argue that the market is so efficient—in other words, stock prices reflect all that is known about a stock and discount information so quickly that finding mispriced stocks is very difficult—that it is extremely difficult to outperform the market on a consistent basis. Many practitioners in the investment field hold that markets are not as efficient as academics believe. Still, you probably won't find too many fund managers who won't acknowledge the difficulty in beating the market.

But even if you believe that it's possible to beat the market regularly, how many mutual-fund managers have the skill to do so? Very few. And the number of mutual-fund managers who truly add value is being spread thinner over an always increasing number of mutual-fund offerings. Indeed, there are now more than 6000 mutual funds. Are all these funds being managed by fund managers who add value? Of course not. Furthermore, performance may be even bleaker over the next decade if the financial markets turn more difficult. After all, it wasn't too hard to show double-digit gains during the last decade when stocks in general were rising at such a rapid rate. However, in an environment where market returns are more in line with historical averages of roughly 11 percent per year for stocks, the disparities between the few effective fund managers and the huge number of mediocre ones will be even more evident.

Also affecting mutual-fund performance is the fact that, in some instances, a mutual fund may have little incentive to go for above-average performance. For example, a fund that accumulates, say, $2 billion in assets may have much more of an incentive to maintain the status quo by focusing on conservative investments. That's because, with $2 billion in assets, fees to the mutual fund could be anywhere from $20 to $40 million every year, even if the fund doesn't make a dime for its shareholders. Thus, preservation of capital rather than aggressive asset appreciation may be the primary objective of the fund manager.

One final factor causing subpar mutual-fund returns has been the huge amount of money flowing into funds in recent years. In many cases, such huge inflows have created problems for fund managers, who are pressured to put these funds to work in stocks. However, especially during periods when stocks are high, huge inflows may force fund managers to abandon investment strategies that were successful when the mutual fund was small or to invest in stocks that may be overpriced and not offering the best upside potential. Some funds have closed their doors to new participants when they perceived fund assets were overwhelming the fund manager's strategy, but the temptation to take in more money because of the annual management fee has caused a number of mutual funds with stellar track records to join the ranks of mediocre performers.

Bottom line: Keep your expectations in check when investing in mutual funds. That way you won't be too disappointed when your fund comes up short.

**From an NLS Perspective.**   *I won't say that no-load stocks, as a group, will outperform no-load mutual funds over time. I will say that investors who ignore no-load stocks for no-load mutual funds may be overlooking some attractive long-term capital-gains performers while relegating their invest-ment funds to subpar performance.*

## Myth 3: My Mutual-Fund Manager Will Protect Me from Bear Markets by Timing the Market

This may be one of the biggest myths of the mutual-fund industry. If you think outperforming the market by picking the best stocks is diffi-cult, it's even more difficult to time the market properly on a sustained basis. Investors who believe their mutual-fund manager can pick stocks *and* time the market need a reality check. First, it's unlikely that your fund manager will successfully call market tops and bottoms over time. But even in the extreme case when a fund manager may have some ability to call market turns, his or her hands may be tied for a variety of reasons. It may be that the fund's policy is to be fully invested at all times, regardless of market conditions. Many mutual funds take the approach that their fund holders invest in order to have exposure to stocks. It's not the job of the fund manager to allocate assets in cash and stocks in order to deal with bear markets. Asset allocation is the job of the fund holder; investing in stocks is the job of the fund manager.

Another reason your fund manager may not try to protect you from a bear market is that it may hurt his or her compensation. Fund man-agers are often paid a base salary and a performance bonus. A manag-er who turns bearish too early and moves money to cash could hurt the fund's performance and, therefore, his or her bonus. The fund manager's risk of turning bearish and being wrong may outweigh the reward of turning bearish and being right.

**From an NLS Perspective.**   *Since you're the "fund manager" with your no-load stocks, you make the decision whether to turn bearish or not. While there's a good chance you'll be wrong if you choose to time the market with your no-load stock investments, at least you're following your own agenda and not the agenda of your fund manager.*

## Myth 4: Investing in No-Load Mutual Funds Is "No-Cost" Investing

Much of the popularity of no-load funds is the fact that they can be bought without a sales fee. However, to say that investing in no-load funds is "no-cost investing" is simply not true. In many cases, the costs of investing in no-load mutual funds are greater than the costs of investing in individual stocks, especially no-load stocks. The problem is that most investors don't realize it, since funds deduct expenses from your holdings—which means you never actually write a check to pay expenses. This may be less obvious, but it is no less painful to portfolio performance.

The sales, or "load," fee is only the tip of the fee iceberg in terms of the costs of investing in mutual funds. I've already discussed fees in Chapter 3, but some of the material bears repeating, given the huge impact that fees have on investment results.

No-load funds have a variety of fees at their disposal to take money from your pockets:

- *Annual management and administrative fees.* These are the fees that all no-load funds charge to manage and administer the assets. Rates differ from one fund group to another and across types of funds. However, it is not uncommon for equity funds, especially those investing in foreign securities, to have annual management fees of well over 1 percent and more than 2 percent in some instances. Administrative fees may include such things as account setup fees, annual account maintenance fees, telephone redemption fees, wire redemption fees, IRA annual maintenance fees, account closeout fees, and check redemption processing fees.

- *12b-1 fees.* A number of no-load mutual funds charge 12b-1 fees to help defray marketing expenses. These fees have become more regulated in recent years, although 12b-1 fees can still consume up to 0.75 percent of your assets.

- *Back-end loads.* Since mutual funds realize that investors don't like up-front load fees, they have become adept at building less conspicuous fees into the system. One such fee is a back-end or redemption fee. Most back-end load fees apply if a fund holder sells shares within 5 years. The fees decline the longer the fund shares are held and usually disappear if the fund is held for longer than 5 or 6 years.

When you add all these fees together, it's quite possible that a no-load mutual fund may be charging you 2 to 3 percent per year in fees.

That translates to annual fees on a $10,000 investment of $200 to $300 per year. That's $200 to $300 on which you'll never earn a dime in the future.

While mutual funds have been dropping "load" fees, management and administrative fees are increasing despite record dollar amounts under management. Logic says that a larger amount of money in a fund would create economies of scale in managing and administering funds, causing fee expense ratios to decline. However, the opposite has occurred. Why? Because fund investors, by and large, have no idea how much they pay in annual fees, thus allowing funds to raise these "hidden" fees aggressively.

Yes, you will avoid a sales fee when investing in no-load mutual funds. But don't believe for a second that investing in no-load mutual funds is truly no-cost investing.

**From an NLS Perspective.**   *How do the costs of investing in no-load stocks compare to the costs of no-load mutual funds? The clear winners are no-load stocks. Not only do you avoid big sales fees on the initial purchase of no-load stocks, but your annual costs to maintain your account are usually zero. All your money works for you each and every year, making no-load stocks the only true "low cost" investing vehicle available to equity investors. Investors should also keep in mind that the cost advantage of no-load stocks versus funds means that a typical no-load mutual fund must outperform a portfolio of no-load stocks by at least 2 percent every year in order to generate the same "after-fee" returns. That gives no-load stocks a big edge in terms of long-term performance.*

## Myth 5: My Portfolio of Mutual Funds Is Properly Diversified

One undeniable advantage mutual funds have over stocks is the ability to diversify with relatively small amounts of money. However, combining different types of mutual funds in a portfolio does not necessarily enhance diversification. Research has shown that fund investments are likely to overlap any time you chase the most popular funds. These funds may be concentrated in similar stock sectors that are relatively "hot" at a particular time. However, when these stocks turn down, it's possible that your portfolio of funds will turn down in unison, which is exactly what you don't want to happen when you diversify.

Another problem with diversification is that investors and fund managers take diversification to extremes. For example, an individual with a large number of general equity mutual funds, whether he or she realizes it, probably is close to "owning the market"—in other words, the portfolio is so diversified and so large that it replicates the entire stock market. At this point, diversification is only costing you money. You'd be better off owning a market-index fund and saving hundreds or even thousands of dollars each year in management fees. The same analysis goes for one stock fund that may own 300 or more individual stocks. At that point, the fund probably is close to being representative of the entire market (or market segment if it's a fund that specializes in, say, small-capitalization stocks), and you'd be better off buying an index fund for that particular market sector and lowering your annual management expenses.

**From an NLS Perspective.**   *Diversifying with no-load stocks is not as complete as diversifying with mutual funds. Still, investors can achieve a reasonable level of diversification with a portfolio of no-load stocks, especially when combined with bonds, money-market instruments, and other investments.*

## Myth 6: My Fund Manager Is an Expert Who Trades Stocks Solely on the Basis of Perceived Value and Appreciation Potential

Assuming any level of expertise about your fund manager may be dangerous to your wealth. The underwhelming performance of most mutual funds suggests that most fund managers do not add value to the investment process. And with talent continually being watered down by the creation of more mutual funds, the "expertise" of fund managers should be questioned even more.

One indication that your fund manager may not be an "expert," at least in investing during bear markets, is the fact that, according to Morningstar, Inc., the mutual-fund research firm, the typical equity fund manager has been running his or her portfolio for roughly 5 years. Given that the equity markets have been trending higher since 1982 without a protracted bear market occurring, very few fund managers have invested during both bear and bull markets. Thus, the jury is still out on how fund managers will perform during the next extended bear market—an issue that ought to be of major concern to mutual-fund investors.

Regarding buy and sell decisions, fund managers presumably buy and sell stocks on the basis of their perceptions of future returns. However, to say that fund managers sell stocks only when they turn negative on their potential may not always be correct. In some cases, fund managers may be forced to sell stock, even though they'd rather not. In fact, a fund manager may know that it's the worst possible time to sell a stock but may have little choice but to do so. Such scenarios usually unfold during sharp market downturns. Keep in mind that most mutual funds are fully or nearly fully invested in securities and hold very small amounts of cash, often 5 percent or less of total fund assets. This cash cushion is used as a source of funds to pay fund holders who redeem shares as well as to pay the fund's operating expenses, such as brokerage costs.

Let's say that a big market drop fuels substantial amounts of liquidations on the part of the fund's investors. The redemptions may exceed the fund's cash cushion. In this instance, the fund manager must raise cash by selling securities. Since large redemptions usually occur during declining markets, fund managers are forced to sell into an environment of falling prices. It's conceivable, indeed likely, that the fund manager would not normally choose to sell the stock at that time. However, the need to raise cash overrides the fund manager's valuation models. In fact, with the stock falling in price, the appropriate investment decision may be to buy more of the stock at its depressed price rather than to sell into the weakness. However, the fund manager's hands are tied because of the need to raise money to pay out to investors who are redeeming shares.

Another reason a mutual-fund manager may sell against his or her better judgment is to get rid of losers and save face with fund holders. Such "window dressing" usually occurs around the end of each quarter, before the quarterly statement is compiled. Let's say IBM undergoes a huge price drop during the quarter, and the fund manager is holding the stock. Even though the stock may be worth holding at its depressed level, the fund manager might sell the shares so he or she doesn't have to include the stock in the fund holders' quarterly report and risk the appearance of looking like a sap.

**From an NLS Perspective.**   *When investing in no-load stocks, you know exactly who the fund manager is (you) and the level of his or her expertise. Furthermore, you have complete freedom in buying and selling stocks. You'll never be forced to sell stocks at potentially the worst possible time in order to raise cash to redeem fund holders.*

## Myth 7: I Know Exactly What Securities My Fund Holds

Knowing what a mutual fund has in its portfolio, if you go solely by the name of the fund, is extremely difficult. A mutual fund can use a certain name if, under normal market conditions, at least 65 percent of its assets are invested in that category. However, that also means that 35 percent of the fund's assets may be invested in totally different instruments carrying perhaps more risk.

But what about the quarterly reports in which the fund lists its holdings? Isn't this a useful source to find out what a fund holds? Perhaps, although this information is often out of date and fairly meaningless. Indeed, in funds with high portfolio turnover, what was reported as a substantial holding in a fund 2 months ago may not even be in the portfolio today.

Well, can't you call the fund manager to find out the fund's top holdings at any given time? The fact is that you'll probably get the runaround if you call your fund to find out its biggest holdings. Most mutual funds are very closemouthed about the securities they hold. Fund managers don't want others—especially big, institutional investors—to know what they are buying or selling, because that information may affect prices.

Finally, even if you know what's in the portfolio, it may not help you to assess the real risk of the fund. Financial derivatives are a popular investment for funds. Derivatives are hybrid securities designed by Wall Street rocket scientists. Many fixed-income funds have been employing derivatives in their portfolios in order to boost returns. The problem is that these newfangled investments have tended to be extremely risky and volatile in the wrong hands. Therefore, even though the overall maturity of your bond fund may be very short— which would make it less susceptible to interest-rate movements—the inclusion of certain financial derivatives may actually make it riskier than you think.

**From an NLS Perspective.**   *You never have to guess what securities are held in your portfolio of no-load stocks. And you can reach the "fund manager" any time you want.*

## Myth 8: Picking No-Load Mutual Funds Is Easier Than Picking Stocks

One of the major selling points of mutual funds is that it's a lot easier to pick a winning fund than a winning stock. All you need to do is look at track records and stick with the top funds. Sounds easy, right?

The reality is that picking mutual funds has become a lot like picking stocks. First, the sheer number of funds presents problems. Sorting through the thousands of mutual funds to find winners is no different than sifting through thousands of stocks to find winners. In fact, it may be more difficult. At least with stocks, you can examine balance sheets and income statements, assess growth prospects of the industry, analyze new products, and so forth. With funds, the only pieces of information to go by are the fund manager—presuming you can even tell who the fund manager is—and the fund's track record. That's it. That's why so much emphasis in picking funds is placed on historical performance.

Muddying the waters are the aggressive promotional campaigns being waged by mutual-fund companies. These ads all focus on fund performance. However, a fund that advertises its impressive 10-year performance may be a fund that has turned in horrible results in the preceding 3-year period. Furthermore, the fund's excellent 10-year track record may have been compiled by a fund manager who is no longer in charge of the fund.

Even if the firm's track record has been impressive, there's no assurance that future results will match past performance. In fact, there's a pretty good chance that this year's top fund will be next year's laggard. John Bogle, the former head of the Vanguard fund group and someone with a vested interest in portraying mutual funds in a positive light, states, "The record is crystal clear that past performance success is rarely the precursor of future success." In his book *Bogle on Mutual Funds* (Irwin Professional Publishing), Bogle shows that a top-20 fund's performance in one year has no systematic relationship to its ranking in the subsequent year. Bogle refers to this as *regressing to the mean*, the powerful tendency for returns on financial assets to regress toward the average following periods of abnormal performance. Bottom line: Picking funds on the basis of historical performance may be no more effective than randomly selecting funds.

So if basing your choice of funds on historical performance is not a surefire way to riches, how are you supposed to pick funds? Mutual-fund companies are spending big bucks on advertising, hoping that you'll pick the fund that fills your mailbox with the most stuff.

In the advertising game, the fund group with the most fund choices usually has the best chance to advertise top performance. That's because the more funds the group has, the more likely one or two of them will be among the top performers. How reliable is mutual-fund advertising in picking future winners? Not very. Still, it's likely that separating the "haves" from the "have nots" in the mutual-fund industry of the future will be which funds have the deepest pockets for advertising or make it easiest to buy their funds.

Another factor that will complicate fund selection is the merger activity which will likely heat up dramatically among mutual funds over the next several years. Low barriers to entry coupled with a slow-down in asset growth will increase competition and lower profit margins in the fund industry. Smaller fund groups will find it difficult to survive and will be acquired, while larger fund groups without a discernible advantage will likely be swallowed up as well. When your fund company is acquired, how will performance of your funds be affected? Should you switch out of the fund? Are new fees being implemented? These issues increase the difficulty of investing in the best mutual funds.

**From an NLS Perspective.** *Picking top-performing no-load stocks, as with no-load mutual funds, is certainly no picnic. However, investors who do their homework have much more information at their disposal to evaluate a no-load stock versus the limited quantitative tools available to analyze mutual funds.*

## Myth 9: It's Easy to Get Out of Mutual Funds at a Moment's Notice

For the most part, mutual funds offer a high degree of liquidity. Investors usually can get in and out of funds relatively quickly and easily. However, that liquidity comes at a price. For example, the ability of investors to redeem shares with a phone call means that funds must maintain at least some cash holdings to cover redemptions. However, such cash may be a drag on results during an up market.

Furthermore, generous selling privileges make trading in and out of funds especially easy. The threat of redemptions may cause a fund manager to invest in the most liquid investments as opposed to investments with better long-term potential but less liquidity. Also, frequent trading of funds generates potentially huge tax liabilities for fund holders—consequences that affect portfolio returns.

And selling mutual funds, under certain circumstances, may not be as instantaneous as you think. Anyone who tried to sell funds during the October 1987 crash knows the potential problems that may occur during dramatic sell-offs. Some of the big mutual-fund families have tested emergency systems in case of huge redemptions. But no one knows for certain how such emergency systems will hold up during a prolonged market meltdown.

**From an NLS Perspective.** *Selling no-load stocks has its own problems in terms of delays. Furthermore, plenty of stock investors couldn't get in* *touch with their brokers to sell stocks during the October 1987 crash. What is encouraging is that several no-load stocks are improving the ability to sell stocks more quickly and cheaply. Also, investors who request shares that accumulate in a no-load stock program in the form of certificates have the ability to sell quickly by taking certificates to the broker of their choice.*

## Myth 10: I Can Depend on the Fund's Directors to Protect My Interests

Corporate governance in mutual funds is similar to corporate governance in publicly traded companies. Just as equity shareholders are owners of the company, fund holders are the owners of the fund. And, just as equity shareholders have a corporate board of directors whose charge it is to protect the interests of stockholders, mutual funds have a board of directors whose job it is to protect fund holders. However, equity investors know all too well that directors are often just a rubber stamp for management, and the same can be said for directors of many mutual funds.

It's the fiduciary responsibility of the directors or trustees to make sure the fund earns acceptable returns while keeping fees reasonable. In addition, directors must satisfy themselves that portfolio managers have the expertise to employ such risky and complicated investments as financial derivatives. Directors are also responsible for making sure that fund management fulfills its responsibility as an active shareholder in terms of corporate governance questions.

How well do directors fulfill their responsibilities? "If you think the boards of ordinary corporations have been lax in doing their job, you should look at the behavior of the boards [of mutual funds]," Warren Buffett was quoted in *Money* magazine. "Almost without exception, they acquiesce in whatever...the sponsors of the funds ask them to do." The lack of accountability is due to a variety of factors:

- Many fund directors pick up nice cash for what amounts to a part-time job. *Money* magazine uncovered several trustees who serve on boards of a number of funds at one fund family, collecting cumulative salaries of well over $100,000 annually. *Money* also found one fund trustee who, by the magazine's estimate, collects roughly $363,000 per year in director's fees. If you were pulling down six figures for a fairly cushy part-time job, would you raise a stink? Probably not.

- Many independent directors have no experience in the mutual-fund field and get their education via fund managers. Thus, their perspectives may be skewed by the agendas of fund management.

Moral of the story: Don't expect fund directors to watch your back. More likely, they're in bed with fund management.

**From an NLS Perspective.** *Because you call the shots when investing in no-load stocks, you don't have outside fund directors consuming profits in the form of bloated salaries.*

## Myth 11: Record Keeping Is Easier with Mutual Funds Than with Individual Stocks

I'm often surprised to hear investors talk about the drudgery of keeping track of their stock investments. This record-keeping issue comes up most often when investors sell stock and have to determine their cost basis of the shares sold for tax purposes.

You also have to keep track each time you buy and sell mutual-fund shares. Yet, for some reason, investors think this is much easier. Some fund families provide assistance in determining the average cost of your fund holdings, a figure that comes in handy at tax time. Still, an investor without record-keeping discipline will have a difficult time keeping track of fund investments. The record-keeping hassle is compounded with funds if you reinvest dividends and are involved in the fund's automatic monthly investment program. By reinvesting dividends and making monthly investments, you increase the number of purchases dramatically, which increases your potential tax headaches when you sell.

**From an NLS Perspective.** *Record keeping is not necessarily a snap with no-load stocks. Frequent purchases of stock through direct-purchase programs make it imperative that you keep the regular statements that are sent by companies. My feeling with record keeping is that, for a disciplined investor, it's no problem. Develop some simple manual or even computer record-keeping system. There are a variety of software packages available to assist you in tracking your stocks. The biggest item to record is the cost basis every time you purchase stocks. If you have gaps in your investment history, you might get help by consulting with the company's transfer agent, who should have a record of your purchase history.*

## Myth 12: Mutual Funds Treat All Shareholders— Both Large and Small— Equally. On the Other Hand, Institutional Investors in Stocks Have Much Lower Commissions and Greater Accessibility to Company Management Than Small Equity Investors

People who think that all mutual funds treat fund holders equally have probably never heard of *hub-and-spoke* funds. Some banks, as well as a few mutual-fund families, offer hub-and-spoke funds for different types of clients. A "hub" is a single portfolio used by the "spoke" funds. Even though each "spoke" is invested in the same "hub" fund—and, therefore, is the exact same portfolio—the spokes may have different fee structures for different groups of investors. For example, one "spoke" may charge investors a 2 percent load fee and 1.5 percent in annual management fees while another spoke may have no load fee and lower annual management expenses. Hub-and-spoke funds discriminate against certain classes of investors who pay more in fees than other investors in the same fund.

**From an NLS Perspective.**   *One of the biggest advantages an institutional stock investor has over a small investor—commission costs as a percentage of total investment—is negated when investing in no-load stocks. In fact, unless a big, institutional investor is willing to have the shares registered in his or her own name as opposed to "street" name, he or she can't even participate in no-load stock programs. Clearly, no-load stocks are one of the very few investment vehicles in which small investors are on equal footing with big investors in terms of investment fees and availability.*

## Myth 13: Investing in Mutual Funds Poses No Particular Tax Considerations That Are Not Common in Any Other Investment

Perhaps the biggest downside to investing in mutual funds is that, in many cases, buying a mutual fund means buying a tax liability.

Investors in funds, especially those with high portfolio turnover, are likely to incur a tax liability at some point in the year. This occurs when the fund manager sells issues that have appreciated, thus turning an "unrealized" gain into a "realized" gain. Since funds with high turnover do a lot of selling, these funds generate a lot of realized gains each year, and these realized gains are distributed to fund holders. When this occurs, current shareholders of the fund incur a tax liability.

The bad part is that *all* fund holders must pay the tax on realized gains that are distributed to them each year. That means that even if you bought the fund in the last month of the year and weren't holding the fund when the big gains were achieved, you still must pay a capital-gains tax on the realized gains if you received them. In fact, even if the value of the fund has dropped since your investment—in other words, you're holding a paper loss in the fund—you still have to pay taxes on realized gains distributed to you.

Even funds with low portfolio turnover cannot escape the tax issue. Mutual funds with low turnover have large unrealized capital gains. While huge unrealized gains are an indication of a fund that has been successful in picking winners, they also pose potential bombshells for new investors in the fund. At some point, the fund will sell these stocks and distribute the "realized" gains to current fund holders. Thus, buying a fund with low turnover may mean that you are also buying a fund with potentially huge "hidden" tax liabilities.

Keep in mind this tax burden is aside from the usual taxes you have to pay on dividend distributions that the fund makes during the year as well as taxes you must pay when selling fund shares at a profit.

The tax issue concerning mutual funds is especially significant at this time given that the markets have been strong for so many years, and a plethora of funds have large unrealized gains. Should fund managers sour on the market and begin selling stock, the size of the distributions of realized gains—and therefore the size of your tax headache—could grow.

Frequent switching among mutual funds within the same fund family and liberal check-writing privileges for some bond funds also present potential tax problems. Being able to switch from one fund to another with just a phone call is a major advertising point of the big fund families. Worried about the stock market? No problem. Just switch your investment from an equity fund to the fund family's money-market fund. Want more exposure to international markets? Simply take some of your money out of that bond fund and invest in the fund family's Pacific Rim fund. The problem, from a tax standpoint, is that every time you switch funds, you incur a tax liability. Indeed, switching money from one fund to another is the same as selling shares in the fund and buying shares in the new fund. If you have a gain on the shares in the fund from which you are switching, you'll have to account for the gain come tax time. Thus, switching privileges are a double-edged sword for investors—more flexibility, but more tax headaches.

And those bond funds that have liberal check-writing features present another tax problem. Investors who write checks against their holdings in a bond fund—not a money-market fund, mind you, but a bond fund—are, in effect, selling fund shares. Any time you sell an investment that is held outside an IRA or other retirement-type account, you incur a potential tax liability. To illustrate the problem, I once knew an investor who was writing checks against his bond fund for everything—groceries, gifts, you name it. You can imagine his shock when he learned that each time he wrote a check against his bond fund, he had to account for the transaction to the IRS.

**From an NLS Perspective.**   *Fund investors are at the mercy of fund managers when it comes to incurring an unwanted tax liability. The fund managers decide when and how much realized gains to distribute. Fund managers also determine what types of stocks to purchase—high-dividend-paying stocks, which create additional tax liabilities for fund holders, or low-dividend-paying stocks. The fact is that fund managers don't necessarily manage the fund with an eye toward tax considerations. That's because mutual funds don't pay taxes—you do. Furthermore, the generous switching and check-writing features have tax consequences as well. However, with no-load stocks, you control your tax destiny. You decide when to realize capital gains. You decide if you want to invest in high-dividend-paying stocks—and incur the tax liability for dividend income—or low-paying or no-paying dividend stocks. You decide when to offset capital gains by taking losses. In short, no-load stock investors control when and how much to pay in taxes on their investments. This control, which is not available in mutual funds, can have huge implications in terms of after-tax investment returns over time.*

## Myth 14: The Mutual-Fund Manager Is Investing in My Best Interests

I've already discussed a few ways that managers may be forced into acting in a way that is contrary to the fund holders' best interests. If fund holders begin redeeming shares en masse, the fund manager may have to sell stocks that he or she would not otherwise sell—stocks whose performance could help fund holders make money—in order to raise money to cash out fleeing investors. In addition, with many managers' compensations based on performance, a manager whose fund is having a good year may have an incentive to protect the fund's gains—and his or her bonus—by moving to cash. However, this move to cash could be detrimental to the best interests of fund holders. Or a fund manager who has underperformed for the year may have an incentive to invest in riskier investments toward the end of the year to try to salvage the fund's performance and his or her bonus.

There are other potential conflicts of interest that arise between fund managers and fund holders.

- *Unethical trading practices.* Mutual-fund managers, especially those of large funds, have incredible power in that their buy and sell decisions can potentially move stocks, at least on a short-term basis. Furthermore, many fund groups encourage their fund managers to trade stocks in order to keep them close to the markets. Being in command of literally billions of dollars and having their own money at risk in the market present the opportunity to trade fund assets to benefit personal accounts. How can this occur? One way is through "front running." *Front running* is the practice whereby a fund manager buys or sells stocks in his or her personal account prior to making the same trades for the mutual fund. For example, the manager of the XYZ fund—a fund with $2 billion in assets— knows that if he buys a lot of a certain small-capitalization, thinly traded stock for the mutual fund, his buying will drive the shares up in price in the short term. Before he buys for the fund, he buys for his own account and is positioned to benefit as the stock rises when he buys for the fund. Front running has been a concern in the brokerage community for years. However, it is only recently that front running became an issue in the mutual-fund industry.

    Another way a fund manager could personally benefit at the expense of fund holders is by accepting money or favors from stock promoters or corporations themselves to purchase or hold a stock in the fund. For example, it's not unusual for fund managers to also be directors of small companies. Through the course of exploring companies, many fund managers become familiar with corporate management. In many cases, the fund managers-directors receive stock options in the companies as payment for being a director.

    By itself, being a fund manager as well as a director of a corporation doesn't necessarily imply a conflict of interest. However, what if the fund manager-director buys the company's stock for the fund, knowing the transaction will drive the price up and make his stock options more valuable? May he be less likely to sell the shares from the portfolio while he's on the board? Wouldn't selling potentially hurt the value of the stock and, therefore, the value of the manager's stock options? And what about insider-trading issues? As a director of the company, the fund manager might be privy to insider knowledge. What if it's bad news? Does he hold the company's stock in the portfolio or sell and break insider-trading rules?

It's also not unusual for fund managers to get a piece of private placements for their own accounts. Private placements of stock often occur before a firm goes public. While there is nothing inherently wrong with a fund manager owning private-placement stock, the opportunity for unethical trading develops once the shares go public. At that point, the fund manager knows that if he or she buys the stock in large quantities for the fund, it will likely increase the value of the shares he or she purchased during the earlier private placement.

Initial public offerings (IPOs) are another area in which potential abuses may occur. Say a fund manager wants a piece of a hot IPO for his personal account. It probably won't hurt his chances of getting some of the offering, as long as the manager agrees to buy some shares of another, not-so-attractive IPO for his mutual fund.

Do mutual-fund groups do anything to prevent abuses from occurring? Most mutual funds have compliance and reporting requirements on the books for their fund managers. In addition, the Investment Company Institute, a fund industry group, has proposed a variety of guidelines for fund managers to follow. How well fund families monitor and enforce these trading restrictions is another story. One can't help but wonder just how vigorously a fund family, especially a small one in which one fund manager oversees most of the fund family's assets, would enforce trading restrictions broken by its star manager.

- *Cross trading within the same fund family.*   *Cross trading* occurs when a money manager shifts securities from one mutual fund to another. Such trades must be reported to fund directors quarterly. In addition, the SEC monitors cross trading that involves illiquid securities to ensure that swaps between funds are made at reasonable prices. When would cross trading abuse occur? Say your fund manager also invests money for institutional investors outside the fund. The fund manager might have an incentive to shift poor-performing investments from favored institutional accounts to the fund, leaving fund holders holding the bag.

- *Soft dollars.*   *Soft dollars* is the practice whereby fund managers run certain trades through brokerage firms in return for certain freebies or premiums. Many brokerage firms provide a variety of computerized research tools for fund managers if they throw enough commissions to the broker. I suppose one could argue that research tools obtained via soft-dollar deals improve the fund manager's ability to pick winners. However, are the soft-dollar "gifts" coming from a brokerage firm whose commission rates may be higher than someone else's? Also, what's stopping the fund manager from personally benefiting from the soft-dollar arrangement by using the premium for his or her own purposes?

**From an NLS Perspective.**  *With no-load stocks, you never have to worry in whose best interests the "manager" is acting.*

## Myth 15: I Can Track the Value of My Mutual Fund Daily in the Newspaper

Given the popularity of mutual funds, most newspapers carry daily net asset values of the funds, but these reported values may be a far cry from the true value of the fund. One reason is that a mutual fund which holds relatively illiquid securities must estimate the value of these securities for net asset value computations. What if the fund's estimates are too high? The value in the newspaper may overstate the fund's true value.

Another problem with daily fund quotes is that there are limited checks and balances to catch most inaccuracies. During one day in 1994, fund giant Fidelity Investments admitted that it had knowingly reported day-old numbers for about 150 funds. *The Wall Street Journal* has reported that some 30 or 40 funds a day confess to the National Association of Securities Dealers (NASD) that they sent in wrong share prices the prior day. An additional 20 or 25 funds simply don't transmit any price at all.

Much of the problem is that, because of the huge number of funds and the growing difficulty of pricing diverse fund investments on a daily basis, mutual-fund companies are finding it difficult to meet the NASD's pricing deadline each day. And the problem is likely to get worse before it gets better because of the continued growth in the number of mutual funds and the increasing complexity of fund investments.

**From an NLS Perspective.**  *Stocks don't suffer from the pricing problems found with mutual funds. Therefore, it's easier for no-load stock investors to track the true value of their holdings on a daily basis.*

## Conclusion

This chapter discusses what I believe are common misconceptions
about mutual funds versus individual stocks, especially no-load
stocks. Do I believe that all mutual-fund managers are guilty of trading for their own accounts at the expense of their fund holders? Of
course not. Nor do I believe that all fund directors are spineless. Nor
that all mutual-fund families care only about asset accumulation at the
expense of performance. Nor that all fund managers use certain brokerage firms because they provide the neatest computer toys.
Nevertheless, history shows that abuses go where the money is, and
there's plenty of money in mutual funds—more than $3 trillion by last
count.

Do mutual funds have a place in a portfolio? Certainly. Mutual
funds provide excellent ways to gain representation in foreign markets, for example. Funds are also good choices for diversifying fixed-
income investments, such as bonds and government securities.
However, to assume that no-load mutual funds are the only game in
town is to overlook the many positive benefits of individual stock
ownership, especially ownership of no-load stocks.

# 5

# Why More No-Load Stocks Are on the Way

An axiom of business is that if demand for a product exists, supply will follow. What the customer wants, the customer eventually gets—if not from one vendor, then from someone else.

This relationship between demand and supply applies to financial products as well. If investors show an interest in new issues, the supply of new issues swells. When investors indicate their interest in tax-exempt and mortgage-backed securities, markets in these instruments explode with offerings. And when investors showed they wanted mutual funds, they got mutual funds—over 6000 of them and still counting.

So what's with no-load stocks?

No-load stocks are a different breed of financial instruments. Strong demand for the product isn't enough. Indeed, for no-load stocks to exist, different constituencies—investors, issuers, transfer agents, regulators, and, to some extent, brokers—all with different agendas must have a meeting of the minds. Building consensus when five distinct factions exist is no easy task.

Fortunately, several developments are under way that will cause the number of no-load stocks to jump dramatically in the years ahead.

This chapter examines the changing dynamics among investors, issuers, regulators, transfer agents, and brokers and how these changes are positively impacting the growth of no-load stocks.

## Demand Side: Individual Investors

One thing is clear—individual investors like no-load stocks. The evidence is overwhelming:

- In the first month of Exxon's no-load stock program, the firm took 50,000 phone calls and opened 25,000 new accounts.

- DQE, which is the holding company for Duquesne Light, opened more than 4000 new accounts in the first year of its no-load stock program. More significantly, 70 percent of those individuals requesting information and an application sent in money.

- In a Harris poll commissioned by the National Association of Investors Corporation, 77 percent of individual investors said that they would be "very or somewhat interested" in programs which would allow them to buy stocks directly from corporations.

- The Direct Stock Purchase Plan Clearinghouse, discussed in Chapters 1 and 2, provides a one-stop source for enrollment information for a growing number of no-load stock plans. In the first 8 months of clearinghouse operations, more than 500,000 enrollment packets were requested by investors on the toll-free hotline number: (800) 774-4117.

- An interesting example of the big investor interest in no-load stocks has to do with an article which ran on the subject in *The Wall Street Journal* in early 1996. At the end of the article, my firm's address was given as a source for a free list of no-load stocks. From that one *Journal* article alone, my company received well over 20,000 written requests for the list of no-load stocks.

- One final piece of evidence indicating investors' attraction to no-load stocks is the success of my first book on direct-purchase plans, *Buying Stocks Without a Broker* (McGraw-Hill). There are over 250,000 copies in print since the book was published at the end of 1991, and demand remains strong.

Clearly, investor demand is not an issue with no-load stocks. Investors, particularly small investors, like no-load stocks and support no-load stock programs when available.

## Supply Side: Corporate Issuers

Corporations hold the key to the supply side, for only corporations can decide to implement no-load stock programs. What potential benefits can a corporation reap from offering a no-load stock? And what are the costs?

## Raising Equity Capital

One of the biggest benefits a no-load stock program provides is a source of cheap equity capital. Firms raise capital in a variety of ways, such as bank loans, bond offerings, and stock offerings. When a company issues new debt or equity, the usual practice is to hire an investment bank to underwrite the offering. The investment bank establishes a syndicate of other investment banks and brokerage houses to help sell the securities to investors. For their work, investment banks receive a cut of the proceeds, usually 3 percent but sometimes up to 7 percent of the deal. For an offering of $50 million, that means the investment bankers' take could be as much as $3 million.

The beauty of a no-load stock program is that the company can bypass the investment banker and go directly to investors to sell stock. Companies have the option of either issuing new shares in their no-load stock program or going into the open market to purchase shares for participants. When firms buy shares on the open market, no new equity capital is created; the firm merely acts as a broker in buying shares for investors. The money that is sent to the company to purchase stock is not kept by the company but instead is used to purchase shares on the open market. When a firm chooses to issue new shares via a no-load stock program, the money sent to the company goes directly into its coffers. This capital can be used to buy equipment, reduce debt, make acquisitions, or fund research. Selling stock in this fashion is attractive to a company because equity can be raised much more cheaply via a no-load stock program than it can via an investment banker.

Philadelphia Suburban offers a good example of a firm's ability to raise funds cheaply through a no-load stock program. Philadelphia Suburban started its no-load stock program for water customers because it needed money for acquisitions and to reduce debt. In 1992 alone, the firm raised more than $24 million through its customer stock purchase plan. (The company has since expanded its no-load stock plan to investors in all 50 states.) The firm estimated its costs to raise these funds at well under 1 percent of the total amount raised—much lower than if the firm had gone through an investment banker.

An indication that no-load stocks are effective tools for raising equity is the large number of electric, water, and natural gas utilities which offer such programs. Utilities need heavy injections of capital in order to operate their businesses. The fact that so many have implemented no-load stock programs indicates the attractiveness of these plans as capital-raising vehicles.

## Mitigating Negative Effects of Stock Issuance

Another attraction of raising equity through no-load stocks is that the negative price effects associated with secondary stock offerings appear to be mitigated.

Studies show that a company's stock price experiences an abnormal negative response to the announcement of new equity offerings. Academics attribute part of this negative response to the existence of what is called *asymmetric information*. When one party with specific information is attempting to transact with another party, to whom that information is not available, the concept of asymmetric information arises. When a company decides to issue new stock in a secondary offering, investors believe that the company has private information and is inclined to overprice the equity offering. Perhaps investors believe that the firm is taking advantage of an overvalued stock or is raising money because its financial situation needs help. Whatever the case, investors, because they are not privy to the information being held by the corporation, may believe the company is issuing stock in its own best interests, a belief that may cause investors to react negatively to the offering.

On the other hand, in a no-load stock program, stock is raised continuously, not in big chunks as is the case in secondary offerings. Since the company is not choosing a specific time to issue stock but is instead offering stock on a continuous basis, the issue of asymmetric information—in effect, investors' concerns over the company's motives for offering stock—is mitigated. Anecdotal evidence seems to bear out the notion that raising money via no-load stock programs does not have a detrimental effect on the company's stock price. Admittedly, more study needs to be done concerning no-load stocks and the impact of dilution and other negatives associated with stock offerings, but early indications are favorable.

## No-Load Programs Save Capital

Not only are no-load stock programs effective for raising capital; they're also good at saving capital. Most investors who participate in a no-load stock program also join the company's dividend reinvestment plan. In dividend reinvestment plans, participants have the company reinvest dividends to buy additional shares of stock. This means that instead of sending dividends to the shareholder, the dividends are kept by the company. These retained dividends are significant over time and can help fund operations.

## Changing Capital-Raising Conditions Favor No-Load Stock Programs

With interest rates extremely low and the stock and bond markets doing well over the last decade, raising capital has been pretty easy for most of corporate America. This relative ease and low cost of raising money via conventional avenues is one reason more companies have not looked seriously at no-load stock programs as equity-raising tools. However, the environment is likely to change over the next decade. In a climate of rising rates and weak financial markets, certain companies will find it much more difficult to raise capital at all, let alone in a cost-effective manner. In this type of environment, the appeal of no-load stock programs as capital-raising vehicles increases dramatically. That's why I believe that the ability of no-load stock programs to raise equity easily and cheaply—and without negatively affecting the stock price—will be one of the major drivers in the growth of these programs over the next decade.

### Cementing Relationships

Another benefit corporations obtain by offering no-load stock programs is to cement relationships with shareholders. Being able to raise equity capital cheaply is not the only reason that the list of no-load stocks is flooded with utility issues. Utility executives understand that, in a regulated industry, it's crucial to have allies among your customers. That's why many utilities offer no-load stock programs to their utility customers. By turning a rate payer into a shareholder, the utility is hopefully turning a potential enemy into an ally, one who may be more receptive when the firm seeks a rate hike.

Utilities also realize that they're in the service business. Service to utility customers takes many forms, such as making sure your lights stay on, responding promptly to your phone call concerning a leaky gas furnace, and even making it easy and convenient for you to buy the utility's stock if interested.

Utilities have another reason for building goodwill with customers via no-load stock programs. As many of you are aware, the days of utilities being monopolies are numbered. The "C" word—competition—is coming to the industry, with many states likely to have "open" utility markets over the next decade. In an environment where customers have a choice, it makes sense for utilities to be building allegiances now with customers in order to have a better chance to retain them when competitors enter the market. Making a current customer a shareholder is an interesting way of perhaps locking up a customer for the long term.

Wisconsin is an excellent example of a state whose electric and natural gas utilities use no-load stock programs as competitive tools. There are no less than six electric and natural gas utilities operating in Wisconsin—Minnesota Power & Light, Wisconsin Energy, WPS Resources, WICOR, Madison Gas & Electric, and Northern States Power—offering residents of the state the ability to buy their initial shares directly.

Another industry in which increased competition is only a matter of time is telephone services. Sweeping telecommunications reform legislation has given way to telecommunications firms competing in all areas of the telephone industry. Indeed, AT&T is positioning itself to become a major player in all local telephone markets, while regional Bell companies are likely to enter long-distance markets. And don't forget cable television companies, which also plan to attack various telecommunications markets. In regional markets where monopoly power is eroding, companies might have a better chance of keeping customers if they can convert customers into shareholders. It's no coincidence that Ameritech and U S West Communications Group are among the telephone companies offering no-load stock plans.

Another industry in which regional markets are being invaded by national competitors is banking. With relaxed interstate banking regulations and increased merger activity, regional banks will find it more difficult to keep customers. Converting current customers into shareholders by offering them no-load stock programs increases the banks' chances. That's probably why banks are well represented among the ranks of no-load stocks.

Companies realize that they not only must compete for retail customers, but also must compete for retail investors. An executive of a natural gas company told me that his interest in direct-purchase programs increases every time he sees a competitor offer a no-load stock program. His point was simple: Why would an investor want to buy the gas company's stock through a broker and pay a hefty commission if he or she could buy a competitor's stock directly from the company and pay little fees? For example, among the oils, Exxon sees Texaco offering a no-load stock program and offers one of its own; Kerr-McGee sees Exxon's and Texaco's programs and launches its own; Mobil sees Kerr-McGee's, Exxon's, and Texaco's programs and starts its own no-load stock plan. Amoco sees its oil competitors offering a plan and jumps on the bandwagon. As more companies from other industries offer no-load programs—and firms within those industries feel increased pressure to compete for retail investors—the number of no-load stock programs could explode.

Improving the corporate image with investors may be another reason to offer a no-load stock program. The evidence is overwhelming that small investors like no-load stock programs. A company that may be suffering from an image problem with investors—perhaps the firm has had a scandal related to executive improprieties or environmental issues—might offer a no-load stock program to repair its image with investors. Exxon started its no-load stock program in March 1992. It's probably no coincidence that the program came just a few years after the *Exxon Valdez* incident. Part of Exxon's motivation may have been to help improve its standing with small investors, who were among the most vocal detractors of the company. Judging from the number of investors who jumped on the no-load stock program, Exxon's strategy seems to have worked.

## Marketing and Competitive Advantage

No-load stocks can be effective marketing tools for companies. In the utilities field, I've already discussed how a no-load stock program might be one way of securing long-term customer loyalty. Certainly in competitive markets, especially in consumer products, a company that turns a consumer into a shareholder has a better chance of having the shareholder buy the firm's products next time he or she goes to the store. McDonald's understands that if you're a shareholder of the company, you're more likely to buy Arch Deluxes than Whoppers. Exxon realizes that the 25,000 new accounts opened in the first month of its no-load stock program represent 25,000 people more predisposed to buying Exxon gasoline and products rather than the competitors'. These 25,000 people also represent a targeted market for the company's credit card.

American Recreation Centers exemplifies a firm using a no-load stock program as a way to compete more effectively. The California-based company operates bowling alleys, primarily in Texas and California. American Recreation understands the synergy between shareholder and consumer as well as anyone. Not only does the firm allow any investor to buy initial shares directly (minimum initial investment is only $100), but the company goes one step further. Those of you who've read my book *Free Lunch on Wall Street* (McGraw-Hill, 1993), are familiar with American Recreation's shareholder perk program. Holders of 500 shares or more are entitled to 5 free games of bowling *per day*—10 if the individual is in a league—at any of the firm's bowling centers. Holders of fewer than 500 shares also receive free games. Making it easy for a person to become a shareholder and then a customer is an excellent way for American Recreation Centers to build goodwill and increase customers in its bowling operations.

## Shareholder Marketing Programs

A study conducted by Capital Analytics Inc. for Automatic Data Processing provides further insight into the potential benefits of shareholder marketing programs. The survey, conducted in March and April of 1993, was based on mail and telephone interviews with 111 investor relations officers and product and brand managers at major firms. Here are some of the more relevant findings of the survey:

- Companies that market to their shareholders as a distinct affinity group are in the minority. One in five of the firms interviewed has a shareholder marketing program. However, a substantial number of firms not running shareholder marketing programs say they are considering them.

- Awareness of shareholder marketing programs is limited. Only one in three companies said it knew of other firms running shareholder marketing programs.

- Companies which have shareholder marketing programs usually have a focus on retail markets, brand-name products, and a greater portion of individual shareholders. These firms are also more likely to encourage participation in direct stock purchase programs.

- Financial firms market to shareholders more actively than any other single industry group.

- Two-thirds of all respondents, irrespective of whether they run shareholder marketing programs, said individual shareholders are a high-priority constituency or have become more important to them over the last 5 years.

- Most shareholder marketing programs concentrate on providing shareholders with product information. Others offer price rebates, product samples, and customer privileges.

- The majority of shareholder marketing programs are implemented as adjuncts to standard shareholder communications rather than stand-alone marketing programs.

- Firms which run shareholder marketing programs largely consider them to be successful. Most also believe the programs are cost-effective, with unit costs the same as or less than those on standard sales.

- Most companies that have considered shareholder marketing programs and rejected them did so because they seemed impractical.

Perhaps the most significant point to come out of the survey was that companies offering shareholder marketing programs felt they were successful in moving product at the same or lower unit costs than other marketing efforts. That's the type of information that usually wakes up marketing and brand managers and could cause companies to take a second look at using a no-load stock program in tandem with a shareholder marketing program.

### Diversifying Shareholder Base

A common complaint from corporate America is the myopic investment vision of institutional investors. If a company fails to meet or exceed earnings estimates each and every quarter, look out. An example of the fierce selling that can hit a stock that disappoints institutional investors occurred in April 1994. At that time, Morton International, the maker of airbags, salt, and specialty chemicals, announced a 46 percent increase in per share profits in the March quarter. How did Wall Street reward the company for its stellar performance? Immediately following the news, the stock fell 10 points—shaving almost $500 million from the company's capitalization in a single day. It seems that the strong earnings were still below some expectations.

Individual investors, on the other hand, are more stable and long-term oriented. Some corporations like small investors because they help stabilize the stock price. For companies which want greater representation of small investors, offering a no-load stock program is an excellent way to draw small investors to its shareholder ranks.

A related benefit is that small investors tend to be more loyal to company management, or at least silent on corporate governance issues. Institutional investors have been rather vociferous in recent years concerning certain corporate matters. A company that is under siege from institutional shareholders might find more friendly faces by boosting the ranks of small investors via a no-load stock program.

Another reason that certain corporations might want to broaden representation among small investors is to help ward off unwanted takeover attempts. A large number of small investors make it more difficult to win proxy battles for control in the case of hostile takeovers.

I'm sure there are some readers who think that there's no way that a contingent of individual investors can take on a hostile suitor with support from institutional investors. Don't tell that to executives of Texaco. The big oil company came under the gun a few years ago when a corporate raider made a run at the company. Texaco's base of individual investors played a critical role in the takeover battle's outcome. This base of small investors helped level the battlefield and was instrumental in Texaco turning back the hostile takeover bid.

Now I'm not saying shareholders were better or worse off because the takeover attempt was put down. The point I'm making is that for corporate executives who believe that their companies are targets of hostile suitors, expanding the number of small investors on the shareholder rolls via no-load stock programs might be the difference between the executives keeping or losing their jobs.

## Continuous Buying Support

Another potential benefit of no-load stock and dividend reinvestment programs is that they facilitate continuous buying activity in the company's stock. Of course, just because a company offers a no-load stock program with wide participation doesn't mean that the buying activity in the program will be enough to keep the stock afloat during a bear market. However, there is something to be said for a stock that has a steady level of buying. Such buying should provide some price support to the shares and contribute to more stable price action.

## Getting Revenge on Wall Street

The relationship between corporate America and Wall Street is like a thirsty man in a desert who stumbles upon a can of warm Tab; he drinks the Tab in order to survive, but he sure wishes something else—anything else—was available.

Corporations and Wall Street have a classic love-hate relationship. Companies rely on investment banks and other Wall Street institutions to assist them in raising capital, hedging financial risk, and completing takeovers and acquisitions. While companies acknowledge their dependence on Wall Street institutions, it doesn't mean they are always happy with the relationship. Indeed, much resentment toward Wall Street exists in corporate America. Corporations, especially those among the hunted, resented the merger and acquisition mania of the 1980s—activity largely driven by Wall Street investment banks. Company CEOs resent having to listen to 20- and 30-year-old pretty faces on Wall Street who've never run anything in their lives telling them how to manage their companies or face the possibility of fending off an unwanted suitor. Companies resent first being told by Wall Street bankers that diversifying via acquisitions was a good idea only to hear the same bankers say only a few years later that restructuring, "deconglomeratizing," was the optimal approach. Companies resent having financial derivatives sold to them by Wall Street pinheads in the name of risk management only to see these investments blow up into red ink when interest rates rise. Company executives resent having to manage their firms from quarter to quarter because not meeting Wall Street's quarterly earnings expectations gets the stock creamed.

Companies also resent the way brokerage firms service "street name" shareholders. All correspondence between companies and individuals who hold shares in street name goes through the broker. Quarterly and annual reports, dividend checks, and proxy statements are all disseminated to street-name accounts via the broker, and brokers charge companies to disseminate this material. The problem is that companies are never sure whether the material ever makes it to street-name accounts. Corporate shareholder services executives have a number of horror stories concerning paying brokers to disseminate quarterly and annual reports or tabulating proxy material only to find out later that the broker overcharged them. One oil executive told me that his firm was charged by a brokerage firm in connection with tabulating proxies. The broker billed on the basis of a 100 percent response by street-name holders to the proxy. However, when the executive reviewed the proxy voting, he saw responses that totaled well below the 100 percent participation for which he was billed. When he balked at paying the bill submitted by the brokerage firm, the broker lowered the bill to reflect the lower participation rate.

For companies seeking revenge on Wall Street institutions, no-load stock programs offer an interesting weapon. With no-load stock programs, companies can raise equity capital without an investment bank while giving small investors the opportunity to buy stock without a broker.

## Costs of No-Load Programs

With all the benefits of no-load stock programs, why aren't more companies offering them? One reason is that no-load stock programs cost money to operate. The ability to invest directly with companies is a big draw for individual investors. The problem is that the company must service these registered investors by preparing and sending them corporate quarterly and annual reports, maintaining their investment records, sending statements and 1099 tax forms, answering phone calls, and providing a host of other service programs to shareholders. To give you an idea of the magnitude of these costs, health-care giant Johnson & Johnson reported that merely by shrinking 18 pages from its 1993 annual report and mailing it third class, the firm saved $400,000.

Shareholder Communications Corp., a shareholder relations consulting firm, surveyed 115 companies on various issues related to the cost of servicing individual investors. The survey indicated that the average cost to service a registered shareholder is nearly $18 per year. The cost breakdown was as follows:

| | |
|---|---|
| Account maintenance | $3.74 |
| Dividend distribution | 1.90 |
| 1099-related costs | 0.34 |
| Annual reports (print and mail) | 5.99 |
| Quarterly reports (per year) | 1.75 |
| Proxy solicitation | 1.82 |
| Other | 2.30 |
| Total | $17.84 per registered investor |

I think it's important to note that one of Shareholder Communications' businesses is to operate odd-lot buyback programs for companies. Thus, it's in Shareholder Communications' best interests to have a survey showing a big cost for servicing investors, because this increases the attractiveness of their services to help companies reduce the number of odd-lot stockholders. Still, companies pay a price for having a large contingent of registered investors in their shareholder ranks. For some companies, the potential cost of servicing the increased number of individual investors as a result of a no-load stock program outweighs the potential benefits.

With that said, there are ways to lower the cost of a no-load stock program. First, with the cost of computing power continuing to fall, administering a no-load stock program in house may not be as expensive as companies think. Furthermore, securities transfer agents, which provide various shareholder record-keeping services for companies, have been aggressively discounting prices in recent years. Therefore, the cost to outsource the administration of a no-load stock program has declined.

Another way companies can defray costs is by charging investors fees to participate in no-load stock programs. (Refer to Chapter 2 for a fuller discussion of fees.) A company that wants a no-load stock program but is afraid of the costs could charge a modest per transaction fee, perhaps $5. This fee would still be well below the investor's cost of buying stock through a broker. An alternative approach would be to set up a fee structure akin to that in the mutual-fund industry. Each year, investors could be charged what would amount to a yearly "management" fee of, say, $5 or $10 to participate in the plan. Again, this fee would be much lower than annual fees associated with other forms of investing, such as mutual funds.

I'm sure most of you don't want fees in no-load stocks. However, if charging a small fee is the difference between a company offering or not offering a plan, I think most investors would agree that paying a fee for the convenience of dealing directly with the company is still far better than paying the high commissions of a broker.

Another way companies can limit the costs of operating no-load stock programs is by providing certain filters to ensure that only committed investors participate. One filter is to keep the minimum initial investment low enough for small investors but high enough to keep out investors who buy only a couple of shares but then never expand their position. Three of the oil issues in the no-load stock group— Exxon, Mobil, and Texaco—require a minimum initial investment of $250; U S West Communications Group, one of the "baby Bells," requires $300. These amounts seem adequately high to discourage "tire kickers" while low enough to permit most small investors to participate. Companies that want a still higher minimum could follow the lead of Advanta, a financial-services concern, which requires $1500 to enroll in the program.

Finally, companies concerned that they'll be stuck with a large number of very small holders who have no intention of increasing their equity holdings could reserve the right to close out accounts where holdings fall below some cutoff point—perhaps 5 or 10 shares—or where accounts have been dormant for more than 1 or 2 years. In this way, the firm won't be stuck with the cost of servicing very small accounts indefinitely.

## Regulatory Hurdles

Overcoming regulatory hurdles is another reason companies are gun-shy about implementing no-load stock programs. Historically, getting a no-load stock program through the regulatory process has been time-consuming. Tom Ross, who runs shareholder relations for DQE, told me it took approximately 8 months to get his company's program approved—and that was one of the quicker approval processes. Fortunately, there have been some key developments over the last 2 years that speed and simplify the regulatory process dramatically. The SEC's role in the growth of no-load stock programs is discussed later in this chapter.

## Other Factors to Consider

A company must consider a number of other factors before implementing a no-load stock program:

- *Does the company need the equity capital?* One of the biggest benefits of a program is to raise equity capital. However, not every company needs additional equity capital. True, a firm can have a no-load stock program that does not issue new shares. Exxon, for example, does not raise new equity with its no-load stock program. Rather, the company goes into the open market to buy shares for participants. Still, a company that doesn't need the capital has one less reason to offer a program.

- *Is the company worried that a no-load stock program would erode a control position in the voting stock?*   Let's say that 55 percent of a company's voting stock is controlled by a single person or voting block. The controlling shareholders might not want to implement a no-load stock program, since their controlling interest could be endangered because of dilution from the issuance of new shares in the program.

- *Can the company exploit the shareholder-consumer relationship?*   A consumer-oriented company, such as McDonald's, has an incentive to expand the number of shareholders via a no-load stock program because shareholders represent potential consumers of the company's products. A maker of heavy construction equipment does not. That's why the list of no-load stocks is dominated by utilities and consumer-related companies.

- *What is the competition doing?*   If a competitor offers a no-load stock program, the company might have to offer one in order to compete effectively for retail investors.

- *What value does the company place on its relationship with Wall Street?* I've had companies tell me that they are reluctant to start no-load stock programs because they are concerned about jeopardizing the relationship with their current investment banker. This might be a consideration for some companies, especially those that raise large amounts of money via secondary offerings and could not duplicate such large-scale capital raising via a no-load stock program.

### Cost-Benefit Analysis

When it's all said and done, a company will offer a no-load stock program only if the benefits outweigh the costs. For many companies, the programs don't make sense. But keep in mind that there are over 10,000 publicly traded companies in the United States. If only 5 percent of those firms initiate no-load stock programs, that's 500 no-load programs. Companies which are naturals to start no-load stock programs because of their businesses and capital needs are highlighted at the end of this chapter.

## Facilitators: Securities Transfer Agents

Securities transfer agents are another key player in the emergence of no-load stock programs. Transfer agents are hired by corporations to handle bookkeeping activities for securities transactions, including dividend reinvestment plans, stock transfers, and other shareholder record-keeping operations. In short, transfer agents make their money servicing a company's registered shareholders.

The securities transfer industry has consolidated over the last decade as a number of firms have sold their transfer operations. Big players are First Chicago Trust of New York, Harris Trust & Savings, American Stock Transfer, Bank of New York, Boston EquiServe, Chase-Mellon Shareholder Services, Key Bank, and Norwest Bank.

The securities transfer business is facing a variety of challenges. First, the business is fairly labor and data processing intensive. Second, clients tend to have limited loyalty and can be extremely sensitive to price. Indeed, a survey of corporations done by *SmartMoney* magazine showed that some firms changed transfer agents three times in a single year. Third, with computing power growing increasingly cheap and software costs declining, many firms have opted to handle transfer operations in house, which provides further pressure on transfer agents.

The upshot is that the securities transfer business is a tough way to make a buck. Competition is keen, profit margins are narrow, and the ability for a corporation to do transfer work in house is increasing.

### Shortened Trade Settlement Period

As if things weren't tough enough, the SEC has added to the transfer agent's woes with its mandate of a "T + 3" settlement period. Since June 1995, security transactions settle 3 days after the trade date. Prior to June 1995, the settlement period was "T + 5"—trades were settled within 5 days after the trade date. The reason that the SEC went to a shortened settlement time is that, in a nutshell, time is risk in the financial markets.

Here's a simple example: Let's say you want to buy 1000 shares of XYZ Corp. at $30 per share. You phone your broker, who executes your trade—1000 shares of XYZ Corp. for $30. At this point, you haven't actually paid for the shares. (There may be some cases when a broker will require prepayment; however, for established customers, payment occurs after the trade is completed.) Prior to June 1995, you had 5 days to pay the broker $30,000 plus commissions. On the second day after the trade is made, XYZ Corp. reports bad earnings and the stock drops 8 points. You've just lost $8000. But you still haven't sent your check to the broker. At this point, you decide to "walk away" from the trade. In other words, you stiff your broker. Now the broker is holding 1000 shares of XYZ Corp. with an $8000 loss.

Admittedly, while brokers are concerned about individual investors stiffing them, a bigger worry is that institutional investors might leave brokers holding the bag on losses of, not $8000, but $800,000 or $8 million. An even bigger concern are financial institutions that, perhaps because of a market crash, become insolvent and can't meet their settlement obligations. That's why many market watchers believe that the T + 3 mandate is just a stopgap measure on the way to a T + 1 settlement period.

You might be wondering what T + 3 has to do with securities transfer agents and no-load stocks. The fact is that, as mentioned, transfer agents make their living by servicing registered stockholders. A T + 3 settlement period, for reasons I'll soon discuss, has reduced the number of registered shareholders dramatically. Therefore, it's in the best interest of transfer agents to promote no-load programs and other direct-purchase programs, because these programs increase the number of registered shareholders. It's probably not an overstatement to say that while individual investors want no-load stocks, transfer agents *need* them.

### Higher Fees for Investors under T + 3

As discussed in Chapter 1, when investors buy stock, the shares are registered either in street name—the name of the brokerage firm—or in their own name. Investors who register shares in their own name go directly onto the company's books as shareholders of record. Transfer agents are usually paid by companies per registered shareholder. The more registered shareholders on a company's books, the more money the transfer agent charges for its services. Securities transfer agents like no-load stock programs because an investor must have the stock registered in his or her name to enroll in these programs. Conversely, securities transfer agents don't like anything that increases the probability that investors will hold stock in street name.

T + 3 is providing plenty of fodder for brokerage firms to push street-name ownership, and that has transfer agents nervous. The more investors who hold shares in street name, the fewer registered shareholders there are on a company's books, and transfer agents need registered shareholders in order to survive.

Individual brokerage firms, as well as the Securities Industry Association (SIA), have been spending big bucks to advertise why street-name ownership is the only way to go in order to ensure on-time settlement. But what if an individual wants to be a registered shareholder? More than likely, he or she will pay dearly for the privilege. Some brokers already charge investors $15 or more to have stock registered in the investor's name and to mail the certificates.

## Direct-Registration System

Securities transfer agents, seeing the possibility of having their market of registered investors decimated by T + 3 and an aggressive advertising program by brokers pushing street-name ownership, have come up with a plan of their own—the direct-registration system (DRS).

DRS is a statement-based form of ownership for all registered investors. The major change is that certificates are not issued automatically to registered shareholders, as they are today. Rather, under DRS, when an individual investor purchases shares and requests to be registered directly, the shares are registered in book-entry form on the books of the company and held in custody by the issuer. Once the shares are registered in book-entry form, a statement is produced by the issuer and sent to the investor. Physical certificates are always available to the investor upon request.

DRS offers many advantages for individual investors:

- Investors have total portability of shares under DRS. Thus, an investor may sell stock through whichever broker he or she prefers.

- Registered investors are not faced with the cost and risk of holding certificates but still have the ability to have physical certificates issued to them if they desire.

- Since shareholders are on the books of the company, quarterly and annual reports as well as dividend checks are sent directly from the company to the shareholders.

From an investor's standpoint, DRS may not seem like much of a change. The only difference is that, instead of receiving stock certificates when becoming a registered shareholder, the investor would receive a statement showing ownership of a certain number of shares. However, from the standpoint of securities transfer agents, DRS is significant because it provides investors with an extremely competitive alternative to street-name ownership that can accommodate a T + 3 or even shorter standard. Full implementation of DRS is scheduled sometime in the second half of 1997.

DRS may be great for transfer agents, but what does it have to do with no-load stocks? It's true that no-load stock programs exist without DRS, and growth of these programs will continue whether or not DRS is fully implemented. Still, because a major aspect of DRS is the ability of investors to buy and sell stock directly through corporations, transfer agents are confident that DRS will help expand the number of no-load stock plans.

### Be Aware of Agendas

Keep in mind that securities transfer agents have a self-serving agenda in seeing that the direct-registration system and more no-load stock programs come into being. I'm sure that individuals within the securities transfer industry feel that it is important to give small investors an alternative to street-name ownership and an easier and cheaper way to buy stocks—items that are accomplished by DRS and no-load stock programs. But transfer agents also realize that DRS and more no-load stock programs mean more registered shareholders. Indeed, I'm sure transfer agents are looking at no-load stock programs as ways to increase their fee-based services.

But even if transfer agents stand to benefit from no-load stock programs, that still doesn't negate the benefits the programs hold for small investors. Fortunately, with transfer agents helping to promote the programs and with the regulatory process dramatically simplified, investors should soon have a greater selection of no-load stocks from which to choose.

## The Opposition: Stockbrokers

An interesting player in the emergence of no-load stocks is the brokerage industry. Obviously, the brokerage community is not interested in seeing no-load stock programs become widely available. No-load stock programs, as well as DRS, forward the notion of direct ownership of stock. Brokers want investors to hold shares in street name so the broker, not the investor, has control over the shares.

### Protecting Its Turf

The brokerage industry's opposition to the development of no-load stocks and DRS is all about protecting its turf. Brokers clearly felt the impact from direct investing in no-load mutual funds and certainly don't want a repeat of history. The unfortunate thing is that investors who are most likely to take advantage of no-load stock programs—by and large, the small investor—aren't the investors brokerage firms want. If brokers did want small investors, they wouldn't be "feeing" them out of the market with inactive account fees, administrative fees, fees for closing accounts, and fees for having certificates sent out.

Such fees, however, have not gone unnoticed even within the brokerage industry. The following is a quote by Benjamin F. Edwards III, chairman of A.G. Edwards & Sons, a major brokerage firm, from *The Wall Street Journal:*

> I worry when we start doing things that help us but don't help the client. In a long bull market, you can charge clients fees, and if every month their account is worth more than the month before, they aren't upset about it. But you get a declining market and every month their accounts are worth less, and they see fees in there, they say, "Why am I paying someone fees to lose my money?"

Of course, talk is cheap, and only time will tell whether the brokerage industry begins to respect the small investor. But if the rapid growth rate in the number of no-load stocks continues, by the time brokers figure out that they need the individual investor, the individual investor may not need them.

## The Gatekeepers: The SEC and State Regulators

Despite the fact that no-load stock programs have been in existence since the early 1980s, the growth of the programs was rather limited prior to 1995. One reason was that it was very difficult for companies to weather the regulatory quagmire to get a program approved by the SEC. Indeed, it was not unusual to take up to 2 years for a company to get its no-load stock program through the SEC. That all changed at the end of 1994.

December 1, 1994, unbeknownst to most investors and members of the business media, may go down as one of the most significant dates in history for individual investors. On that day, the Securities and Exchange Commission issued its long-awaited comments concerning no-load stock programs. In a nutshell, the SEC handed down two rulings which made it much easier for companies to implement plans in a timely fashion.

The first ruling was the issuance of a "no-action letter" to First Chicago Trust of New York pertaining to a "bank-sponsored" no-load stock program. In addition to the no-action letter, the SEC issued a class-action exemption to rule 10b-6 to the Securities Transfer Association. This exemption permits any company which has a "registered" no-load stock program to follow a preapproved model plan.

Further regulatory relief came in September 1995 when all bank transfer agents received permission to market their own "bank-sponsored" no-load stock programs to clients.

As you look at these rulings, it is important to distinguish between a "bank-sponsored" no-load stock plan and a "registered" no-load stock plan. If a firm plans to raise money through its no-load stock program, it must file a registered no-load stock plan. A registered no-load stock plan provides greater flexibility in terms of a firm's ability to advertise the program. A bank-sponsored plan is a plan created by the transfer agent for its clients. The plan is run exclusively by the transfer agent, with little involvement from the company. Bank-sponsored no-load stock programs have various restrictions on their ability to advertise the plans to investors.

The SEC's rulings, in effect, make it much easier and faster for companies to implement plans. Now, with these "model" no-load stock plans already approved at the SEC level, a company can have a plan up and running in as little as 2 or 3 months. Say AT&T, which is one of First Chicago Trust Company of New York's clients, wanted to offer a no-load stock program. The firm could offer its own registered program or choose the "off the shelf" bank plan provided by First Chicago Trust.

With the regulatory approval process much less onerous, it is not surprising that growth of no-load stock plans exploded in 1995 and 1996. My guess is that you will see further regulatory refinements made governing no-load stock programs over the next several years. For example, I would expect to see an increased ability for companies to advertise no-load stock programs.

### Blue-Sky Laws

In order for an investment to be sold to investors in specific states, it must pass each state's blue-sky laws. Thus, no-load stock programs not only must pass scrutiny by federal regulators but must get the go-ahead from state regulators as well. Because of blue-sky laws and the tighter restrictions some states have relative to others, some no-load stock programs are not available to residents in certain states. Fortunately, the trend over the last 2 years has been for companies to blue-sky their stock plans in every state.

### The Next No-Load Stocks?

If more no-load stock programs are on the way, which companies are the most likely to offer new programs? The following firms represent excellent candidates for no-load stock programs:

**Sprint.**  Sprint is currently the third-largest provider of long-distance services. When you're in third place, you have to try harder. One way to expand the potential pool of long-distance users quickly is via a no-load stock program. Sprint spends big bucks each year to market its long-distance services. If Sprint could add, say, 30,000 new investors via a no-load stock program and convert just 10 percent of those to new long-distance customers, the no-load stock program would quickly pay for itself. Also, turning existing telephone customers into shareholders means that a competitor might have a harder time winning the business. Another reason Sprint makes a good candidate is that it is beefing up its presence as a player in the information highway. Expanding its local, long-distance, and telecommunications operations requires large amounts of money—money that could be raised via a no-load stock program. Sprint already has a dividend reinvestment plan. But the ability for investors to make their initial purchases directly could have a major impact on expanding the number of participants.

For much the same reasons, AT&T could benefit from a no-load stock program.

**SBC Communications.**  SBC Communications, formerly Southwestern Bell, is one of the regional Bells. In addition to local telephone service, the firm has extensive cellular operations. The regulatory climate is changing dramatically for SBC Communications. Not only will the firm soon be competing in the long-distance market, but the company will also experience increased competition in its local telephone markets. A shifting regulatory and competitive environment makes relationships with end users even more important. An increasingly competitive environment requires more money for marketing expenses and customer services. A no-load stock program could meet both these needs by solidifying relationships and enhancing customer relations while raising capital in the process. A no-load stock program for other baby Bells would be a natural as well.

**Edison International.**  Edison International is the parent company of Southern California Edison, one of the country's largest electric utilities. A tough regulatory climate, rising competition in its regional markets, and the need for large amounts of capital to fund its operations are items that could be addressed by offering a no-load stock program. With approximately 11 million people living in its service region, Edison International could have a very successful no-load stock program even if it were offered only to residents in its service region. Such a program would not be costly to market—a statement in the customer's monthly utility bill might suffice—and would likely raise large amounts of money.

**Philip Morris Companies.**   Talk about a company with an image problem. Saddam Hussein gets better "PR" than Philip Morris Companies. A no-load stock program would provide a variety of benefits. Perhaps it would be a way to alter or at least tone down the negative image some small investors have toward the company. Exxon wasn't a crowd favorite after its *Exxon Valdez* incident, but plenty of small investors apparently changed their minds toward the company by taking advantage of its no-load stock program in 1992. Philip Morris is still a "name" stock and might see similar success with a no-load stock program. Furthermore, since cigarette companies are relegated pretty much to advertising on sunken ships now that other advertising outlets have been closed off, expanding the list of shareholders through a direct-purchase program for first-time buyers would provide a new market that could be reached via direct mail. And this market could be targeted for the company's nontobacco products as well. Finally, with some institutional investors grumbling about the company's unwillingness to spin off its cigarette operations, it may be time for Philip Morris executives to increase their allies. Individual investors tend to side with management: In a Harris poll of individual investors, 78 percent think that top management should have the most influence on corporate decision making versus just 26 percent who believe institutional investors should have a major influence on the company. Allowing investors to make first-time purchases directly would be a way to add small investors to the shareholder ranks in order to build support for management's decisions.

Another company with an image problem and a strong presence with the consumer is Kmart. A no-load stock program—perhaps one supplemented by various shareholder perks in the form of discounts on products at the stores—makes sense for this laggard retailer.

**America Online.**   America Online is the largest on-line computer service company in the country. A no-load stock program would provide America Online with several benefits. First, given its strong consumer presence, bringing in more shareholders who potentially would use the firm's on-line services is a plus. What may be even more beneficial is how a no-load stock program and America Online might be combined to promote an on-line stock market down the road.

Suffice it to say that America Online has the perfect vehicle for not only getting the word out about a no-load stock program but also effecting transactions. Wouldn't it be convenient to purchase America Online directly from the company using its own on-line service?

Wouldn't it be great to be able to purchase other stocks that way? Isn't America Online in an interesting position to prosper from such a service, given that it's already touching 6 million people? Doesn't its international customer base provide some interesting possibilities for promoting a global on-line stock market? A no-load stock program could be the first step in the development of a national and, indeed, global on-line stock market that could be used by individuals buying from one another as well as directly from companies both in the United States and around the world.

Other companies in the on-line world that offer interesting candidates for no-load stock programs include Netscape Communications, a leading provider of software for the Internet, and Microsoft, the computer giant that is making a big push into the Internet world. Wouldn't it be exciting to be able to load up on your computer Netscape's or Microsoft's software and have an icon on your screen asking if you would like to purchase stock directly from the companies? Indeed, such an icon could be part of any software program marketed by any software supplier. Given the fact that the software industry is rapidly becoming a consumer-products industry, it would make sense for software concerns to want to build lasting relationships with end users by turning those consumers into shareholders.

**Lands' End.**   A no-load stock program for Lands' End would be an excellent way for the company to build its mailing list. Catalog sellers, such as Lands' End, know the value of a name and would be able to exploit the marketing possibilities afforded by a no-load stock program. Other catalog and direct-mail companies in similar positions are The Limited and Spiegel.

**Ben & Jerry's Homemade.**   Ben & Jerry's has a different agenda than a lot of companies. Sure, the company wants to be profitable. But its community involvement and social agendas give it an interesting angle on which to exploit a no-load stock program. Of course, no-load stock participants would be natural targets for marketing and couponing efforts for the company's ice cream. But a no-load stock program would perhaps bring on more supporters of the firm's social agenda. Ben & Jerry's is no stranger to no-load stock programs—the first stock offering of the company was directed exclusively at residents of Vermont. Now that the company has grown nationally in scope, perhaps a no-load stock program available to individuals across the country is in order.

Companies in the competitive consumer products and services markets are good candidates for no-load stock programs because every new participant represents a potential lifetime customer. PepsiCo, Wendy's International, and Coca-Cola would make great no-load stocks, as would firms in the leisure and entertainment markets, such as Carnival cruise lines and hotel and gambling concerns like Promus Hotel and Circus Circus Enterprises. American Express could perhaps build its charge and credit card customer bases via a no-load stock program.

## A Perfect World Revisited

You might recall that in this book's introduction, I talked about a perfect world for small investors, one in which you could go into a McDonald's or Wal-Mart and buy stock along with a hamburger or bug spray. Unfortunately, a perfect world does not exist in many regards. Today, investing for the small investor still means finding a broker and paying a hefty commission.

But change is coming, and the major catalyst for change is the emergence of no-load stock plans. More responsive regulators and growing corporate awareness of the benefits of offering no-load stock plans have fueled dramatic growth in the number of plans in the last 2 years. But if these plans grow like I think they will, we've seen only the tip of the iceberg.

# 6
# Directory of No-Load Stocks

This book has introduced a new and exciting investment opportunity—no-load stocks. The book has examined the birth of no-load stocks, emerging trends in the no-load stock world, investment strategies using no-load stocks, the pros and cons of no-load stocks versus mutual funds, and the reasons more no-load stocks are on the way. While I hope you have found the information interesting and useful, you and I know that the main reason you bought the book is that you want to know what no-load stocks are available and which ones make the best investments. This chapter answers both these questions.

## About the Directory

Each no-load stock review is divided into six sections:

- Company and Stock Information
- Performance Rating
- Performance History
- Plan Specifics
- Corporate Profile
- Investment Advice

### Company and Stock Information

This section is self-explanatory. Each listing features the stock exchange on which the issue trades (NYSE: New York Stock Exchange; ASE: American Stock Exchange; NASDAQ: Nasdaq National Market) and the stock symbol. Also, some listings have two phone numbers—

the number of the corporation and the number of the firm's transfer agent that administers the plan. Obviously, if a toll-free number is given, try that number first to request information and an enrollment packet.

## Performance Rating

A performance rating has been assigned to every no-load stock. The highest rating is five stars (*****), with the lowest rating being one star (*). The ratings are based on a variety of criteria. Financial strength was one of the major determinants. A firm with solid finances has the ability to weather ups and downs in the economy and business cycle. Because no-load investing is investing for the long term, strong finances provide the necessary staying power.

Earnings and dividend records also affected the performance rating. A company with steadily rising profits and dividends usually is a company with a steadily rising stock price over time.

The stability and growth prospects of the company's industry were taken into account. I prefer companies in growth industries, and the ratings reflect this bias.

I realize that many of you may be novice investors, perhaps just now making your first entrée into the stock market. I tried to take that into account when assigning ratings. Thus, if I err in a rating, my guess is that it will be on the conservative side. Indeed, I gave very few five-star ratings.

## Performance History

This section will probably be the most closely read—and the most misinterpreted. The performance histories, which are given for every stock on which data were available, show what a $1000 investment at the end of 1985 would have become 10 years later. The returns include reinvested dividends. (I'd like to thank Standard & Poor's for the use of its total-return data.)

For comparison purposes, the Standard & Poor's 500, with reinvested dividends, returned 300 percent during the time period.

Now, before all of you go out and buy a no-load stock that posted huge gains over the last decade, it's important to remember that past performance is no guarantee of future results. As already discussed in these pages, the best performers one year are not necessarily the best performers the next.

Finally, the returns of stocks in general were extremely atypical during the 10-year period. Such strong market returns are not likely to be duplicated in the next 10 years, a trend that will have a dampening effect on most individual stock's performance.

I guess what I'm trying to say is that, while I think performance histories provide important information, they should not be used for divining the future or relied on exclusively for stock selection.

## Plan Specifics

The plan specifics provide in detail various features of the company's no-load stock and dividend reinvestment plan (DRIP). Remember that once you enroll in the no-load stock program, you can take advantage of the various features of the company's dividend reinvestment plan, such as optional cash payments (OCP) and automatic investment services.

One feature to which readers should pay special attention is the eligibility requirement for each plan. In some cases, companies may place certain restrictions on who can participate in the no-load stock program. These restrictions, if any, are addressed in the section on plan specifics. *Please read eligibility requirements carefully.*

Keep in mind that, even if you don't qualify for a firm's no-load stock program, you can still enroll in its dividend reinvestment plan once you have become a shareholder of record. For example, Duke Power is a five-star electric utility. Unfortunately, only residents of the states of North and South Carolina may make initial purchases directly. However, any other investor who acquires one share of stock and has the share registered in his or her name—not street name—is eligible to join the company's dividend reinvestment plan and make optional cash payments. If you see a company that interests you but you don't qualify to buy your initial shares directly, contact the company to determine how many shares you need to own in order to join the DRIP (in most cases it will be just one share). Below are explanations of some common no-load stock and DRIP features:

- Some plans permit partial dividend reinvestment. This option allows participants to receive dividends on part of the shares held in the plan while reinvesting dividends on the remainder.

- Optional cash payments (OCP) are the voluntary payments that participants may make directly into the plans in order to purchase additional shares. For example, Exxon allows OCPs of a minimum of $50 to a maximum of $100,000 per year. Each listing indicates how frequently OCPs are invested by the company.

- In many cases, companies charge no fees for purchases made in the plans, although most charge a nominal fee when selling shares from the plans. Fees are addressed in the plan specifics.

- A growing number of no-load stocks have IRA options in their plans. This option allows participants to make investments directly with the company, and these investments are put into an IRA that is administered by the company or its agent. If a firm offers an IRA option, it will be listed in the plan specifics.

- Automatic investment services are becoming a popular feature of no-load stock and DRIP programs. These services provide a mechanism for investors to make optional cash payments automatically by having money taken each month from a bank account. If a company offers automatic investment services, it will be listed in the plan specifics.

- A few companies with no-load stocks provide a little something extra for investors by buying stock at a discount to the market price. This discount is usually applied only to shares purchased with reinvested dividends. Companies with discounts are earmarked in the plan specifics.

- If a company has an outside agent administering its plan, the agent's name and phone number are given.

- Each listing provides the monthly dividend payment dates for the stock. While most no-load stock investors reinvest their dividends, some investors like to receive at least some of their dividends in cash and thus may find this listing particularly helpful in generating income from their no-load stock investments. The information is especially useful for building a portfolio in which dividends are paid every month.

## Corporate Profile

This section provides a snapshot of the company's business and operating environments.

## Investment Advice

This section gives my specific opinion and advice on the stock. Am I always going to be right? Of course not. But at least I'm objective.

## An Important Reminder

I said this at the beginning of the book, but it bears repeating. Companies frequently change features of their no-load stock and dividend reinvestment plans. Fortunately, all companies offering no-load stock and DRIP plans must prepare a prospectus explaining all details of the program. Always request a copy of a plan prospectus—and make sure you read it when you get it—before investing.

ABT Building Products Corp.
NASDAQ: ABTC
One Neenah Center, Suite 600
Neenah, WI 54956-3070
(414) 751-8611 • (800) 774-4117

ABTCO

Performance Rating: * * *

## Performance History: Not available.

## Plan Specifics

- Initial purchase is available to investors in all 50 states ($250 minimum initial investment).
- OCP: $50 to $100,000 per year.
- No discount.
- OCP is invested weekly.
- Automatic investment services are available.
- Purchasing fees are $1.50 plus 8 cents per share when purchasing with automatic monthly debit; $5 plus 8 cents per share when purchasing via check. Selling costs are $10 plus 8 cents per share.
- Plan Administrator: Harris Trust (800) 286-9178.
- The company does not pay a dividend.

## Corporate Profile

ABT Building Products manufactures specialty building products used in the remodeling, repair, and new residential construction markets.

## Investment Advice

ABT Building Products is an interesting issue among no-load stocks. The firm does not pay a dividend, which is unusual but likely to become more common among the ranks of no-load stocks. In terms of investment quality, it's hard to get too excited about companies whose business is tied so closely to interest rates. Still, the firm's decent track record over the years and relatively small size — annual sales are less than $300 million — should afford the firm reasonable growth prospects. The other factor in the company's favor is its lack of attention on Wall Street. The stock is not widely followed, which could be a plus should ABT continue to post decent results and investors start to notice these shares.

**ADVANTA**

Advanta Corp.
NASDAQ: ADVNB
Welsh and McKean Rds.
Spring House, PA 19477
(215) 444-5335 • (800) 774-4117

Performance Rating: * * * *

## Performance History: Not available.

## Plan Specifics

- Initial purchase is available to investors in all 50 states ($1,500 minimum initial investment).
- Partial dividend reinvestment is available.
- Up to 5 percent discount on reinvested dividends and OCPs.
- OCP: $50 to $3,000 per month. Investors wanting to invest more than $3,000 per month may call (800) 299-3150 for a waiver.
- OCP is invested monthly.
- There are no purchasing fees. Selling fees are $15 plus 12 cents per share.
- Investors must own at least 25 shares to reinvest dividends.
- Plan Administrator: ChaseMellon Shareholder Investment Service (800) 225-5923.
- Dividends are paid March, June, September, and December.

## Corporate Profile

Advanta is a major marketer of consumer financial services. The bulk of revenues are generated from the issuance of MasterCard and Visa credit cards. Products are sold via direct mail and telemarketing.

## Investment Advice

Advanta has been an excellent performer for investors since bottoming at approximately $3 per share in 1991. It is unlikely the firm will be able to post the type of returns that characterized the stock in the first half of the '90s. Still, Advanta has carved out a nice niche in its markets and should continue to perform at least as well as the general market going forward.

Aegon N.V.
  NYSE: AEG
c/o Morgan Guaranty Trust Co., PO Box 9073
Boston, MA 02205
(800) 749-1687 • (800) 774-4117

Performance Rating: * * * *

## Performance History: Not available.

## Plan Specifics

- Initial purchase is available to investors in all states except Texas, Oregon, and North Dakota ($250 minimum initial investment).
- Partial dividend reinvestment is available.
- No discount.
- OCP: $50 to $100,000 per year.
- OCP is invested weekly.
- Automatic investment services are available.
- Annual administration fee of $15 must accompany initial stock purchase and may be paid with a credit card.
- Purchasing and selling fees include a transaction fee of $5, plus brokerage commissions of approximately 12 cents per share.
- Investors will be assessed a brokerage commission of 12 cents per share to reinvest dividends.
- Shares may be sold via the telephone.
- Plan Administrator: Morgan Guaranty Trust Co. (800) 749-1687.
- Dividends are paid in June and October.

## Corporate Profile

Aegon N.V., based in the Netherlands, is a major international insurance company. The firm's Aegon USA unit is the largest foreign-owned insurance company operating in the U.S. The firm's primary product line includes life insurance and various financial services.

## Investment Advice

Aegon's impressive performance of recent years leaves these shares vulnerable during market dips. Also, interest-rate and currency fluctuations could impact these shares. Nevertheless, the firm's track record ranks with the best of U.S. insurers. Investors should have some representation overseas, and these shares are an acceptable holding.

AFLAC, Inc.
NYSE: AFL
1932 Wynnton Rd.
Columbus, GA 31999
(800) 227-4756 • (706) 323-3431

| Performance Rating: * * * * |

## Performance History

- $1,000 invested on 12/31/85 was worth $6,080 on 12/31/95 — a 508 percent increase in 10 years.

## Plan Specifics

- Initial purchase is available to investors in all 50 states ($750 minimum initial investment).
- Partial dividend reinvestment is available.
- No discount.
- OCP: $50 to $120,000 per year.
- OCP is invested twice monthly.
- There are no purchasing fees. Selling costs are modest brokerage commissions.
- Automatic investment services are available.
- Dividends are paid March, June, September, and December.

## Corporate Profile

AFLAC is a leading seller of supplemental cancer insurance policies. Business in Japan brings in the lion's share of revenues (roughly 80 percent). This niche business has served the firm well over the years, with per-share profits rising every year but one since 1981.

## Investment Advice

AFLAC should do at least as well as the overall market. Steady earnings and dividend growth should fuel investor support. The company's performance, despite sluggishness in the Japanese economy in recent years, speaks well of the firm's ability to prosper even during less than ideal conditions in its major market. I would have no problem owning these shares in a portfolio.

AirTouch Communications, Inc.
   NYSE: ATI
One California St.
San Francisco, CA 94111
(415) 658-2000 • (800) 233-5601

| Performance Rating: * * * * |
| --- |

## Performance History: Not available. ——————————

## Plan Specifics ——————————————————————

- Initial purchase is available to investors in all 50 states ($500 minimum initial investment).
- No discount.
- OCP: $100 to $10,000 per transaction.
- OCP is invested at least weekly.
- The firm charges $7.50 plus brokerage commissions of 10 cents per share for each purchase and sale of shares.
- Plan Administrator: Bank of New York (800) 233-5601.
- The company does not pay a dividend.

## Corporate Profile ——————————————————

AirTouch Communications provides cellular-telephone services throughout the U.S. The firm was formerly part of Pacific Telesis, the regional Bell company. The company has important markets in Europe and Asia. AirTouch has posted good results in recent years. There is still ample penetration prospects for cellular-telephone services in the U.S. International markets, too, offer good growth potential.

## Investment Advice ——————————————————

Cellular-telephone stocks are rarely cheap. However, for investors willing to accept some price volatility, AirTouch has interesting growth potential. These shares aren't for conservative investors, but I would feel comfortable owning them in the growth portion of a no-load stock portfolio.

American Recreation Centers, Inc.
NASDAQ: AMRC
11171 Sun Center Dr., Suite 120
Rancho Cordova, CA 95670
(916) 852-8005 • (800) 522-6645

> **Performance Rating: \* \***

## Performance History

- $1,000 invested on 12/31/85 was worth $1,782 on 12/31/95 — a 78 percent increase in 10 years.

## Plan Specifics

- Initial purchase is available to investors in all 50 states ($100 minimum initial investment).
- Partial dividend reinvestment is not available.
- No discount.
- OCP: $25 to $5,000 per month.
- OCP is invested monthly.
- There are no purchasing fees. Selling fees include brokerage commissions and other expenses.
- Plan Administrator: ChaseMellon Shareholder Investment Service (800) 522-6645.
- Dividends are paid January, April, July, and October.

## Corporate Profile

American Recreation Centers operates bowling alleys, predominantly in California and Texas. The company sold its interest in Right Start, Inc., a direct-mail marketer of infant and children's products in 1995.

## Investment Advice

American Recreation Centers is one of the smaller no-load stocks and certainly one of the more aggressive issues in the group. The stock's inability over the years to sustain price advances is a negative. I can't give the company more than two stars due to its spotty track record.

American Water Works Company, Inc.
  NYSE: AWK
1025 Laurel Oak Rd., PO Box 1770
Voorhees, NJ 08043
(609) 346-8200 • (800) 736-3001

> **Performance Rating: * * * ***

## Performance History

- $1,000 invested on 12/31/85 was worth $3,812 on 12/31/95 — a 281 percent increase in 10 years.

## Plan Specifics

- Initial purchase is available for customers of the utility ($100 minimum initial investment).
- Partial dividend reinvestment is available.
- No discount.
- OCP: $100 to $5,000 per month.
- OCP is invested monthly.
- There are no purchasing fees. Selling fees include brokerage commission, transfer taxes, and a handling charge.
- Plan Administrator: First National Bank of Boston (800) 736-3001.
- Dividends are paid February, May, August, and November.

## Corporate Profile

American Water Works supplies water to six million people in 21 states. The largest revenue contribution states are Pennsylvania and New Jersey. Geographic diversity helps lessen volatility from extreme weather conditions in any one area. The firm's finances are solid, which has allowed the company to be active on the acquisition front. The modest payout ratio — per-share dividends divided by per-share earnings — means dividends have ample room to expand.

## Investment Advice

American Water Works offers an attractive issue among utilities. Geographic diversification is a plus, as are growth opportunities via acquisitions. These shares are a suitable holding in any portfolio.

Ameritech Corp.
NYSE: AIT
30 S. Wacker Dr.
Chicago, IL 60606
(888) 752-6248 • (312) 750-5353 • (800) 774-4117

Performance Rating: * * * * *

## Performance History

■ $1,000 invested on 12/31/85 was worth $5,354 on 12/31/95 — a 435 percent increase in 10 years.

## Plan Specifics

■ Initial purchase is available to investors in all 50 states ($1,000 minimum or automatic monthly withdrawals of at least $100). Initial cash investment will be charged $10 plus 10 cents per share.
■ Partial dividend reinvestment is available.
■ No discount.
■ OCP: $100 to $150,000 per year.
■ OCP is invested at least weekly.
■ Purchasing costs are brokerage commissions, any applicable transfer taxes, and a $5 service fee ($1 service fee if made with automatic monthly deductions). Fees to reinvest dividends are maximum of $3 per quarter. Selling fees are $10 plus brokerage commissions.
■ Automatic investment services are available.
■ Shares may be sold via the telephone.
■ IRA option is available ($35 annual fee).
■ Participants may establish a stock-secured loan or line of credit, backed by shares held on deposit.
■ Plan Administrator: First Chicago Trust-NY (888) 752-6248.
■ Dividends are paid February, May, August, and November.

## Corporate Profile

Ameritech provides local telephone service in Illinois, Indiana, Michigan, Ohio, and Wisconsin. The firm also has a cellular phone operation.

## Investment Advice

Ameritech is one of the strongest players among the regional Bells and is situated nicely to prosper in tomorrow's telecommunications markets. These shares are an attractive portfolio holding.

Amoco Corp.
NYSE: AN
200 E. Randolph Dr.
Chicago, IL 60601
(800) 821-8100 • (800) 446-2617 • (800) 774-4117

---

**Performance Rating: * * * * ***

---

## Performance History

- $1,000 invested on 12/31/85 was worth $3,491 on 12/31/95 — a 249 percent increase in 10 years.

## Plan Specifics

- Initial purchase is available to investors in all 50 states ($450 minimum initial investment). One-time enrollment fee of $8.50.
- Partial dividend reinvestment is not available.
- No discount.
- OCP: $50 to $150,000 per year.
- OCP is invested at least weekly.
- Purchasing fees are 5 percent of amount invested ($3 maximum) plus brokerage commissions. Selling costs are $10 service charge plus 12 cents per share.
- Automatic investment services are available ($1 charge per ACH transaction).
- Shares may be sold via the telephone.
- Plan Administrator: First Chicago Trust-NY (800) 446-2617.
- Dividends are paid March, June, September, and December.

## Corporate Profile

Amoco is one of the largest energy companies in the country. The bottom line has given a good performance in the last few years. Cost controls and improved prices for natural gas and oil should help the bottom line going forward. The above-average yield is another plus.

## Investment Advice

Amoco is one of the top energy issues in the market. Strong finances and solid positions in the oil and natural gas market should lead to above-average total returns for these shares. The stock, with its decent yield and respectable appreciation prospects, is a solid holding.

Amway Japan Ltd.
  NYSE: AJL
c/o Morgan Guaranty Trust Co., PO Box 9073
Boston, MA 02205
(800) 749-1687 • (800) 774-4117

Performance Rating: * * *

## Performance History: Not available.

## Plan Specifics

- Initial purchase is available to investors in all states except North Dakota, Oregon, and Texas ($250 minimum initial investment).
- Partial dividend reinvestment is available.
- No discount.
- OCP: $50 to $100,000 per year.
- OCP is invested weekly.
- Automatic investment services are available.
- Annual administration fee of $15 must accompany initial stock purchase and may be paid with a credit card.
- Purchasing and selling fees include a transaction fee of $5, plus brokerage commissions of approximately 12 cents per share.
- Investors will be assessed a brokerage commission of 12 cents per share to reinvest dividends.
- Shares may be sold via the telephone.
- Plan Administrator: Morgan Guaranty Trust Co. (800) 749-1687.
- Dividends are paid May and December.

## Corporate Profile

Amway Japan is the exclusive distributor in Japan for Amway's consumer products. The firm had nearly one million distributors at the end of fiscal 1995. Housewares, personal care, and nutrition products account for the majority of revenues. Per-share profits have moved higher since 1992.

## Investment Advice

Amway Japan has been publicly traded only since 1994, so the trading history of the company's American Depositary Receipts (ADRs) is rather limited. The ADRs have done well in the last few years, and the expected earnings growth should provide some support to these shares. The stock is an interesting way to give your portfolio exposure to Japan.

Arrow Financial Corp.
NASDAQ: AROW
250 Glen St., PO Box 307
Glens Falls, NY 12801
(518) 793-4121 • (718) 921-8200

> **Performance Rating: * * ***

## Performance History

- $1,000 invested on 12/31/85 was worth $2,498 on 12/31/95 — a 150 percent increase in 10 years.

## Plan Specifics

- Initial purchase is available to investors in all 50 states ($300 minimum initial investment).
- Partial dividend reinvestment is not available.
- No discount.
- OCP: $50 to $10,000 per quarter.
- OCP is invested monthly.
- There are no purchasing fees. Selling fees include brokerage commissions.
- Plan Administrator: American Stock Transfer & Trust Co. (718) 921-8200.
- Dividends are paid March, June, September, and December.

## Corporate Profile

Arrow Financial is a holding company for Glens Falls National Bank & Trust, Saratoga National Bank & Trust, and Green Mountain Bank. The company has posted decent results in recent years. The stock has trended higher during that time.

## Investment Advice

Arrow has gotten its house in order in recent years. Still, there are other banking issues among the list of no-load stocks — Regions Financial comes to mind — that I think are superior. To be sure, these shares are not without some appeal, especially as takeover activity heats up in the banking group. Still, investors should not have a large exposure to the stock.

**ATLANTIC
ENERGY**

Atlantic Energy, Inc.
NYSE: ATE
6801 Black Horse Pike, PO Box 1334
Pleasantville, NJ 08232
(609) 645-4506

Performance Rating: * *

## Performance History

- $1,000 invested on 12/31/85 was worth $2,851 on 12/31/95 — a 185 percent increase in 10 years.

## Plan Specifics

- Initial purchase is available to investors in all 50 states ($250 minimum initial investment).
- Partial dividend reinvestment is available on shares held in certificate form.
- No discount.
- OCP: up to $100,000 per year.
- OCP is invested monthly.
- Purchasing and selling fees may include brokerage commissions when stock is purchased or sold on the open market.
- Automatic investment services are available.
- Dividends are paid January, April, July, and October.

## Corporate Profile

Atlantic Energy is the holding company for Atlantic City Electric, which supplies electricity in a 2,700 square mile area in southern New Jersey. The firm has entered into a merger agreement with Delmarva Power. Dividend growth will be modest or nonexistent.

## Investment Advice

I'm not enamored with the utility's dividend-growth prospects. In fact, a good argument could be made that, should earnings falter, a dividend cut is not out of the question. I think there are better opportunities elsewhere in the utility sector.

Atmos Energy Corp.
NYSE: ATO
PO Box 650205
Dallas, TX 75265-0205
(800) 382-8667 • (800) 543-3038 • (800) 774-4117

| Performance Rating: * * * * |

## Performance History

- $1,000 invested on 12/31/85 was worth $3,830 on 12/31/95 — a 283 percent increase in 10 years.

## Plan Specifics

- Initial purchase is available to investors in all 50 states ($200 minimum initial investment).
- Partial dividend reinvestment is available.
- 3 percent discount on reinvested dividends.
- OCP: $25 to $100,000 per year.
- OCP is invested weekly.
- There are no purchasing fees. Selling costs are brokerage commissions, a $5 fee, and any other costs of sale.
- Automatic investment services are available.
- IRA option is available.
- Plan Administrator: Bank of Boston (800) 543-3038.
- Dividends are paid March, June, September, and December.

## Corporate Profile

Atmos Energy is a leading provider of natural-gas services in Colorado, Missouri, Kentucky, Louisiana, Kansas, and Texas. Residential customers account for roughly 50 percent of total sales.

## Investment Advice

Atmos Energy will be affected by interest-rate movements in line with utilities in general. However, the firm offers one of the better holdings in the group. Solid finances, steady dividend growth, and a competitive market position should translate into above-average total returns. The stock is a quality holding in any portfolio.

Augat, Inc.
NYSE: AUG
89 Forbes Blvd., PO Box 448
Mansfield, MA 02048
(508) 543-4300 • (617) 575-3400

| Performance Rating: * * * |
| --- |

## Performance History

- $1,000 invested on 12/31/85 was worth $815 on 12/31/95 — a 19 percent decrease in 10 years.

## Plan Specifics

- Initial purchase may be made directly from the company by residents in 42 states ($250 minimum initial investment). One-time $5 service fee for new accounts.
- Partial dividend reinvestment is available.
- No discount.
- OCP: $100 to $100,000 per year.
- OCP is invested weekly.
- There are no purchasing fees. Selling fees are a maximum of $10 plus 15 cents per share.
- Automatic investment services are available.
- Plan Administrator: First National Bank of Boston (617) 575-3400.
- Dividends are paid February, May, August, and November.

## Corporate Profile

Augat produces various electrical connection devices, wiring systems, and communications products. Profits have been extremely uneven over the years. Nevertheless, the company's communications business has good growth prospects over the next several years. With annual sales of roughly $600 million, Augat is still small enough to post decent earnings growth over time.

## Investment Advice

Augat's stock price has been trending sideways for several years. Wall Street needs to see further evidence of a sustained earnings turnaround before it is likely to return to these shares in full force. Still, the next 10 years should be much kinder to Augat shareholders than the last 10.

Banco Santander, S.A.
  NYSE: STD
c/o Morgan Guaranty Trust Co., PO Box 9073
Boston, MA 02205
(800) 749-1687 • (800) 774-4117

> Performance Rating: * * *

## Performance History: Not available.

## Plan Specifics

- Initial purchase is available to investors in all states except North Dakota, Oregon, and Texas ($250 minimum initial investment).
- Partial dividend reinvestment is available.
- No discount.
- OCP: $50 to $100,000 per year.
- OCP is invested weekly.
- Automatic investment services are available.
- Annual administration fee of $15 must accompany initial stock purchase and may be paid with a credit card.
- Purchase and selling costs include a transaction fee of $5, plus brokerage commissions of approximately 12 cents per share.
- Investors will be assessed a brokerage commission of approximately 12 cents per share to reinvest dividends.
- Shares may be sold via the telephone.
- Plan Administrator: Morgan Guaranty Trust Co. (800) 749-1687.
- Dividends are paid February, May, August, and November.

## Corporate Profile

Banco Santander is the largest bank in Spain. The firm conducts banking operations in some 30 countries. The company has expanded via acquisitions. The stock has picked up backing over the last year due, in part, to improving profits.

## Investment Advice

Banco Santander registered a nice price breakout in 1996 and appears poised to head higher. Admittedly, it is somewhat difficult to evaluate foreign banks, which is one reason for the three-star rating. However, these shares have interesting potential going forward, especially as the firm penetrates new geographic markets.

Bancorp Hawaii, Inc.
NYSE: BOH
130 Merchant St.
Honolulu, HI 96813
(808) 537-8239 • (800) 509-5586

> **Performance Rating:** * * * *

## Performance History

- $1,000 invested on 12/31/85 was worth $5,230 on 12/31/95 — a 423 percent increase in 10 years.

## Plan Specifics

- Initial purchase is available to residents of the state of Hawaii ($250 minimum initial investment).
- Partial dividend reinvestment is available.
- No discount.
- OCP: $25 to $5,000 per quarter.
- OCP is invested monthly.
- There are no purchasing fees. Selling fees are brokerage commissions, a service fee, and any applicable taxes.
- Plan Administrator: Continental Stock Transfer (800) 509-5586.
- Dividends are paid March, June, September, and December.

## Corporate Profile

Bancorp Hawaii is a bank holding company for Bank of Hawaii, the largest commercial bank in the state. The firm has offices in several South Pacific islands plus the Far East. Over the long term, growth in the Pacific Rim has potentially big implications for Bancorp Hawaii given its presence in this market.

## Investment Advice

Bancorp Hawaii has a leadership position in an economy that should do reasonably well. Its operations in the South Pacific are a plus. The company's strong finances, healthy dividend growth, and favorable earnings prospects give these shares above-average total-return potential. Although only Hawaii residents may make initial purchases directly, the stock would be a worthwhile holding for any investor.

Bard (C.R.), Inc.

  NYSE: BCR
730 Central Ave.
Murray Hill, NJ 07974
(908) 277-8000 • (800) 828-1639 • (800) 446-2617

> **Performance Rating: * * * ***

## Performance History

■ $1,000 invested on 12/31/85 was worth $3,465 on 12/31/95 — a 247 percent increase in 10 years.

## Plan Specifics

■ Initial purchase is available to investors in all 50 states ($250 minimum initial investment). Initial investments will entail a $15 transaction fee plus 3 cents per share brokerage fee.
■ Partial dividend reinvestment is available.
■ No discount.
■ OCP: $25 minimum, no maximum.
■ OCP is invested at least weekly.
■ Purchasing fees are 5 percent of OCP (maximum $10) plus brokerage commissions. Selling costs are $15 plus 12 cents per share brokerage commission.
■ Automatic investment services are available ($1 charge).
■ Shares may be sold via the telephone.
■ Plan Administrator: First Chicago Trust-NY (800) 828-1639.
■ Dividends are paid February, May, August, and November.

## Corporate Profile

Bard produces balloon angioplasty catheters and other types of cardiac catheters. The firm also manufactures a variety of urological products, including Foley catheters and incontinent products.

## Investment Advice

Bard is a solid holding in the health-care sector. Granted, the stock will have trouble repeating the strong performance of recent years. Still, new products and positions in markets destined for good growth due, in part, to demographic trends should help these shares at least keep pace with the overall market.

Barnett Banks, Inc.
NYSE: BBI
Shareholder Services Dept., PO Box 40789
Jacksonville, FL 32203-0789
(904) 791-7668 • (800) 328-5822

> **Performance Rating: \* \* \* \***

## Performance History

- $1,000 invested on 12/31/85 was worth $2,796 on 12/31/95 — a 180 percent increase in 10 years.

## Plan Specifics

- Initial purchase is available to investors in all 50 states ($250 minimum initial investment).
- Partial dividend reinvestment is available.
- No discount.
- OCP: $25 to $10,000 per month.
- OCP is invested twice per month.
- There are no purchasing fees. Selling fees include brokerage commissions.
- IRA option is available.
- Automatic investment services are available.
- Preferred dividends may be reinvested for additional common stock.
- Plan Administrator: First Chicago Trust-NY (800) 328-5822.
- Dividends are paid January, April, July, and October.

## Corporate Profile

Barnett Banks is Florida's largest bank holding company. The company's location in the Southeast should provide above-average earnings growth. In addition, its active acquisition program should spur growth.

## Investment Advice

Barnett Banks offers a worthwhile holding among banking stocks. Its location is a plus. For representation in the financial-services sector, the stock is an acceptable investment.

Bob Evans Farms, Inc.
  NASDAQ: BOBE
Stock Transfer Dept.
3776 S. High St., PO Box 07863
Columbus, OH 43207
(614) 492-4950 • (800) 272-7675

Performance Rating: * * * *

## Performance History

- $1,000 invested on 12/31/85 was worth $2,389 on 12/31/95 — a 139 percent increase in 10 years.

## Plan Specifics

- Initial purchase may be made directly from the company by residents in 32 states ($50 minimum initial investment).
- Partial dividend reinvestment is available.
- No discount.
- OCP: $10 to $10,000 per month.
- OCP is invested twice monthly.
- There are no purchasing fees. Selling fees may include brokerage commissions.
- Automatic investment services are available.
- Dividends are paid March, June, September, and December.

## Corporate Profile

Bob Evans operates a chain of nearly 400 restaurants, with the largest number in Ohio. Per-share profits have generally trended higher over the years. However, in 1995 profits were hurt partly by high sausage prices as well as a downturn that affected the restaurant industry in general. Over the long term, continued outlet expansion should help return profits to the growth track.

## Investment Advice

The performance of Bob Evans stock has been fairly dismal over the last year, and it may take some time for these shares to rebound. However, despite the competitive industry conditions that are likely to continue, Bob Evans has a proven concept and ample room to expand geographically. Thus, the four-star performance rating is more a bet on prospects 3-5 years out and not so much the stock's expected performance over the next 12 months.

Boston Edison Co.
NYSE: BSE
800 Boylston St.
Boston, MA 02199
(617) 424-2000 • (800) 736-3001

Performance Rating: * * *

## Performance History

- $1,000 invested on 12/31/85 was worth $2,663 on 12/31/95 — a 166 percent increase in 10 years.

## Plan Specifics

- Initial purchase may be made by customers of the utility ($500 minimum initial investment).
- Partial dividend reinvestment is available.
- No discount.
- OCP: $50 to $40,000 per year.
- OCP is invested monthly.
- There are no purchasing fees. Selling costs include transaction fee (maximum $15 charge), brokerage commissions, and transfer tax.
- Plan Administrator: First National Bank of Boston (800) 736-3001.
- Dividends are paid February, May, August, and November.

## Corporate Profile

Boston Edison supplies electricity to the city of Boston and surrounding communities. Commercial customers represent roughly 50 percent of total sales. Nuclear energy accounts for more than 40 percent of fuel sources. The dividend has shown good growth in recent years, although more modest dividend growth is expected going forward.

## Investment Advice

Boston Edison is an unexciting choice in the utility sector. Long-term appreciation prospects appear limited. Furthermore, finances are a cut below other utilities.

**BRE**

BRE Properties, Inc.
NYSE: BRE
One Montgomery St., Telesis Tower, Suite 2500
San Francisco, CA 94104-5525
(415) 445-6530 • (800) 368-8392 • (800) 774-4117

> **Performance Rating: * * ***

## Performance History: Not available. ─────────

## Plan Specifics ─────────────────────────────

- Initial purchase is available to investors in all 50 states ($500 minimum initial investment).
- Partial dividend reinvestment is available.
- No discount.
- OCP: $100 to $10,000 per month. Waivers may be obtained for investing more than $10,000 per month by calling (415) 445-6530.
- OCP is invested at least weekly.
- There are no purchasing fees. Selling costs are $15 plus 12 cents per share.
- Automatic investment services are available.
- Plan Administrator: ChaseMellon Shareholder Investment Service (800) 368-8392.
- Dividends are paid March, June, September, and December.

## Corporate Profile ─────────────────────────

BRE Properties, a real estate investment trust, operates industrial and rental properties. Properties include rental apartments. The bulk of properties are located in the western part of the country. The company merged with Real Estate Investment Trust of California in 1996.

## Investment Advice ─────────────────────────

BRE has had a decent run over the last two years. The issue has above-average total-return potential for the REIT group, although investors should not have a large exposure to the REIT field due to its sensitivity to interest rates.

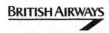

British Airways PLC
  NYSE: BAB
c/o Morgan Guaranty Trust Co., PO Box 9073
Boston, MA 02205
(800) 749-1687 • (800) 774-4117

> Performance Rating: * * * *

## Performance History: Not available. ───────────

## Plan Specifics ───────────────────────────

- Initial purchase is available to investors in all states except Texas, Oregon, and North Dakota ($250 minimum initial investment).
- Partial dividend reinvestment is available.
- No discount.
- OCP: $50 to $100,000 per year.
- OCP is invested weekly.
- Automatic investment services are available.
- Annual administrative fee of $15 must accompany initial stock purchase and may be paid with a credit card.
- Purchasing and selling fees include a transaction fee of $5, plus brokerage commissions of approximately 12 cents per share.
- Investors will be assessed a brokerage commission of 12 cents per share to reinvest dividends.
- Shares may be sold via the telephone.
- Plan Administrator: Morgan Guaranty Trust Co. (800) 749-1687.
- Dividends are paid February and August.

## Corporate Profile ──────────────────────────

This United Kingdom-based concern operates one of the largest airline systems in the world. The firm has equity stakes in a variety of airlines, including USAir.

## Investment Advice ──────────────────────────

I've never been a huge fan of airline stocks for long-term investors due to the competitive nature of the industry and usual lack of earnings stability for airline companies. Nevertheless, British Airways seems to be able to fend off the problems that afflict other carriers. I give the stock four stars, although I would not want to have an overly large exposure to the airline industry.

British Telecommunications PLC
NYSE: BTY
c/o Morgan Guaranty Trust Co., PO Box 9073
Boston, MA 02205
(800) 749-1687 • (800) 774-4117

| Performance Rating: * * * * |

## Performance History: Not available.

## Plan Specifics

- Initial purchase is available to investors in all states except Texas, Oregon, and North Dakota ($250 minimum initial investment).
- Partial dividend reinvestment is available.
- No discount.
- OCP: $50 to $100,000 per year.
- OCP is invested weekly.
- Automatic investment services are available.
- Annual administration fee of $15 must accompany initial stock purchase and may be paid with a credit card.
- Purchasing and selling costs include a transaction fee of $5, plus brokerage commissions of approximately 12 cents per share.
- Investors will be assessed a brokerage commission of approximately 12 cents per share to reinvest dividends.
- Shares may be sold via the telephone.
- Plan Administrator: Morgan Guaranty Trust Co. (800) 749-1687.
- Dividends are paid February and September.

## Corporate Profile

British Telecommunications provides various telecommunications services in the United Kingdom. The firm has developed a number of alliances with foreign carriers, including MCI Communications.

## Investment Advice

British Telecommunications has traded sideways for several years. Wall Street seems a bit unsure how the changing global telecommunications market will affect these shares. However, the company has a solid franchise in an important international market and the ability to become a major player on a global scale.

Brooklyn Union Gas Co.
NYSE: BU
One MetroTech Center
Brooklyn, NY 11201
(718) 403-3334 • (800) 328-5090

> **Performance Rating: * * * * ***

## Performance History

- $1,000 invested on 12/31/85 was worth $3,576 on 12/31/95 — a 258 percent increase in 10 years.

## Plan Specifics

- Initial purchase is available to customers of the company ($250 minimum initial investment).
- Partial dividend reinvestment is available.
- No discount.
- OCP: $25 to $100,000 per year.
- OCP is invested monthly.
- There are no purchasing fees. Selling costs are brokerage commissions.
- Shareholders of preferred stock and registered bonds may reinvest dividends and interest payments in additional common shares.
- Dividends are paid February, May, August, and November.

## Corporate Profile

Brooklyn Union Gas is a leading provider of natural-gas services in and around New York City, including the boroughs of Brooklyn, Staten Island, and Queens. Finances are solid, and dividend growth should at least match the industry average. Over the long term, penetration of non-regulated markets in the natural-gas sector should spark growth.

## Investment Advice

Brooklyn Union Gas is one of the better natural-gas utilities in the market. The firm has shown the ability to prosper despite a relatively mature service region. The stock is a first-rate portfolio holding for income-oriented investors.

*Cadbury Schweppes*

Cadbury Schweppes PLC
  NYSE: CSG
c/o Morgan Guaranty Trust Co., PO Box 9073
Boston, MA 02205
(800) 749-1687 • (800) 774-4117

> **Performance Rating: * * ***

## Performance History: Not available.

## Plan Specifics

- Initial purchase is available to investors in all states except Texas, Oregon, and North Dakota ($250 minimum initial investment).
- Partial dividend reinvestment is available.
- No discount.
- OCP: $50 to $100,000 per year.
- OCP is invested weekly.
- Automatic investment services are available.
- Annual administrative fee of $15 must accompany initial stock purchase and may be paid with a credit card.
- Purchasing and selling costs include a transaction fee of $5, plus brokerage commissions of approximately 12 cents per share.
- Investors will be assessed a brokerage commission of approximately 12 cents per share to reinvest dividends.
- Shares may be sold via the telephone.
- Plan Administrator: Morgan Guaranty Trust Co. (800) 749-1687.
- Dividends are paid June and December.

## Corporate Profile

Cadbury Schweppes is a major provider of confectionery products and beverages. This United Kingdom-based company derives more than 40 percent of sales and profits from the United Kingdom. Brand names include Cadbury, Dr. Pepper, Seven Up, Canada Dry, Sunkist, and A&W.

## Investment Advice

Cadbury Schweppes will likely be only an average performer over time. While I generally like consumer-products companies, the firm's second-tier market positions make the company's long-term earnings power uninspiring.

Capstead Mortgage Corp.

**CAPSTEAD**    NYSE: CMO

2711 N. Haskell Ave., Ste. 900

Dallas, TX 75204

(214) 874-2323 • (800) 527-7844

| Performance Rating: * * * |

## Performance History

- $1,000 invested on 12/31/85 was worth $5,169 on 12/31/95 — a 417 percent increase in 10 years.

## Plan Specifics

- Initial purchase is available to investors in all 50 states ($250 minimum initial investment).
- Partial dividend reinvestment is available.
- May offer up to 5 percent discount on reinvested dividends and OCPs.
- OCP: $50 to $10,000 per month.
- OCP is invested monthly.
- There are no purchasing fees. Selling costs are brokerage commissions and a $5 service charge.
- Automatic investment services are available.
- Plan Administrator: Society National Bank (800) 527-7844.
- Dividends are paid March, June, September, and December.

## Corporate Profile

Capstead Mortgage generates income from servicing mortgage loans. The firm also invests in mortgage-backed securities. The company's business is dependent on interest rates, which lends a fair amount of volatility to the earnings stream. Still, these shares seem to be one of the better firms in this group.

## Investment Advice

I've never been a huge fan of mortgage-investment companies, as their earnings stream and stock prices react violently to interest-rate movements. Capstead Mortgage has not been immune to such volatility over the years. Nevertheless, these shares seem a cut above the usual players in this industry and are worth a look from investors.

Carolina Power & Light Co.
NYSE: CPL
PO Box 1551
Raleigh, NC 27602
(919) 546-6111 • (800) 633-4236

| Performance Rating: * * * * |
| --- |

## Performance History

- $1,000 invested on 12/31/85 was worth $4,226 on 12/31/95 — a 323 percent increase in 10 years.

## Plan Specifics

- Initial purchase is available to utility customers living in North and South Carolina ($20 minimum initial investment).
- Partial dividend reinvestment is available.
- No discount.
- OCP: $20 to $2,000 per month.
- OCP is invested monthly.
- Purchasing and selling fees include brokerage commissions.
- Automatic investment services are available.
- Plan Administrator: Wachovia Bank (800) 633-4236.
- Dividends are paid February, May, August, and November.

## Corporate Profile

Carolina Power & Light provides electric power to more than one million customers in parts of North and South Carolina. Major industries in the firm's growing service region include textiles and chemicals. The company should continue to show dividend increases on the order of 2-3 percent.

## Investment Advice

Carolina Power & Light has a number of things going for it, such as a strong service region and decent finances. The firm's nuclear exposure — nuclear energy accounts for more than 40 percent of fuel mix — could scare some investors. However, the stock has reasonable total-return potential.

®

Carpenter Technology Corp.
NYSE: CRS
101 West Bern St.
Reading, PA 19612-4662
(610) 208-2000 • (800) 822-9828 • (800) 446-2617

Performance Rating: * * * *

## Performance History

- $1,000 invested on 12/31/85 was worth $3,814 on 12/31/95 — a 281 percent increase in 10 years.

## Plan Specifics

- Initial purchase is available to investors in all 50 states ($500 minimum initial investment). Investors will be charged $10 plus 10 cents per share on the initial investment. There are no fees for additional purchases.
- Partial dividend reinvestment is available.
- No discount.
- OCP: $25 to $125,000 per year.
- OCP is invested at least weekly.
- Selling costs are $10 plus 12 cents per share.
- Shares may be sold via the telephone.
- Plan Administrator: First Chicago Trust-NY (800) 446-2617.
- Dividends are paid March, June, September, and December.

## Corporate Profile

Carpenter Technology produces various specialty steels and electronic alloys. Stainless steel products account for more than 50 percent of total sales. Despite a presence in a fairly cyclical industry, Carpenter has done a good job of posting higher profits over the years.

## Investment Advice

While I generally don't care for steel producers, Carpenter Technology is no ordinary steel company. A focus on specialty products, decent finances, and a dividend stream that is likely to increase over time give these shares ample appeal. I would feel comfortable owning the stock in a portfolio.

Cascade Natural Gas Corp.
NYSE: CGC
222 Fairview Ave. North
Seattle, WA 98109
(206) 624-3900 • (800) 524-4458

> **Performance Rating: \* \* \***

## Performance History

- $1,000 invested on 12/31/85 was worth $5,193 on 12/31/95 — a 419 percent increase in 10 years.

## Plan Specifics

- Initial purchase is available to residential customers of the company in Washington and Oregon ($250 minimum initial investment).
- Partial dividend reinvestment is available.
- No discount.
- OCP: $50 to $20,000 per year.
- OCP is invested monthly.
- There are no purchasing fees. Selling fees are applicable brokerage commissions and transfer taxes.
- Plan administrator: Bank of New York (800) 524-4458.
- Dividends are paid February, May, August, and November.

## Corporate Profile

Cascade Natural Gas distributes natural gas in communities in Washington and Oregon. Residential and commercial customers account for one-half of total revenues. Major industries in the company's service region produce pulp, paper, plywood, and industrial chemicals. The service region is experiencing nice growth. The downside to rapid growth, however, is the fact that the company must service growth via capacity additions, and that requires capital spending.

## Investment Advice

Clean-burning natural gas has environmental advantages over other fuel sources. Still, I'm neutral on these shares. Investors should not expect a duplication of the strong returns posted over the last decade.

Centerior Energy Corp.
NYSE: CX
PO Box 94661
Cleveland, OH 44101-4661
(800) 433-7794

Performance Rating: * *

## Performance History

- $1,000 invested on 12/31/85 was worth $883 on 12/31/95 — a 12 percent decrease in 10 years.

## Plan Specifics

- Initial purchase is available to customers of the utility ($10 minimum initial investment).
- Partial dividend reinvestment is available.
- No discount.
- OCP: $10 to $40,000 per year.
- OCP is invested monthly.
- Minimal fees for purchasing and selling.
- IRA option is available.
- Preferred dividends may be reinvested for additional common shares.
- Dividends are paid February, May, August, and November.

## Corporate Profile

Centerior Energy was formed in 1986 via the merger of the Cleveland Electric Illuminating Company and Toledo Edison. The firm serves 2.6 million people in a combined service area of 4,200 square miles. The firm has received a takeover offer from Ohio Edison.

## Investment Advice

Even when utilities were going strong, Centerior Energy lagged. With its high rates, the firm will find it difficult to compete in the utility markets of the future. The poor dividend record is yet another negative. I would avoid these shares.

Central & South West Corp.
NYSE: CSR
PO Box 660164
Dallas, TX  75266-0164
(800) 527-5797 • (800) 774-4117

Performance Rating: * * * *

## Performance History

- $1,000 invested on 12/31/85 was worth $3,771 on 12/31/95 — a 277 percent increase in 10 years.

## Plan Specifics

- Initial purchase is available to investors in all 50 states ($250 minimum initial investment).
- Partial dividend reinvestment is available.
- No discount.
- OCP: $25 to $100,000 per year.
- OCP is invested weekly.
- Investors will pay a small brokerage fee on shares purchased in the open market. Selling fees are modest brokerage charges.
- Automatic investment services are available.
- Dividends are paid February, May, August, and November.

## Corporate Profile

Central & South West provides utility service to more than 1.6 million people in an area covering 152,000 square miles — Arkansas, Louisiana, Oklahoma, and Texas. The firm also owns an intrastate natural-gas transmission company, a developer of nonutility power projects, and a leasing business. The company has increased dividends annually for 45 years — one of only two companies on the New York Stock Exchange to have such an uninterrupted history of dividend increases. The firm is expanding overseas via the acquisition of Seeboard PLC, a British utility.

## Investment Advice

Central & South West offers an interesting choice in the utility field. The company's growing nonregulated operations and overseas expansion enhance appeal. I like these shares as a growth selection in the utility sector.

Central Fidelity Banks, Inc.
NASDAQ: CFBS
1021 E. Cary St.
Richmond, VA 23219
(804) 697-6942 • (800) 293-2327

| Performance Rating: * * * * |
|---|

## Performance History

- $1,000 invested on 12/31/85 was worth $4,043 on 12/31/95 — a 304 percent increase in 10 years.

## Plan Specifics

- Initial purchase is available to residents of Maryland, North Carolina, and Virginia ($100 minimum initial investment).
- Partial dividend reinvestment is available.
- No discount.
- OCP: $25 to $10,000 per month.
- OCP is invested monthly.
- There are no purchasing fees. Selling fees are brokerage commissions.
- Automatic investment services are available.
- Direct deposit of dividends is available.
- Dividends are paid January, April, July, and October.

## Corporate Profile

Central Fidelity Banks is one of Virginia's largest banking organizations. Profits have historically shown good upside momentum. Dividends, too, have expanded at a healthy rate. The firm is positioned to expand its presence via acquisitions. Given the takeover activity in the banking field and Central Fidelity's presence in a reasonably good growth region, these shares have to be considered a takeover candidate as well.

## Investment Advice

Central Fidelity should do at least as well as the average banking issue. The stock represents a worthwhile total-return issue in the group.

## Central Hudson Gas & Electric Corp.
### NYSE: CNH
284 South Ave.
Poughkeepsie, NY 12601-4879
(914) 452-2000 • (800) 428-9578

**Central Hudson**

| Performance Rating: * * |

## Performance History

- $1,000 invested on 12/31/85 was worth $2,292 on 12/31/95 — a 129 percent increase in 10 years.

## Plan Specifics

- Initial purchase is available to customers of the utility ($100 minimum initial investment).
- Partial dividend reinvestment is available.
- No discount.
- OCP: $25 to $10,000 per quarter.
- OCP is invested quarterly.
- There are no purchasing fees. Selling fees include brokerage commissions.
- Plan Administrator: First Chicago Trust-NY (800) 428-9578.
- Dividends are paid February, May, August, and November.

## Corporate Profile

Central Hudson Gas & Electric supplies electricity to more than 250,000 customers in the Hudson River Valley of New York. Electric sales account for approximately 80 percent of revenues. Residential and commercial customers account for approximately 72 percent of revenues. Coal is the company's largest fuel source. The company has had its problems in recent years, affected by the downsizing of IBM, a major corporate customer.

## Investment Advice

Central Hudson would not be my first choice for a utility investment. The issue has some upside potential in line with the long-term potential of the electric-utility sector. However, investors would probably do better looking elsewhere.

Central Maine Power Co.
NYSE: CTP
83 Edison Dr.
Augusta, ME 04336
(800) 695-4267

Performance Rating: * *

## Performance History

- $1,000 invested on 12/31/85 was worth $2,119 on 12/31/95 — a 112 percent increase in 10 years.

## Plan Specifics

- Initial purchase is available to customers of the company residing in Maine ($25 minimum initial investment).
- Partial dividend reinvestment is available.
- No discount.
- OCP: $10 to $40,000 per year.
- OCP is invested monthly.
- There are no purchasing fees. Selling fees include brokerage commissions.
- Automatic investment services are available.
- Dividends are paid January, April, July, and October.

## Corporate Profile

Central Maine Power provides electricity to about 500,000 customers. Residential users account for roughly 40 percent of total revenues. The fuel mix includes nuclear, cogeneration/small power products, and oil and hydro. Major industrial customers have businesses in pulp and paper, chemicals, and ship building. Weak earnings fueled a dividend cut in 1994.

## Investment Advice

The relatively weak performance for Central Maine over the last decade versus the big gains by other utilities reflects the subpar quality of these shares. With the likelihood of little or no dividend growth over the next few years and continued regulatory and costs concerns, these shares have below-average prospects.

Central Vermont Public Service Corp.
   NYSE: CV
77 Grove St.
Rutland, VT 05701
(802) 747-5406 • (800) 354-2877

> **Performance Rating: \* \* \***

## Performance History

■ $1,000 invested on 12/31/85 was worth $1,867 on 12/31/95 — an 87 percent increase in 10 years.

## Plan Specifics

■ Initial purchase is available to investors in certain states ($250 minimum initial investment).
■ Partial dividend reinvestment is not available.
■ No discount.
■ OCP: $100 to $6,000 per quarter.
■ OCP is invested monthly.
■ Purchasing and selling fees include brokerage commissions.
■ Dividends are paid February, May, August, and November.

## Corporate Profile

Central Vermont Public Service supplies electricity to customers in Vermont and New Hampshire. Residential and commercial/industrial customers make up nearly 80 percent of total revenues. Sources of power are primarily nuclear and hydro. The company's Catamount Energy unit invests in nonregulated energy-related projects. Per-share profits have been flat over the last five years, and earnings could remain erratic in the near term.

## Investment Advice

There's nothing particularly stellar about Central Vermont Public Service. Growth of nonregulated businesses is a plus. However, dividend growth prospects are unappealing, and the firm's service region will likely see only limited growth.

**CMS ENERGY**

CMS Energy Corp.
NYSE: CMS
Investor Services Dept.
212 W. Michigan Ave.
Jackson, MI 49201
(517) 788-1868 • (800) 774-4117

> Performance Rating: * * *

## Performance History

- $1,000 invested on 12/31/85 was worth $4,655 on 12/31/95 — a 366 percent increase in 10 years.

## Plan Specifics

- Initial purchase is available to investors in all 50 states ($500 minimum initial investment).
- Partial dividend reinvestment is available.
- No discount.
- OCP: $25 to $120,000 per year.
- OCP is invested monthly.
- There are no purchasing fees. Selling costs are brokerage commissions.
- Automatic investment services are available.
- Preferred stock is eligible for reinvestment for CMS Energy common shares.
- Dividends are paid February, May, August, and November.

## Corporate Profile

CMS Energy is the largest provider of electricity in Michigan and one of the largest electric utilities in the country. The firm generates more than 45 percent of fuel from coal, with nuclear accounting for more than 10 percent. CMS had its problems in the mid-'80s, when the utility omitted its dividend. In recent years, however, the stock has rebounded in line with many utilities, and dividend growth has been solid.

## Investment Advice

CMS has improved its position in recent years. Still, finances are below average for the group, and the firm's service region does not have dynamic growth potential. The stock's dividend-growth prospects are the main allure of these shares.

COMSAT Corp.
NYSE: CQ
6560 Rock Spring Dr.
Bethesda, MD 20817
(301) 214-3200 • (800) 524-4458

Performance Rating: * * * *

## Performance History

■ $1,000 invested on 12/31/85 was worth $1,552 on 12/31/95 — a
55 percent increase in 10 years.

## Plan Specifics

■ Initial purchase is available to investors in all 50 states ($250
minimum initial investment).
■ Partial dividend reinvestment is not available.
■ No discount.
■ OCP: $50 to $10,000 per month.
■ OCP is invested monthly.
■ There are no purchasing fees. Selling costs include a $5 fee plus 6 cents
per share.
■ Plan Administrator: Bank of New York (800) 524-4458.
■ Dividends are paid March, June, September, and December.

## Corporate Profile

COMSAT furnishes international communication and information
services. It provides voice, video, and data services to customers worldwide by fixed and mobile technologies. The company is a major owner
and user of the global INTELSAT satellite network.

## Investment Advice

Although COMSAT has been a sluggish stock in recent years, the issue
could be a winner for investors over the next decade. Telecommunications markets are likely to be some of the fastest-growing sectors during
that time. The wild card is increased competition and technological
obsolescence. Restructuring opportunities could bring investors back to
these shares. The stock would add some spice to a no-load stock portfolio, but only a limited exposure is suggested.

Connecticut Energy Corp.
NYSE: CNE
PO Box 1540
Bridgeport, CT 06601
(203) 382-8156 • (800) 736-3001

Performance Rating: * * * *

## Performance History

- $1,000 invested on 12/31/85 was worth $3,475 on 12/31/95 — a 248 percent increase in 10 years.

## Plan Specifics

- Initial purchase is available to customers of the utility ($250 minimum initial investment).
- Partial dividend reinvestment is available.
- No discount.
- OCP: $50 to $50,000 per year.
- OCP is invested monthly.
- There are no purchasing fees. Selling fees include brokerage commissions, a service charge, and transfer taxes.
- IRA option is available.
- Automatic investment services are available.
- Plan Administrator: Boston EquiServe (800) 736-3001.
- Dividends are paid March, June, September, and December.

## Corporate Profile

Connecticut Energy is a holding company engaged in the retail distribution of natural gas to over 152,000 customers in 22 Connecticut communities through its principal subsidiary, Southern Connecticut Gas. Finances are in good shape. Connecticut Energy, through its predecessor companies, has paid cash dividends on its common stock since 1850, the longest consecutive dividend payment record of any utility or nonfinancial company listed on the New York Stock Exchange.

## Investment Advice

Connecticut Energy offers a suitable holding in a portfolio. The company's long-term dividend record is impressive, and the firm's focus on the residential market is a plus. Enhancing appeal is the IRA option available in the dividend reinvestment plan.

Connecticut Water Service, Inc.
NASDAQ: CTWS
93 W. Main St.
Clinton, CT 06413
(860) 669-8630 • (800) 426-5523

| Performance Rating: * * * |
| --- |

## Performance History

■ $1,000 invested on 12/31/85 was worth $2,876 on 12/31/95 — a 188 percent increase in 10 years.

## Plan Specifics

■ Initial purchase is available to customers of the utility ($100 minimum initial investment).
■ Partial dividend reinvestment is available.
■ No discount.
■ OCP: $25 to $1,000 per month.
■ OCP is invested monthly.
■ There are no purchasing fees. Selling costs are $5 service fee plus brokerage commissions.
■ IRA option is available.
■ Plan Administrator: Boston EquiServe (800) 426-5523.
■ Dividends are paid March, June, September, and December.

## Corporate Profile

Connecticut Water provides water services in more than 30 Connecticut towns. Profits have generally trended higher. More stringent regulations are opening opportunities for financially sound water utilities to expand via acquisitions, and Connecticut Water will likely be a player in the takeover market.

## Investment Advice

Connecticut Water has given a good account of itself over the last year or so. While my preference among no-load stocks in the water utility sector is Philadelphia Suburban, these shares are likely to keep pace with the average water utility.

Conrail, Inc.
NYSE: CRR
Two Commerce Square
Philadelphia, PA 19101
(215) 209-4000 • (800) 243-7812

| Performance Rating: * * * * |
| --- |

## Performance History: Not available.

## Plan Specifics

- Initial purchase is available to investors in all 50 states ($250 minimum initial investment). $15 enrollment fee.
- Partial dividend reinvestment is available.
- No discount.
- OCP: $50 to $120,000 per year.
- OCP is invested at least weekly.
- Purchasing fees include 5 percent of purchase amount (maximum $10) plus applicable brokerage commissions. Selling costs are $15 processing fee plus 12 cents per share brokerage commission.
- Investors will be assessed a fee of 5 percent of the amount of dividends to be reinvested (maximum $3) plus applicable brokerage commissions.
- Automatic investment services are available ($1 service charge).
- Shares may be sold via the telephone.
- Plan Administrator: First Chicago Trust-NY (800) 243-7812.
- Dividends are paid March, June, September, and December.

## Corporate Profile

Conrail operates a rail network of some 11,000 miles located primarily in midwestern and northeastern states. Coal, chemicals, and autos account for the bulk of shipments. Takeover activity has swirled around these shares.

## Investment Advice

Conrail has been a solid performer over the years. Profits should continue to trend higher. However, given takeover developments in these shares, investors should defer buying.

Crown American Realty Trust

**NYSE: CWN**

Pasquerilla Plaza

Johnstown, PA 15907

(814) 536-4441 • (800) 278-4353 • (800) 774-4117

---

| **Performance Rating: * *** |
| --- |

## Performance History: Not available.

## Plan Specifics

- Initial purchase is available to investors in all 50 states ($100 minimum initial investment).
- Partial dividend reinvestment is available.
- No discount.
- OCP: $100 to $5,000 per quarter.
- OCP is invested monthly.
- There are no purchasing fees. Investors will incur brokerage fees when selling shares from the plan.
- Plan Administrator: American Stock Transfer & Trust Co. (800) 278-4353.
- Dividends are paid March, June, September, and December.

## Corporate Profile

Crown American Realty is a real estate investment trust specializing in enclosed shopping malls. The firm owns properties in a number of states, with its largest geographic exposure in Pennsylvania. Anchor stores at its malls include Sears, Kmart, and The Bon Ton. The firm's business has been affected by an uneven retailing climate in recent years and the woes at Kmart.

## Investment Advice

Weak finances, interest-rate sensitivity, and setbacks at some anchor stores make these shares relatively unattractive. Investors would do well focusing attention elsewhere.

**CSR**

CSR Limited
NASDAQ: CSRLY
c/o Morgan Guaranty Trust Co., PO Box 9073
Boston, MA 02205
(800) 749-1687 • (800) 774-4117

> **Performance Rating: * ***

## Performance History: Not available. ——————

## Plan Specifics ——————————————————

- Initial purchase is available to investors in all states except North Dakota, Oregon, and Texas ($250 minimum initial investment).
- Partial dividend reinvestment is available.
- No discount.
- OCP: $50 to $100,000 per year.
- OCP is invested weekly.
- Automatic investment services are available.
- Annual administration fee of $15 must accompany initial stock purchase and may be paid with a credit card.
- Purchase and sell fees include a transaction fee of $5, plus brokerage commissions of approximately 12 cents per share.
- Investors will be assessed a brokerage commission of 12 cents per share to reinvest dividends.
- Shares may be sold via the telephone.
- Plan Administrator: Morgan Guaranty Trust Co. (800) 749-1687.
- Dividends are paid August and December.

## Corporate Profile ——————————————————

CSR is a diversified concern based in Australia. The company is involved in the milling, refining, and marketing of sugar; the production of building materials; and the mining of various natural resources.

## Investment Advice ——————————————————

Admittedly, information on CSR is rather limited. The company's bottom line has historically reflected the cyclical nature of its markets. This issue would not be my first choice for overseas representation.

Dassault Systemes S.A.
 NASDAQ: DASTY
c/o Morgan Guaranty Trust Co., PO Box 9073
Boston, MA 02205
(800) 749-1687 • (800) 774-4117

| Performance Rating: * * * |

## Performance History: Not available.

## Plan Specifics

- Initial purchase is available to investors in all states except Texas, Oregon, and North Dakota ($250 minimum initial investment).
- No discount.
- OCP: $50 to $100,000 per year.
- OCP is invested weekly.
- Automatic investment services are available.
- Annual administration fee of $15 must accompany initial stock purchase and may be paid with a credit card.
- Purchasing and selling fees include a transaction fee of $5, plus brokerage commissions of approximately 12 cents per share.
- Investors will be assessed a brokerage commission of 12 cents per share to reinvest dividends.
- Shares may be sold via the telephone.
- Plan Administrator: Morgan Guaranty Trust Co. (800) 749-1687.
- The company does not pay a dividend.

## Corporate Profile

Dassault Systemes, headquartered in France, develops computer-aided design/computer-aided manufacturing software. The company's American Depositary Receipts (ADRs) began trading June 1996.

## Investment Advice

Dassault Systemes has done reasonably well during its short trading life. While it is difficult to recommend these shares due to their limited trading history, the stock is one to watch given the long-term potential of the company's markets.

Dean Witter, Discover & Co.

*DEAN WITTER ● DISCOVER*　NYSE: DWD

Two World Trade Center, 56th Floor

New York, NY 10048

(800) 622-2393 • (800) 228-0829

> **Performance Rating: \* \* \* \***

## Performance History: Not available.

## Plan Specifics

- Initial purchase is available to investors in all 50 states ($1,000 minimum initial investment).
- Partial dividend reinvestment is available.
- No discount.
- OCP: $100 to $40,000 per year.
- OCP is invested twice monthly.
- There are no purchasing fees. Selling costs include brokerage commissions and $5 service charge.
- Plan Administrator: Dean Witter Trust Co. (800) 622-2393.
- Dividends are paid January, April, July, and October.

## Corporate Profile

Dean Witter is a major player in the investment securities and credit-card businesses. Credit services account for slightly more than half of total sales and profits. Profits have jumped sharply in recent years, spurred by growth in the credit-card business and strong financial markets.

## Investment Advice

Dean Witter offers one of the better issues in the financial-services industry. While the stock will be dependent to a certain extent on the financial markets, investors should do well owning these shares over the next 3-5 years.

Delta Natural Gas Co., Inc.
NASDAQ: DGAS
3617 Lexington Rd.
Winchester, KY 40391
(606) 744-6171 • (800) 837-2755

**Performance Rating: * * ***

## Performance History

- $1,000 invested on 12/31/85 was worth $3,355 on 12/31/95 — a 236 percent increase in 10 years.

## Plan Specifics

- Initial purchase is available to residents of Kentucky ($100 minimum initial investment).
- Partial dividend reinvestment is available.
- No discount.
- OCP: $25 to $50,000 per year.
- OCP is invested monthly.
- There are no purchasing fees. Must go through own broker to sell shares.
- Plan Administrator: Fifth Third Bank (800) 837-2755.
- Dividends are paid March, June, September, and December.

## Corporate Profile

Delta Natural Gas provides natural-gas distribution services in central and southeastern Kentucky. Residential customers account for nearly half of total revenues. Dividends have shown modest growth in recent years. The company's profit stream has been inconsistent over the last few years.

## Investment Advice

With the many quality natural-gas issues (Atmos Energy, Energen, Piedmont Natural Gas) that offer no-load stock programs, Delta Natural Gas does not rank as a top choice in the group.

 Dominion Resources, Inc.
NYSE: D
PO Box 26532
Richmond, VA 23261
(800) 552-4034

> **Performance Rating: * * * ***

## Performance History

- $1,000 invested on 12/31/85 was worth $3,303 on 12/31/95 — a 230 percent increase in 10 years.

## Plan Specifics

- Initial purchase is available to investors in all 50 states ($250 minimum initial investment). The company will waive the $250 minimum if an investor agrees to automatic monthly payments of $40 or more.
- Partial dividend reinvestment is available.
- No discount.
- OCP: $40 to $100,000 per quarter.
- OCP is invested twice monthly.
- There are no purchasing fees. Selling fees include brokerage commissions.
- Automatic investment services are available.
- Dividends are paid March, June, September, and December.

## Corporate Profile

Dominion Resources is a holding company for Virginia Electric & Power, which provides electric service to parts of Virginia and North Carolina. The region's economy includes government installations and technology companies. Residential users account for approximately 45 percent of total revenues. Primary fuels are nuclear and coal.

## Investment Advice

Dominion Resources would be a worthwhile holding in a portfolio. Dividend growth should at least match the industry average. Finances are strong and should fund customer growth. While the stock will not likely match its impressive performance of the last 10 years, its total returns should be in the upper half of all utilities.

DQE
  NYSE: DQE
PO Box 68
Pittsburgh, PA 15230-0068
(800) 247-0400 • (412) 393-6167

Performance Rating: * * * *

## Performance History

- $1,000 invested on 12/31/85 was worth $5,229 on 12/31/95 — a 423 percent increase in 10 years.

## Plan Specifics

- Initial purchase is available to investors in all 50 states ($100 minimum initial investment plus a $5 one-time account setup fee).
- Partial dividend reinvestment is available.
- No discount.
- OCP: $10 to $60,000 per year.
- OCP is invested monthly.
- Purchasing fees are nominal brokerage commissions. Selling fees are brokerage commissions and any handling fee.
- Preferred dividends may be reinvested for common shares.
- Automatic investment services are available.
- Dividends are paid January, April, July, and October.

## Corporate Profile

DQE is the holding company whose principal subsidiary is Duquesne Light. Its service territory of approximately 800 square miles in southwestern Pennsylvania has a population of 1.5 million. Nuclear power generates roughly 25 percent of electricity. Coal accounts for the remainder.

## Investment Advice

DQE offers a decent utility holding among no-load stocks with open enrollment. Total returns should at least match the industry average.

**DTE Energy**

DTE Energy Co.
NYSE: DTE
PO Box 33380
Detroit, MI 48232
(800) 551-5009 • (800) 774-4117

> **Performance Rating: \* \* \***

## Performance History

- $1,000 invested on 12/31/85 was worth $4,564 on 12/31/95 — a 356 percent increase in 10 years.

## Plan Specifics

- Initial purchase is available to investors in all 50 states ($100 minimum initial investment).
- Partial dividend reinvestment is available.
- No discount.
- OCP: $25 to $100,000 per year.
- OCP is invested monthly.
- Purchasing fees are $1 per purchase administrative charge plus brokerage commissions. Selling costs are brokerage fees.
- Preferred dividends may be reinvested for additional common shares.
- Dividends are paid January, April, July, and October.

## Corporate Profile

DTE Energy is the holding company for Detroit Edison. The firm provides electricity services to southeastern Michigan. The auto industry is a major industrial customer. The firm's primary fuel source is coal, with approximately 10 percent of electricity generated by nuclear fuel.

## Investment Advice

Given the company's dependence on commercial and industrial customers (more than 60 percent of total revenues), these shares are vulnerable to new competition in an era of deregulation in the utility field. DTE has taken measures to nail down current industrial customers. Nevertheless, this company will be tested in the utility markets of tomorrow.

Duke Power Co.
NYSE: DUK
Attn: Investor Relations Dept., PO Box 1005
Charlotte, NC 28201-1005
(800) 488-3853

| Performance Rating: * * * * * |

## Performance History

- $1,000 invested on 12/31/85 was worth $4,463 on 12/31/95 — a 346 percent increase in 10 years.

## Plan Specifics

- Initial purchase is available to residents of North Carolina and South Carolina ($25 minimum initial investment).
- Partial dividend reinvestment is available.
- No discount.
- OCP: $25 to $20,000 per quarter.
- OCP is invested monthly.
- There are no purchasing fees. Selling fees include brokerage commissions.
- Preferred dividends may be reinvested for additional common shares.
- Automatic investment services are available.
- Dividends are paid March, June, September, and December.

## Corporate Profile

Duke Power sells electricity in portions of North Carolina and South Carolina. Residential customers account for roughly one-third of total revenues; commercial and industrial, 53 percent. Power sources are primarily nuclear and coal. Duke Power's service area should grow at an above-average rate. The company's rates are on the low side, which puts it in a good position to fend off increased competition down the road.

## Investment Advice

Investors who live in North Carolina and South Carolina should take advantage of the firm's no-load stock program. Strong dividend-growth prospects, an attractive service region, and above-average appreciation prospects relative to the rest of the industry make this issue an excellent holding. Investors who cannot buy their initial shares directly should still consider joining the firm's dividend reinvestment plan after making initial purchases through a broker.

Duke Realty Investments, Inc.
NYSE: DRE
8888 Keystone Crossing, Ste. 1200
Indianapolis, IN 46240
(800) 278-4353 • (800) 774-4117 • (317) 574-3531

Realty Investments

| Performance Rating: * * * |
| --- |

## Performance History: Not available. ————————

## Plan Specifics ——————————————————————

- Initial purchase is available to investors in all 50 states ($250 minimum initial investment).
- Partial dividend reinvestment is not available.
- 4 percent discount on reinvested dividends.
- OCP: $100 to $5,000 per month.
- OCP is invested monthly.
- There are no purchasing fees. Selling fees include brokerage commissions.
- Automatic investment services are available.
- Plan Administrator: American Stock Transfer & Trust Co. (800) 278-4353.
- Dividends are paid February, May, August, and November.

## Corporate Profile ————————————————————

Duke Realty Investments provides leasing and management services for a variety of properties. The firm has a diversified portfolio of properties, including industrial, office, and retail space. The company has expanded at a rapid clip in recent years. The stock has been a good performer in recent years relative to the average real estate investment trust.

## Investment Advice ————————————————————

Duke Realty offers a worthwhile choice for investors who want to diversify their portfolios to include real estate. The stock will be vulnerable to interest-rate movements but has good total-return potential.

**TheEastern
Company**

Eastern Company
ASE: EML
112 Bridge St.
Naugatuck, CT 06770
(203) 729-2255 • (800) 633-3455

**Performance Rating: \* \***

## Performance History

- $1,000 invested on 12/31/85 was worth $2,969 on 12/31/95 — a 197 percent increase in 10 years.

## Plan Specifics

- Initial purchase is available to investors in all 50 states ($250 minimum initial investment). One-time enrollment fee of $5.
- Partial dividend reinvestment is available.
- No discount.
- OCP: $50 to $150,000 per year.
- OCP is invested weekly.
- There are no purchasing fees. Selling costs are brokerage commissions and maximum $10 service fee.
- Automatic investment services are available.
- Plan Administrator: The First National Bank of Boston (800) 633-3455.
- Dividends are paid March, June, September, and December.

## Corporate Profile

Eastern manufactures locks and security hardware. The firm's products are used in the mining and security businesses. Eastern is one of the smaller no-load stocks, with annual revenues of less than $100 million. Profits have been uneven over the last several years. Dividend growth has been either modest or nonexistent since 1991. The company has received takeover overtures in the past, which enhances speculative appeal.

## Investment Advice

Eastern's stock has been a fairly lackluster performer over the years. Price action, takeover speculation aside, is likely to be uneventful going forward.

**Endesa**

Empresa Nacional de Electricidad S.A.
NYSE: ELE
c/o Morgan Guaranty Trust Co., PO Box 9073
Boston, MA 02205
(800) 749-1687 • (800) 774-4117

Performance Rating: * * * *

## Performance History: Not available.

## Plan Specifics

- Initial purchase is available to investors in all states except North Dakota, Oregon, and Texas ($250 minimum initial investment).
- Partial dividend reinvestment is available.
- No discount.
- OCP: $50 to $100,000 per year.
- OCP is invested weekly.
- Automatic investment services are available.
- Annual administration fee of $15 must accompany initial stock purchase and may be paid with a credit card.
- Purchasing and selling costs include a transaction fee of $5, plus brokerage commissions of approximately 12 cents per share.
- Investors will be assessed a brokerage commission of approximately 12 cents per share to reinvest dividends.
- Shares may be sold via the telephone.
- Plan Administrator: Morgan Guaranty Trust Co. (800) 749-1687.
- Dividends are paid January and July.

## Corporate Profile

Empresa Nacional is Spain's largest producer of electricity. Commercial and industrial users comprise roughly 70 percent of total revenues. The firm has expanded its position in Europe via investments in Germany and Portugal.

## Investment Advice

Empresa Nacional has been a good performer for investors, and the company's long-term prospects remain attractive. Fluctuations in currency exchange rates will affect profits and the stock price. Nevertheless, these shares provide an interesting way for a utility investor to diversify a portfolio overseas.

**ΞNΞRGΞN**
          Energen Corp.
           NYSE: EGN
          2101 Sixth Ave. N.
          Birmingham, AL 35203
          (800) 286-9178 • (800) 774-4117

> **Performance Rating: * * * * ***

## Performance History

- $1,000 invested on 12/31/85 was worth $3,821 on 12/31/95 — a 282 percent increase in 10 years.

## Plan Specifics

- Initial purchase is available to investors in all 50 states ($250 minimum initial investment).
- Partial dividend reinvestment is available.
- No discount.
- OCP: $25 to $100,000 per year.
- OCP is invested monthly.
- There are no purchasing fees. Selling costs are brokerage commissions and transfer taxes.
- Automatic investment services are available.
- Plan Administrator: Harris Trust and Savings Bank (800) 286-9178.
- Dividends are paid March, June, September, and December.

## Corporate Profile

Energen is the largest natural-gas distributor in Alabama. The firm is also involved in oil and gas production via its Taurus Exploration unit. The company is expanding its exploration and production business, which will likely lend some volatility to the earnings stream. Dividends have increased annually since 1982.

## Investment Advice

Energen has one of the better track records in the natural-gas utility sector. Investors who want representation among natural-gas utilities should preference these shares.

Enova Corp.
NYSE: ENA
101 Ash St.
San Diego, CA 92101
(619) 696-2020 • (800) 821-2550 • (800) 307-7343

> **Performance Rating: \* \* \***

## Performance History

- $1,000 invested on 12/31/85 was worth $3,337 on 12/31/95 — a 234 percent increase in 10 years.

## Plan Specifics

- Initial purchase is available to investors in all 50 states ($250 minimum initial investment or automatic monthly investments of at least $25). One-time enrollment fee of $15.
- Partial dividend reinvestment is available.
- No discount.
- OCP: $25 to $150,000 per year.
- OCP is invested at least weekly.
- There are no purchasing fees. Selling costs are brokerage commissions and a $10 fee.
- Automatic investments services are available.
- Shares may be sold via the telephone.
- Participants may establish a stock-secured loan or line of credit, backed by shares held on deposit.
- Plan Administrator: First Chicago Trust-NY (800) 307-7343.
- Dividends are paid January, April, July, and October.

## Corporate Profile

Enova is the holding company for San Diego Gas & Electric. Natural gas, nuclear, and purchased power account for the bulk of fuel sources. Enova's rates are fairly competitive with other utilities in the state, which should be a plus when "open" utility markets come to California. Dividend growth should be about average for the industry. The company has agreed to merge with Pacific Enterprises.

## Investment Advice

Enova has reasonable total-return potential. However, I don't find these shares particularly attractive relative to some other utilities offering no-load stock plans, such as Wisconsin Energy and WPS Resources.

Enron Corp.
NYSE: ENE
1400 Smith St.
Houston, TX 77002
(713) 853-6161 • (800) 446-2617 • (800) 662-7662

> **Performance Rating: * * ***

## Performance History

■ $1,000 invested on 12/31/85 was worth $5,095 on 12/31/95 — a 410 percent increase in 10 years.

## Plan Specifics

■ Initial purchase is available to investors in all 50 states ($250 minimum initial investment). Company charges a $17 set-up fee plus brokerage charges.
■ Partial dividend reinvestment is available.
■ No discount.
■ OCP: $25 to $120,000 per year.
■ OCP is invested weekly.
■ There are no purchasing fees. Selling costs are $15 plus brokerage fees.
■ Automatic investment services are available ($1 fee).
■ Stock may be sold via the telephone.
■ Plan Administrator: First Chicago Trust-NY (800) 446-2617.
■ Dividends are paid March, June, September, and December.

## Corporate Profile

Enron operates the nation's largest natural-gas pipeline. The firm is also engaged in oil and gas exploration and production. The company has laid out fairly aggressive growth goals, which could generate investor interest should these goals be met.

## Investment Advice

Enron has enjoyed decent investor support over the years. Overseas expansion opportunities should boost the bottom line. Still, the historical volatility of the earnings stream over the last decade makes it difficult for me to give these shares more than three stars.

Entergy Corp.
NYSE: ETR
PO Box 61000
New Orleans, LA 70161
(504) 576-4218 • (800) 333-4368 • (800) 225-1721

| Performance Rating: * * |
|---|

## Performance History: Not available.

## Plan Specifics

- Initial purchase is available to investors in all 50 states ($1,000 minimum initial investment).
- Partial dividend reinvestment is available.
- Up to 3 percent discount on OCPs.
- OCP: $100 to $3,000 per month. The $3,000 per month maximum may be waived pursuant to a request approved by Entergy.
- OCP is invested monthly.
- Purchasing fees are $5 per transaction. Selling costs are $15 plus 12 cents per share brokerage commissions.
- Plan Administrator: ChaseMellon Shareholder Investment Service (800) 333-4368.
- Dividends are paid March, June, September, and December.

## Corporate Profile

Entergy provides electricity services to parts of Arkansas, Texas, Louisiana, and Mississippi. Nuclear power accounts for approximately 30 percent of fuel generation. Residential customers make up about 36 percent of total revenues. Finances are a cut below the average utility. Furthermore, dividend growth has been nonexistent in recent years.

## Investment Advice

Entergy carries a higher risk than some other utilities. Investors would do well to focus attention on higher-quality electric utilities.

Equitable Companies
NYSE: EQ
787 Seventh Ave.
New York, NY 10019
(800) 437-8736 • (800) 774-4117

Performance Rating: * * * *

## Performance History: Not available.

## Plan Specifics

- Initial purchase is available to investors in all 50 states ($500 minimum initial investment).
- Partial dividend reinvestment is not available.
- No discount.
- OCP: $50 to $50,000 per year.
- OCP is invested weekly.
- There are no purchasing fees. Selling costs are brokerage commissions, a $10 service fee, and any other cost of sale.
- Automatic investment services are available.
- Plan Administrator: First Chicago Trust-NY (800) 437-8736.
- Dividends are paid March, June, September, and December.

## Corporate Profile

Equitable Companies has positions in two industries — insurance products and financial services. The firm's Equitable Life Assurance Society of the U.S. is one of the largest U.S. life insurance companies. In the financial-services sector, the firm has ownership positions in Alliance Capital Management, a major investment adviser, and Donaldson, Lufkin & Jenrette, a major Wall Street firm. Profits have benefited from strong demand for annuities and surging financial markets in recent years. While quarterly comparisons may be more difficult over time due to a likely slowdown in the equity markets, the company's bottom line should maintain its upward trend.

## Investment Advice

While the stock's sensitivity to interest rates and the stock and bond markets enhances volatility, long-term potential should be above average. Investors should feel comfortable holding these shares in their portfolios.

Exxon Corp.
  NYSE: XON
PO Box 160369
Irving, TX 75016-0369
(800) 252-1800 • (214) 444-1000

> **Performance Rating: * * * * ***

## Performance History

- $1,000 invested on 12/31/85 was worth $4,635 on 12/31/95 — a 364 percent increase in 10 years.

## Plan Specifics

- Initial purchase is available to investors in all 50 states ($250 minimum initial investment).
- Partial dividend reinvestment is available.
- No discount.
- OCP: $50 to $100,000 per year.
- OCP is invested weekly.
- There are no purchasing fees. Selling fees include a $5 administrative charge plus brokerage commissions.
- IRA option is available ($20 annual administrative fee).
- Automatic investment services are available.
- Plan Administrator: Bank of Boston (800) 252-1800.
- Dividends are paid March, June, September, and December.

## Corporate Profile

Exxon is a leading oil company. Foreign exploration, production, and refining operations account for more than 50 percent of total profits. The firm has small operations in chemicals and coal. Profits have generally trended higher over the years. Over the long term, higher oil prices should help profits.

## Investment Advice

Exxon is one of the top no-load stocks. Its "user-friendly" no-load stock program, with such options as IRA, weekly investments, and automatic investment services, enhances the appeal of these shares. Among no-load stocks in the oil group, Exxon is the most attractive. I'm a participant in the plan and recommend these shares for any investor.

Fiat S.P.A.
   NYSE: FIA
c\o Morgan Guaranty Trust Co., PO Box 9073
Boston, MA 02205
(800) 749-1687 • (800) 774-4117

| Performance Rating: * * |
|---|

## Performance History: Not available.

## Plan Specifics

- Initial purchase is available to investors in all states except North Dakota, Oregon, and Texas ($250 minimum initial investment).
- Partial dividend reinvestment is available.
- No discount.
- OCP: $50 to $100,000 per year.
- OCP is invested weekly.
- Automatic investment services are available.
- Annual administration fee of $15 must accompany initial stock purchase and may be paid with a credit card.
- Purchasing and selling costs include a transaction fee of $5, plus brokerage commissions of approximately 12 cents per share.
- Investors will be assessed a brokerage commission of approximately 12 cents per share to reinvest dividends.
- Shares may be sold via the telephone.
- Plan Administrator: Morgan Guaranty Trust Co. (800) 749-1687.
- Dividends are paid in August.

## Corporate Profile

Fiat is one of the largest automakers in Europe. This Italy-based company also has interests in agricultural and construction equipment, publishing, financial services, and insurance. Per-share profits have been extremely uneven over the last several years.

## Investment Advice

Fiat's track record has been mediocre, and the company's mature markets make it difficult to generate the type of growth that catches Wall Street's eye.

*First Commercial Corporation*

# First Commercial Corp.
## NASDAQ: FCLR
400 W. Capitol Ave.
Little Rock, AR 72201
(501) 371-7000 • (501) 371-6716 • (800) 482-8410

> **Performance Rating:** * * * *

## Performance History

- $1,000 invested on 12/31/85 was worth $8,481 on 12/31/95 — a 748 percent increase in 10 years.

## Plan Specifics

- Initial purchase is available to investors in all 50 states ($500 minimum initial investment).
- Partial dividend reinvestment is not available.
- 5 percent discount on reinvested dividends.
- OCP: $25 to $2,500 per quarter.
- OCP is invested monthly.
- There are no purchasing fees. Participants must go through own broker to sell shares.
- Dividends are paid January, April, July, and October.

## Corporate Profile

First Commercial owns banks in Arkansas, Texas, and Tennessee. The firm has grown in recent years via acquisitions, and this growth strategy will likely continue. Earnings have trended higher over the last several years. The stock price has benefited from the solid bottom line growth and the stock market's penchant for banks. Dividends have grown at a healthy clip, and dividend growth should continue.

## Investment Advice

First Commercial will not likely match the strong gains of the last decade. Still, this is one of the better banking issues offering a no-load stock. The takeover activity in the banking field enhances speculative appeal.

First USA, Inc.

# FIRST USA
NYSE: FUS
1601 Elm St.
Dallas, TX 75201
(214) 849-2000 • (800) 524-4458

> **Performance Rating:** * * * *

## Performance History: Not available.

## Plan Specifics

- Initial purchase is available to investors in all states except North Carolina, North Dakota, and Vermont ($1,000 minimum initial investment).
- Partial dividend reinvestment is available.
- Up to 5 percent discount on reinvested dividends and OCPs.
- OCP: $100 to $3,000 per month. OCPs in excess of $3,000 may be made with permission of the company by calling (214) 849-3700.
- OCP is invested monthly.
- Purchasing fees include $1.50 service fee plus applicable brokerage commissions. Selling fees are $5 administrative fee plus applicable brokerage commission.
- Plan Administrator: Bank of New York (800) 524-4458.
- Dividends are paid February, May, August, and November.

## Corporate Profile

First USA is one of the largest issuers of Visa and MasterCard credit cards. The firm also has operations in the payment-processing business. The company sells its cards primarily through direct marketing and affinity marketing programs. Per-share profits, fueled by the steady demand for credit cards, have grown at a dramatic rate since 1992. Dividend growth has followed the upward earnings path. Long term, the increasingly competitive credit card market may crimp earnings growth. Still, the bottom line should show ample gains.

## Investment Advice

First USA is an excellent holding for investors who want participation in the credit card market. The stock will show periodic volatility, especially during periods of rising charge write-offs. Still, long-term appreciation potential should be well above average.

**FLORIDA
PROGRESS**
CORPORATION

Florida Progress Corp.
NYSE: FPC
Investor Services
PO Box 33028
St. Petersburg, FL 33733-8028
(800) 352-1121 • (813) 824-6400

Performance Rating: * * * *

## Performance History

- $1,000 invested on 12/31/85 was worth $3,197 on 12/31/95 — a 220 percent increase in 10 years.

## Plan Specifics

- Initial purchase is available to residents of the state of Florida ($100 minimum initial investment).
- Partial dividend reinvestment is available.
- No discount.
- OCP: $10 to $100,000 per year.
- OCP is invested monthly.
- Purchasing and selling fees include brokerage commissions and other fees.
- Dividends are paid March, June, September, and December.

## Corporate Profile

Florida Progress owns Florida Power, which provides electric service to over 1.2 million customers. The firm also has operations in coal mining, transportation, financial services, and real estate development. Residential customers account for roughly 47 percent of total revenues. The energy mix is approximately 45 percent coal, 16 percent oil, 17 percent nuclear, and 22 percent purchased and other. Florida Progress, like most utilities, is trying to get its costs under control. Florida has generally been a reasonable regulatory state, which is a plus.

## Investment Advice

Florida Progress has worthwhile total-return prospects. Florida residents who desire to add to the income portion of a portfolio should consider taking advantage of the company's no-load stock program.

## General Growth Properties, Inc.

GENERAL GROWTH PROPERTIES, INC.    NYSE: GGP
55 W. Monroe, Suite 3100
Chicago, IL 60603-5060
(312) 551-5000 • (888) 291-3713 • (800) 774-4117

> **Performance Rating: * * ***

## Performance History: Not available.

## Plan Specifics

- Initial purchase is available to investors in all 50 states ($200 minimum initial investment, plus $15 enrollment fee). The firm will waive the $200 initial minimum investment if an investor agrees to automatic monthly investments of at least $50.
- Partial dividend reinvestment is available.
- No discount.
- OCP: $50 to $125,000 per quarter.
- OCP is invested weekly.
- Investors will be assessed a fee of 4 percent of the purchase amount (maximum $2.50) for each reinvested dividend.
- Purchasing fees are $5 for each OCP plus 5 cents per share brokerage commission. Selling costs are $10 plus 15 cents per share brokerage commission.
- Automatic investment services are available ($3 processing fee).
- Shares may be sold via the telephone.
- Plan Administrator: Norwest Shareowner Services (888) 291-3713.
- Dividends are paid January, April, July, and October.

## Corporate Profile

General Growth Properties, which began trading publicly in 1993, owns and operates regional shopping centers. The acquisition of Homart Development made the company the largest shopping center owner, manager, and developer in the U.S.

## Investment Advice

General Growth has a decent track record of earnings and dividend growth. Real estate investment trusts are vulnerable to rising interest rates and declines in retail spending. Thus, investors should not have a large exposure to these shares.

## Grand Metropolitan PLC
### NYSE: GRM
c/o Morgan Guaranty Trust Co., PO Box 9073
Boston, MA 02205
(800) 749-1687 • (800) 774-4117

> **Performance Rating: \* \* \***

## Performance History: Not available. ―――――――

## Plan Specifics ――――――――――――――――――

- Initial purchase is available to investors in all states except North Dakota, Oregon, and Texas ($250 minimum initial investment).
- Partial dividend reinvestment is available.
- No discount.
- OCP: $50 to $100,000 per year.
- OCP is invested weekly.
- Annual administration fee of $15 must accompany initial stock purchase and may be paid with a credit card.
- Purchasing and selling costs include a transaction fee of $5, plus brokerage commissions of approximately 12 cents per share.
- Investors will be assessed a brokerage commission of approximately 12 cents per share to reinvest dividends.
- Automatic investment services are available.
- Shares may be sold via the telephone.
- Plan Administrator: Morgan Guaranty Trust Co. (800) 749-1687.
- Dividends are paid April and October.

## Corporate Profile ―――――――――――――――――

Grand Metropolitan PLC, based in the United Kingdom, produces various distilled spirits (Smirnoff vodka, Baileys Original Irish Cream), makes foods (Pillsbury products, Haagen-Dazs ice cream), and owns restaurants (Burger King). Business in the U.S. accounts for more than 50 percent of total revenues.

## Investment Advice ―――――――――――――――――

Even with well-known brand names, Grand Metropolitan has been unable to show sustained upward earnings. The company's far-reaching operations lend themselves to restructurings and asset sales — the type of events usually rewarded on Wall Street. However, without such developments, these shares are likely only to track the market.

Green Mountain Power Corp.
NYSE: GMP
25 Green Mountain Dr.
South Burlington, VT 05402
(802) 864-5731 • (800) 647-4273

| Performance Rating: * * |

## Performance History

■ $1,000 invested on 12/31/85 was worth $2,837 on 12/31/95 — a
  184 percent increase in 10 years.

## Plan Specifics

■ Initial purchase is available to residents of Vermont ($50 minimum
  initial investment).
■ Partial dividend reinvestment is available.
■ 5 percent discount on reinvested dividends.
■ OCP: $50 to $40,000 per year.
■ OCP is invested monthly.
■ There are no purchasing fees. Selling costs are brokerage commissions.
■ Plan Administrator: Chemical Bank (800) 647-4273.
■ Dividends are paid March, June, September, and December.

## Corporate Profile

Green Mountain Power provides electric utility services in Vermont.
Hydropower and nuclear account for the bulk of electricity generation.
One-third of total revenues come from residential customers. The
company's dividend growth has been meager or nonexistent over the
last four years.

## Investment Advice

Green Mountain Power has been an uneventful performer over the
years. With limited dividend-growth prospects and a fairly mature
service region, these shares have little appeal.

GUIDANT

Guidant Corp.
NYSE: GDT
111 Monument Circle, 29th Floor
Indianapolis, IN 46204
(800) 537-1677 • (800) 317-4445

Performance Rating: * * * *

## Performance History: Not available.

## Plan Specifics

- Initial purchase is available to investors in all 50 states ($250 minimum initial investment). Initial purchase fees are $15 plus 3 cents per share.
- Partial dividend reinvestment is available.
- No discount.
- OCP: $50 to $150,000 per year.
- OCP is invested at least weekly.
- Purchasing fees are 5 percent of the amount invested (maximum $7.50) plus brokerage commissions. Selling costs are $15 plus 12 cents per share.
- Fees to reinvest dividends are a processing fee of 5 percent of the dividend up to a maximum of $3 plus applicable brokerage commissions.
- Automatic investment services are available ($1 charge per transaction).
- Shares may be sold via the telephone.
- Plan Administrator: First Chicago Trust-NY (800) 317-4445.
- Dividends are paid March, June, August, and November.

## Corporate Profile

Guidant, spun off by Eli Lilly in 1995, manufactures products used in cardiac rhythm management and coronary disease treatment. The firm is a leader in various coronary angioplasty markets. The company's bottom line has shown impressive growth in recent years.

## Investment Advice

Guidant's high-growth markets will attract competitors over time, which will impact the firm's double-digit profit margins. Still, the company has a solid market niche and excellent long-term appreciation potential.

Hawaiian Electric Industries, Inc.
  NYSE: HE
PO Box 730
Honolulu, HI 96808-0730
(808) 543-5662 • (808) 532-5841

> **Performance Rating: * * ***

## Performance History

- $1,000 invested on 12/31/85 was worth $2,840 on 12/31/95 — a 184 percent increase in 10 years.

## Plan Specifics

- Initial purchase is available to investors in all 50 states ($100 minimum initial investment).
- Partial dividend reinvestment is available.
- No discount.
- OCP: $25 to $100,000 per year.
- OCP is invested twice monthly.
- There are no purchasing fees. Selling fees include brokerage commissions and a $10 service charge.
- Charge of $0.50 per quarter to reinvest dividends.
- Automatic investment services are available.
- Preferred dividends may be reinvested for common shares.
- Dividends are paid March, June, September, and December.

## Corporate Profile

Hawaiian Electric Industries is a public utility holding company providing electric service to nearly all of Hawaii's population. Residential customers account for roughly one-third of revenues. The primary fuel source is oil. A nonutility subsidiary is American Savings Bank.

## Investment Advice

The likelihood of modest dividend growth limits the appeal of these shares. The nonutility unit enhances growth prospects but also lends some volatility to the earnings stream. Performance going forward will likely be average at best.

**Hillenbrand Industries**

Hillenbrand Industries, Inc.
NYSE: HB
700 State Route 46 East
Batesville, IN 47006
(800) 286-9178 • (800) 774-4117 • (800) 445-4802

| Performance Rating: * * * * |
| --- |

## Performance History: Not available. ───────────

## Plan Specifics ──────────────────────────

- Initial purchase is available to investors in all 50 states ($250 minimum initial investment).
- Partial dividend reinvestment is available.
- No discount.
- OCP: $100 to $50,000 per year.
- OCP is invested at least weekly.
- Purchasing fees are $5 plus 10 cents per share. Selling costs are $10 plus 10 cents per share.
- Automatic investment services are available.
- Plan Administrator: Harris Trust Company (800) 445-4802.
- Dividends are paid February, April, July, and October.

## Corporate Profile ──────────────────────

Hillenbrand Industries is a leading maker of burial caskets. The firm also manufactures various hospital supplies, including hospital beds. Profits had shown good growth prior to 1995. However, an increasing cost-conscious hospital industry dampened sales of hospital supplies. The company's businesses should benefit from the "graying of America." Still, Wall Street is unlikely to return to these shares in full force until more evidence of a sustained earnings turnaround is seen.

## Investment Advice ──────────────────────

I give Hillenbrand a four-star rating, not so much for its potential over the next 12 months, but for its 3-5 year prospects. In that time, I expect the bottom line to get on track and the stock price to move higher.

Home Depot, Inc.
  NYSE: HD
2727 Paces Ferry Road
Atlanta, GA 30339
(800) 730-4001 • (800) 774-4117 • (770) 433-8211

> **Performance Rating: * * * * ***

## Performance History

- $1,000 invested on 12/31/85 was worth $39,820 on 12/31/95 — a 3,882 percent increase.

## Plan Specifics

- Initial purchase is available to investors in all 50 states ($250 minimum initial investment). There is a one-time enrollment fee of $5.
- Partial dividend reinvestment is not available.
- No discount.
- OCP: $25 to $100,000 per year.
- OCP is invested weekly.
- Purchasing fees are 5 percent of the amount invested (maximum $2.50) plus 5 cents per share for cash payments, automatic debits, and reinvested dividends. Selling fees are $5 plus 15 cents per share.
- Automatic investment services are available.
- Plan Administrator: Bank of Boston (800) 730-4001.
- Dividends are paid March, June, September, and December.

## Corporate Profile

Home Depot operates a chain of more than 400 building-supply and home-accessories stores. Steady store expansion should help profits continue to move higher at a rapid clip. Finances are strong and should handily fund future growth.

## Investment Advice

Home Depot's stock registered a huge advance over the last decade, although price action in recent years has slowed a bit. While future price action is unlikely to match the heady gains of the late '80s and early '90s, investors in these shares should still expect to see healthy capital gains over the next several years. The issue is one of the premier retailers among no-load stocks.

Home Properties of NY, Inc.
NYSE: HME
850 Clinton Square
Rochester, NY 14604
(716) 546-4900 • (800) 774-4117 • (800) 278-4353

| Performance Rating: * * * |
| --- |

## Performance History: Not available. ─────────

## Plan Specifics ─────────────────

- Initial purchase is available to investors in all 50 states ($2,000 minimum initial investment).
- Partial dividend reinvestment is available (must reinvest dividends on at least 100 shares).
- 3 percent discount on reinvested dividends and OCPs.
- OCP: $50 to $5,000 per month. Investors may request a waiver to invest more than the $5,000 monthly maximum by calling (716) 546-4900.
- OCP is invested monthly.
- There are no purchasing fees. Selling fees are brokerage commissions.
- Plan Administrator: American Stock Transfer & Trust Co. (800) 278-4353.
- Dividends are paid February, May, August, and November.

## Corporate Profile ─────────────────

Home Properties is a real estate investment trust that concentrates its real estate operations on housing for mature residents. The firm's properties are located primarily in upstate New York. The stock began trading publicly in 1994.

## Investment Advice ─────────────────

Home Properties has done reasonably well over the last year or so. The company's focus on housing for seniors makes it an interesting demographic play. Still, investors should expect a fair amount of volatility with these shares.

Houston Industries, Inc.
NYSE: HOU
Investor Services Dept., PO Box 4505
Houston, TX 77210
(713) 629-3000 • (800) 231-6406 • (800) 774-4117

**Performance Rating: \* \* \***

## Performance History

- $1,000 invested on 12/31/85 was worth $3,688 on 12/31/95 — a 269 percent increase in 10 years.

## Plan Specifics

- Initial purchase is available to investors in all 50 states ($250 minimum initial investment).
- Partial dividend reinvestment is available.
- No discount.
- OCP: $50 to $120,000 per year.
- OCP is invested twice monthly.
- There are no purchasing fees unless shares are purchased on the open market. Selling costs are brokerage commissions.
- Houston Industries' debentures, first mortgage bonds, and preferred stock are eligible for reinvestment for common stock.
- Dividends are paid March, June, September, and December.

## Corporate Profile

Houston Industries is a utility holding company. The firm's Houston Lighting & Power Company is the nation's ninth-largest electric utility. The company sold its cable television operations in 1995. Commercial and industrial users account for nearly 60 percent of total revenues. Power requirements are derived primarily from gas and coal. The company also has exposure to nuclear power.

## Investment Advice

Houston Industries has only average prospects over the next few years. Dividend growth will likely be small or nonexistent. Expansion overseas offers one source of potential interest in these shares. Nevertheless, the stock would not be my first choice among electric utilities.

Idaho Power Co.
NYSE: IDA
PO Box 70
Boise, ID 83707
(800) 635-5406

> **Performance Rating: \* \* \***

## Performance History

- $1,000 invested on 12/31/85 was worth $2,555 on 12/31/95 — a 156 percent increase in 10 years.

## Plan Specifics

- Initial purchase is available to residential customers of the company ($10 minimum initial investment).
- Partial dividend reinvestment is available.
- No discount.
- OCP: $10 to $15,000 per quarter.
- OCP is invested quarterly.
- Purchasing fees are approximately 4 cents per share when shares are purchased on the open market. The plan permits investors to sell up to 99 shares when terminating the account.
- Dividends are paid February, May, August, and November.

## Corporate Profile

Idaho Power supplies electricity to a 20,000-square-mile area encompassing parts of southern Idaho, eastern Oregon, and northern Nevada. Hydroelectric and coal are the primary fuels. The biggest contributors to revenues are commercial and industrial customers, together accounting for roughly 39 percent of total sales.

## Investment Advice

Idaho Power has a few things going for it, such as a fast-growing service region. However, the need for external financing to service its growing region could put a strain on finances. On balance, the stock will likely track the average utility holding.

IES Industries, Inc.
NYSE: IES
200 First St. SE
Cedar Rapids, IA 52401
(800) 247-9785 • (800) 774-4117

| Performance Rating: * * * |

## Performance History

- $1,000 invested on 12/31/85 was worth $2,720 on 12/31/95 — a 172 percent increase in 10 years.

## Plan Specifics

- Initial purchase is available to customers of the utility ($25 minimum initial investment).
- Partial dividend reinvestment is available.
- No discount.
- OCP: $25 to $120,000 per year.
- OCP is invested monthly.
- There are no purchasing fees. Selling costs include brokerage commissions.
- Dividends are paid January, April, July, and October.

## Corporate Profile

IES Industries supplies electricity and natural gas in communities in Iowa. The firm has agreed to merge with WPL Holdings. Residential customers account for approximately 37 percent of total revenues. Coal accounts for about half of the fuel source, with nuclear and purchased power accounting for the remainder. The firm's nonutility operations include rail and barge services.

## Investment Advice

IES is not a particularly noteworthy selection in the utility group, especially in light of the pending acquisition.

Illinova Corp.
 NYSE: ILN
Attn: Shareholder Services
500 S. 27th St.
Decatur, IL 62525-1805
(800) 800-8220 • (800) 750-7011

Performance Rating: * * *

## Performance History

■ ⸂1,000 invested on 12/31/85 was worth $2,142 on 12/31/95 — a 114 percent increase in 10 years.

## Plan Specifics

■ Initial purchase is available to investors in all 50 states ($250 minimum initial investment).
■ Partial dividend reinvestment is available.
■ No discount.
■ OCP: $25 to $60,000 per year.
■ OCP is invested twice monthly.
■ There are no purchasing fees. Selling costs are brokerage commissions and other fees.
■ Automatic investment services are available.
■ Preferred dividends are eligible for reinvestment for common shares.
■ Dividends are paid February, May, August, and November.

## Corporate Profile

Illinova provides electricity and natural-gas services to customers in Illinois. More than 60 percent of fuel generation is coal. The firm cut its dividend in the late '80s. However, dividend growth has been above average in recent years.

## Investment Advice

Illinova has solid dividend-growth prospects. However, finances are average at best, and the growth potential of its service region is limited. There are better utilities among those offering no-load stock plans.

Imperial Chemical Industries PLC
   NYSE: ICI
c/o Morgan Guaranty Trust Co., PO Box 9073
Boston, MA 02205
(800) 749-1687 • (800) 774-4117

| Performance Rating: * * * * |
|---|

## Performance History: Not available.

## Plan Specifics

- Initial purchase is available to investors in all states except North Dakota, Oregon, and Texas ($250 minimum initial investment).
- Partial dividend reinvestment is available.
- No discount.
- OCP: $50 to $100,000 per year.
- OCP is invested weekly.
- Annual administration fee of $15 must accompany initial stock purchase and may be paid with a credit card.
- Purchase and selling costs include a transaction fee of $5, plus brokerage commissions of approximately 12 cents per share.
- Investors will be assessed a brokerage commission of approximately 12 cents per share to reinvest dividends.
- Automatic investment services are available.
- Shares may be sold via the telephone.
- Plan Administrator: Morgan Guaranty Trust Co. (800) 749-1687.
- Dividends are paid May and October.

## Corporate Profile

   Imperial Chemical Industries is a United Kingdom-based producer of chemicals, plastics, and paints. The United Kingdom accounts for a little over one-third of total sales. Earnings should show good growth in 1997.

## Investment Advice

   Imperial Chemical's exposure to cyclical markets may cause periodic volatility in the earnings stream and stock price. Still, the firm has attractive positions in its primary markets and ample earning power. These shares would be an acceptable holding in most portfolios.

**Integon Corporation**

Integon Corp.
NYSE: IN
PO Box 3199
Winston-Salem, NC 27102-3199
(910) 770-2000 • (800) 826-3978 • (800) 446-2617

| Performance Rating: * * * |
|---|

## Performance History: Not available.

## Plan Specifics

- Initial purchase is available to investors in all 50 states ($500 minimum initial investment). There is an enrollment fee of $7.50.
- Partial dividend reinvestment is available.
- No discount.
- OCP: $50 to $120,000 per year.
- OCP is invested twice monthly.
- There are no purchasing fees. Selling fees are $10 plus 12 cents per share brokerage commission.
- Automatic investment services are available.
- Shares may be sold via the telephone.
- Plan Administrator: First Chicago Trust-NY (800) 446-2617.
- Dividends are paid March, June, September, and December.

## Corporate Profile

Integon underwrites auto insurance for high-risk drivers. The firm has been expanding geographically in the last few years. As major insurance carriers tighten their underwriting requirements, Integon's market should grow. The bottom line should trend upward over the next several years.

## Investment Advice

While I can give Integon only three stars at this time due partly to its mixed track record, I think these shares have interesting potential over the next 2-3 years. More aggressive investors may want to give these shares a second look.

**Interchange Financial Services Corp.**
ASE: ISB
Park 80 West/Plaza Two
Saddle Brook, NJ 07662
(201) 703-2265 • (212) 509-4000

**Performance Rating: \* \* \***

## Performance History

- $1,000 invested on 12/31/85 was worth $2,094 on 12/31/95 — a 109 percent increase in 10 years.

## Plan Specifics

- Initial purchase is available to investors in all 50 states ($100 minimum initial investment).
- Partial dividend reinvestment is not available.
- No discount.
- OCP: $25 to no maximum (must be in multiples of $10).
- OCP is invested monthly.
- Purchasing and selling fees are brokerage commissions.
- Plan Administrator: Continental Stock Transfer & Trust Co. (212) 509-4000.
- Dividends are paid January, April, July, and October.

## Corporate Profile

Interchange Financial Services operates banks in New Jersey. Residential real estate is the firm's biggest source of loans. Profits have picked up nicely in the last few years. The total number of shares outstanding is less than 3 million.

## Investment Advice

Interchange's relatively small size makes these shares a logical takeover candidate. While I prefer Regions Financial among no-load regional banks, these shares have reasonable speculative appeal.

Interstate Power Co.
NYSE: IPW
PO Box 769, 1000 Main St.
Dubuque, IA 52004-0769
(319) 582-5421

Performance Rating: * * *

## Performance History

■ $1,000 invested on 12/31/85 was worth $3,131 on 12/31/95 — a 213 percent increase in 10 years.

## Plan Specifics

■ Initial purchase is available to utility customers ($50 minimum initial investment).
■ Partial dividend reinvestment is available.
■ No discount.
■ OCP: $25 to $2,000 per month.
■ OCP is invested monthly.
■ Purchasing and selling costs may include brokerage commissions.
■ Dividends are paid March, June, September, and December.

## Corporate Profile

Interstate Power provides utility services to customers in Iowa, Minnesota, and Illinois. The service area is primarily rural, although the firm does have a sizable exposure to industrial and commercial users. Electricity services generate more than 80 percent of total revenues, with natural-gas services accounting for the remainder. Coal is the primary fuel source. The firm is planning to merge with WPL Holdings and IES Industries.

## Investment Advice

There is nothing particularly noteworthy about Interstate to warrant investment, particularly in light of its pending merger. Dividend growth will likely be minimal.

**INVESTORS**
FINANCIAL SERVICES CORP.

Investors Financial Services Corp.
NASDAQ: IFIN
89 South St.
Boston, MA 02111
(617) 330-6700 • (888) 333-5336

> **Performance Rating: * * ***

## Performance History: Not available. ——————————

## Plan Specifics ————————————————————————

- Initial purchase is available to investors in all 50 states ($250 minimum initial investment plus a $10 service fee and 10 cents per share).
- Dividend reinvestment is not available.
- No discount.
- OCP: $100 minimum, no maximum.
- OCP is invested at least weekly.
- Purchasing fees are $5 plus 10 cents per share. Selling costs are $15 plus 12 cents per share.
- Automatic investment services are available ($2 fee plus 10 cents per share).
- Shares may be sold via the telephone.
- Plan Administrator: First Chicago Trust-NY (888) 333-5336.
- Dividends are paid February, May, August, and November.

## Corporate Profile ————————————————————————

Investors Financial provides asset administration services for the financial-service industry. Services include accounting, transfer work, performance measurement, and mutual-fund administration. Profits have been rising in recent years.

## Investment Advice ————————————————————————

I'm giving these shares only 3 stars due to their limited trading history — the stock has been trading publicly only since November 1995. However, the company's markets have good growth potential which should help the firm's bottom line and stock price.

IPALCO Enterprises, Inc.
NYSE: IPL
Shareholder Services
PO Box 798
Indianapolis, IN 46206-0798
(317) 261-8394 • (888) 847-2526 • (800) 774-4117

Performance Rating: * * * * *

## Performance History

■ $1,000 invested on 12/31/85 was worth $3,777 on 12/31/95 — a 278 percent increase in 10 years.

## Plan Specifics

■ Initial purchase is available to investors in all 50 states ( $250 minimum initial investment).
■ Partial dividend reinvestment is available.
■ No discount.
■ OCP: $25 to $100,000 per year.
■ OCP is invested twice monthly.
■ There are no purchasing fees unless shares are purchased on the open market. Selling costs are brokerage commissions.
■ Automatic investment services are available.
■ Dividends are paid January, April, July, and October.

## Corporate Profile

IPALCO Enterprises is the holding company for Indianapolis Power & Light, an electric utility servicing Indianapolis and surrounding areas. The company's primary fuel source is coal. Indiana generally offers a positive regulatory environment, which has been a plus for the company. The firm is a low-cost producer, which puts it in a solid competitive position.

## Investment Advice

IPALCO is one of the better electric utilities in the market. A positive regulatory climate, stellar finances, and above-average dividend-growth prospects make these shares a solid choice for income investors.

Johnson Controls, Inc.

JOHNSON     NYSE: JCI
CONTROLS    Shareholder Services
PO Box 591
Milwaukee, WI 53201-0591
(414) 228-2363 • (800) 828-1489

Performance Rating: * * * *

## Performance History

- $1,000 invested on 12/31/85 was worth $3,861 on 12/31/95 — a 286 percent increase in 10 years.

## Plan Specifics

- Initial purchase is available to investors in all 50 states ($50 minimum initial investment).
- Partial dividend reinvestment is available.
- No discount.
- OCP: $50 to $15,000 per quarter.
- OCP is invested monthly.
- There are no purchasing fees. Selling fees include brokerage commissions. There is a $5 service charge for termination.
- Plan Administrator: Firstar Trust Co. (800) 828-1489.
- Dividends are paid March, June, September, and December.

## Corporate Profile

Johnson Controls has operations in four primary markets. The biggest division in terms of revenues and profits is automotive. This unit manufactures seats and seating components. The controls segment, accounting for one-third of sales, manufactures, installs, and services control systems for nonresidential buildings. The plastics and batteries units comprise the remainder of sales and profits.

## Investment Advice

Johnson Controls is a quality company with strong market positions in its primary markets. The cyclical bent to its business could cause earnings to be erratic on a quarterly basis. Nevertheless, profits should trend higher over the long term, which should aid the stock price.

Kellwood Co.
NYSE: KWD
600 Kellwood Parkway
Chesterfield, MO 63017
(314) 576-3100 • (800) 321-1355

> Performance Rating: * * *

## Performance History

- $1,000 invested on 12/31/85 was worth $2,584 on 12/31/95 — a 158 percent increase in 10 years.

## Plan Specifics

- Initial purchase is available to investors in all 50 states ($100 minimum initial investment).
- Partial dividend reinvestment is available.
- No discount.
- OCP: $25 to $3,000 per month.
- OCP is invested monthly.
- There are no purchasing fees. Selling fees include brokerage commissions. There is a termination fee of $5.
- Plan Administrator: KeyCorp Shareholder Services (800) 321-1355.
- Dividends are paid March, June, September, and December.

## Corporate Profile

Kellwood is a leading marketer, merchandiser, and manufacturer of apparel. The company's products are sold in more than 25,000 stores in the U.S., Mexico, and Canada. Sales to Sears accounted for only 8 percent of total revenues in fiscal 1995, down from 50 percent in fiscal 1985. Kellwood has grown rapidly through acquisitions, and further moves on this front are expected.

## Investment Advice

Kellwood is carving out a growing niche in the retail apparel sector. Retailers tend to run hot and cold on Wall Street, and investors may have to accept some volatility with these shares. However, the stock has interesting turnaround potential.

Kerr-McGee Corp.
NYSE: KMG
PO Box 25861
Oklahoma City, OK 73125
(405) 270-3582 • (800) 786-2556 • (800) 395-2662

> **Performance Rating: * * * ***

## Performance History

- $1,000 invested on 12/31/85 was worth $2,548 on 12/31/95 — a 155 percent increase in 10 years.

## Plan Specifics

- Initial purchase is available to investors in all 50 states ($750 minimum initial investment).
- Partial dividend reinvestment is not available.
- No discount.
- OCP: $10 to $3,000 per quarter.
- OCP is invested monthly.
- No fees for purchasing or selling shares.
- Plan Administrator: Liberty Bank & Trust Co. of Oklahoma City (800) 395-2662.
- Dividends are paid January, April, July, and October.

## Corporate Profile

Kerr-McGee is involved in a variety of natural-resources markets. The firm conducts oil and natural-gas activities. The company also operates major coal and chemical businesses.

## Investment Advice

Kerr-McGee provides a way to play a variety of natural-resources markets. To be sure, the firm's track record is not exactly stellar. Still, restructuring of its business portfolio and better prospects for its production and exploration activities should help these shares post decent returns. The stock is a suitable selection for more aggressive investors.

Lucent Technologies, Inc.
NYSE: LU
600 Mountain Ave.
Murray Hill, NJ 07974
(888) 582-3686 • (908) 582-8500

Performance Rating: * * * * *

## Performance History: Not available. ─────────────

## Plan Specifics ──────────────────────────

- Initial purchase is available to investors in all 50 states ($1,000 minimum initial investment or automatic monthly withdrawals of at least $100). There is a $7.50 one-time enrollment fee.
- Partial dividend reinvestment is available.
- No discount.
- OCP: $100 to $50,000 per year.
- OCP is invested at least weekly.
- Purchasing fees are 10 percent of the amount invested (maximum $2) plus 10 cents per share. Selling costs are $10 plus 10 cents per share.
- Automatic investment services are available.
- IRA option is available ($30 first year, $35 annually thereafter).
- Plan Administrator: Bank of New York (888) 582-3686.
- Dividends are paid February, May, August, and November.

## Corporate Profile ─────────────────────────

Lucent Technologies, spun off from AT&T in 1996, is one of the world's largest providers of telecommunications equipment. More than 50 percent of 1995 revenues came from the sale of systems for network operators. Research and development activities are conducted through its Bell Laboratories unit.

## Investment Advice ─────────────────────────

I think Lucent will flourish now that it is no longer under AT&T's wings. The firm is in the position to sell its products to any and all telecommunications concerns. Granted, competition will likely be intense in these markets going forward. However, Lucent should remain a major global player. I own the stock and recommend the issue for any investor.

Madison Gas & Electric Co.
NASDAQ: MDSN
133 S. Blair St., PO Box 1231
Madison, WI 53701-1231
(608) 252-7000 • (800) 356-6423

> **Performance Rating: * * * ***

## Performance History

- $1,000 invested on 12/31/85 was worth $3,550 on 12/31/95 — a 255 percent increase in 10 years.

## Plan Specifics

- Initial purchase is available to investors in all 50 states ($50 minimum initial investment).
- Partial dividend reinvestment is available.
- No discount.
- OCP: $25 to $25,000 per quarter.
- OCP is invested monthly.
- Purchasing fees are approximately 8 cents per share brokerage commission when shares are purchased on the open market. Selling costs are approximately 8 cents per share.
- Dividends are paid March, June, September, and December.

## Corporate Profile

Madison Gas & Electric provides electricity (more than 60 percent of total revenues) and gas (approximately 40 percent) to Madison, Wisconsin and surrounding areas. The company's service region has been receiving its share of notoriety as one of the best places in the country to live. Thus, service-region growth should be above average over the next few years. The firm has consistently raised its dividend, and growth in the payout should continue.

## Investment Advice

The state of Wisconsin is home to several top-notch electric utilities offering no-load stock plans. Madison Gas & Electric has good finances and decent dividend-growth potential. I would feel comfortable owning these shares in a portfolio.

Mattel, Inc.
NYSE: MAT
333 Continental Blvd.
El Segundo, CA 90245-5012
(888) 909-9922 • (310) 252-2000

> **Performance Rating: * * * ***

## Performance History

- $1,000 invested on 12/31/85 was worth $7,639 on 12/31/95 — a 664 percent increase in 10 years.

## Plan Specifics

- Initial purchase is available to investors in all 50 states ($500 minimum initial investment). A service charge of $10 will be deducted from the initial investment.
- Partial dividend reinvestment is not available.
- No discount.
- OCP: $100 to $100,000 per year.
- OCP is invested weekly.
- Purchasing fees are $5 plus 8 cents per share. Selling costs are $10 plus 15 cents per share.
- Automatic investment services are available ($2.50 fee per transaction).
- Plan Administrator: First National Bank of Boston (888) 909-9922.
- Dividends are paid January, April, July, and October.

## Corporate Profile

Mattel is a leading producer of children's toys. Top sellers include Barbie dolls, Fisher-Price toys, Frisbees, and Hot Wheels. Despite the fickle nature of the toy industry, Mattel has posted a nice record of higher profits over the years. The stock has done well, posting a higher high every year since 1988.

## Investment Advice

Although these shares may be on the volatile side, Mattel represents a solid choice in a more speculative industry group. The stock would be a worthwhile choice for introducing a child or grandchild to the stock market.

McDonald's Corp.
NYSE: MCD
McDonald's Plaza
Oak Brook, IL 60521
(630) 623-7428 • (800) 228-9623 • (800) 774-4117

| Performance Rating: * * * * * |
| --- |

## Performance History

- $1,000 invested on 12/31/85 was worth $5,508 on 12/31/95 — a 451 percent increase in 10 years.

## Plan Specifics

- Initial purchase is available to investors in all 50 states ($1,000 minimum initial investment or automatic monthly investments of at least $100). Enrollment fee is $5.
- Partial dividend reinvestment is available.
- No discount.
- OCP: $100 to $250,000 per year.
- OCP is invested at least weekly.
- Need 25 shares to open an account through transfer.
- Purchasing fees are $5 plus 10 cents per share. Selling fees are $10 plus 10 cents per share. Brokerage fees for buying and selling are capped at $5.
- $3 annual account administrative fee.
- Automatic investment services are available ($1 per transaction).
- IRA option is available ($35 annual administrative fee).
- Shares may be sold via the telephone.
- Plan Administrator: First Chicago Trust-NY (800) 621-7825.
- Dividends are paid March, June, September, and December.

## Corporate Profile

McDonald's is a leader in the fast-food industry. The firm has more than 16,000 outlets in the U.S. and overseas. International operations account for more than half of operating profits.

## Investment Advice

McDonald's will go through periodic bouts of selling on Wall Street as investors become concerned about growth prospects. However, continued overseas expansion should help the bottom line move higher. I own these shares and recommend them for any portfolio.

**MDU RESOURCES**

MDU Resources Group, Inc.
NYSE: MDU
400 N. Fourth St.
Bismarck, ND 58501
(701) 222-7900 • (800) 813-3324

> **Performance Rating: * * * ***

## Performance History

- $1,000 invested on 12/31/85 was worth $2,805 on 12/31/95 — a 181 percent increase in 10 years.

## Plan Specifics

- Initial purchase is available to residents of North Dakota, South Dakota, Montana, and Wyoming ($50 minimum initial investment).
- Partial dividend reinvestment is available.
- No discount.
- OCP: $50 to $5,000 monthly.
- OCP is invested monthly.
- There are no purchasing fees. Selling costs are brokerage commissions and any other costs of sale.
- Automatic investment services are available.
- Plan Administrator: Norwest Shareowner Services (800) 813-3324.
- Dividends are paid January, April, July, and October.

## Corporate Profile

MDU Resources provides electricity and gas services to North and South Dakota, Montana, and Wyoming. The firm is also involved in oil and gas production and coal mining. The company's nonutility businesses provide a relatively large part of overall profits. Dividends have grown annually since 1990.

## Investment Advice

MDU Resources offers an interesting play in the utility sector due to its rather large nonutility operations. The stock's dividend growth is likely to be only average. The stock should at least match the performance of the typical utility holding.

MidAmerican Energy Co.

**MidAmerican**      NYSE: MEC
ᴇɴᴇʀɢʏ
666 Grand Ave., PO Box 9244
Des Moines, IA 50306-9244
(515) 242-4310 • (800) 247-5211

Performance Rating: * * *

## Performance History: Not available.

## Plan Specifics

- Initial purchase is available to investors in all 50 states ($250 minimum initial purchase).
- Partial dividend reinvestment is available.
- No discount.
- OCP: $25 to $10,000 per month.
- OCP is invested monthly.
- Purchasing and selling fees are approximately 5 cents per share.
- Dividends are paid March, June, September, and December.

## Corporate Profile

MidAmerican Energy provides electricity and natural gas to parts of Iowa, Illinois, Nebraska, and South Dakota. The firm was formed through the merger of Midwest Resources and Iowa-Illinois Gas & Electric. The firm's nonregulated units include oil and gas, energy marketing, and financial management businesses.

## Investment Advice

MidAmerican Energy has rather lackluster prospects going forward. The company may be able to surprise analysts if the benefits of the merger exceed expectations. Still, until the merged company has established more of a track record, investors should probably look elsewhere.

Minnesota Power & Light Co.
NYSE: MPL
30 W. Superior St.
Duluth, MN 55802-2093
(218) 722-2641 • (800) 535-3056 • (800) 774-4117

| Performance Rating: * * * |
| --- |

## Performance History

- $1,000 invested on 12/31/85 was worth $2,730 on 12/31/95 — a 173 percent increase in 10 years.

## Plan Specifics

- Initial purchase is available to investors in all 50 states ($250 minimum initial investment).
- Partial dividend reinvestment is available.
- No discount.
- OCP: $10 to $100,000 per year.
- OCP is invested monthly.
- There are no purchasing fees. Selling fees are $5. The plan permits investors to sell up to 99 shares once a year.
- Some preferred dividends may be reinvested for additional common shares.
- Dividends are paid March, June, September, and December.

## Corporate Profile

Minnesota Power provides utility services primarily in Minnesota and Wisconsin. Coal is the major power source. The firm has a big exposure to industrial customers, which makes it somewhat vulnerable to increased competition in its markets. The firm has been expanding its non-utility businesses, which enhances growth prospects but also boosts potential earnings volatility.

## Investment Advice

Minnesota Power's total-return potential is not likely to be especially noteworthy over the next 2-3 years. Investors would likely be better off with higher-rated utilities.

**Mobil**

Mobil Corp.
  NYSE: MOB
3225 Gallows Rd.
Fairfax, VA 22037-0001
(800) 648-9291 • (703) 849-3000

| Performance Rating: * * * * * |
|---|

## Performance History

■ $1,000 invested on 12/31/85 was worth $5,806 on 12/31/95 — a 481 percent increase in 10 years.

## Plan Specifics

■ Initial purchase is available to investors in all 50 states ($250 minimum initial purchase).
■ Partial dividend reinvestment is not available.
■ No discount.
■ OCP: $10 to $7,500 per month.
■ OCP is invested weekly.
■ There are no purchasing fees. Selling fees include brokerage commissions plus a $5 service charge.
■ IRA option is available.
■ Plan Administrator: ChaseMellon Shareholder Investment Service (800) 648-9291.
■ Dividends are paid March, June, September, and December.

## Corporate Profile

Mobil is a major integrated oil company. The firm also has a presence in the chemicals industry. Despite the volatility of oil markets in general, Mobil has traditionally been a profitable oil company. Dividends have been rising in recent years, and the firm's healthy cash flow should ensure continued gains in the dividend.

## Investment Advice

Mobil offers solid representation in the oil sector. Diversified operations, strong cash flow, and good dividend-growth prospects enhance the potential of these shares. The company's no-load stock program, which includes an IRA option, is attractive as well.

Montana Power Company
NYSE: MTP
40 E. Broadway
Butte, MT 59701-9394
(406) 723-5421 • (800) 245-6767

> **Performance Rating: \* \* \***

## Performance History

- $1,000 invested on 12/31/85 was worth $2,677 on 12/31/95 — a 168 percent increase in 10 years.

## Plan Specifics

- Initial purchase is available to investors in 17 states ($100 minimum initial investment).
- Partial dividend reinvestment is available.
- No discount.
- OCP: $10 to $60,000 per year.
- OCP is invested monthly.
- There are no purchasing fees. Selling fees include brokerage commissions, and any applicable taxes.
- Automatic investment services are available.
- Preferred dividends may be reinvested for additional common shares.
- Dividends are paid February, May, August, and November.

## Corporate Profile

Montana Power provides electric and natural gas services. Coal, hydro, and purchased power account for the firm's fuel mix. The company's nonutility operations include coal mining, oil and natural-gas exploration, and telecommunications. Montana Power's nonutility businesses have helped to boost profits over the years.

## Investment Advice

Montana Power has appeal given its large nonutility operations. However, these operations also increase the potential volatility of these shares. The stock is best suited for more aggressive utility investors.

Morton International, Inc.
NYSE: MII
100 N. Riverside Plaza
Chicago, IL 60606-1596
(800) 990-1010 • (800) 774-4117 • (800) 446-2617

> **Performance Rating: * * * * ***

## Performance History: Not available. ———————————

## Plan Specifics ——————————————————————————

- Initial purchase is available to investors in all 50 states ($1,000 minimum initial investment). Initial purchases will be charged a $10 fee plus brokerage commissions.
- Partial dividend reinvestment is available.
- No discount.
- OCP: $50 to $60,000 per year.
- OCP is invested at least weekly.
- Purchasing fees for OCPs are 5 percent of the amount invested (maximum $10) and 12 cents per share. Selling fees are $15 plus 12 cents per share.
- Minimum dividend reinvestment fee of 3 percent of the amount to be reinvested or $2.50, whichever is smaller, plus brokerage fees.
- Shares may be sold via the telephone.
- Automatic investment services are available.
- IRA option is available.
- Plan Administrator: First Chicago Trust-NY (800) 446-2617.
- Dividends are paid March, June, September, and December.

## Corporate Profile ——————————————————————

   Morton International has positions in three markets: specialty chemicals, salt, and automotive airbags. Driving growth in recent years has been the firm's airbag business. The company is merging its airbag business with a foreign competitor. The surviving entity will consist of the salt and specialty chemicals business.

## Investment Advice ——————————————————————

   Morton International is a solid holding for any investor. The stock has done well over the last five years, and further upward price action should continue.

**National Fuel Gas Company**

National Fuel Gas Company
NYSE: NFG
10 Lafayette Square
Buffalo, NY 14203
(716) 857-7022 • (800) 648-8166

| Performance Rating: * * * * |
| --- |

## Performance History

- $1,000 invested on 12/31/85 was worth $4,027 on 12/31/95 — a 303 percent increase in 10 years.

## Plan Specifics

- Initial purchase is available to customers of the company ($200 minimum initial investment).
- Partial dividend reinvestment is not available.
- No discount.
- OCP: $25 to $5,000 per month.
- OCP is invested monthly.
- There are no purchasing fees. Selling fees include brokerage commissions, any transfer tax, and a $15 bank service fee.
- Plan Administrator: ChaseMellon Shareholder Investment Service (800) 648-8166.
- Dividends are paid January, April, July, and October.

## Corporate Profile

National Fuel Gas is an integrated natural-gas company. The firm's pipeline and storage unit transports and stores natural gas for the local user market as well as markets in northeastern U.S. The company owns and operates 30 underground natural-gas storage fields. The company's nonregulated activities include oil and gas exploration, a sawmill and kiln business, and a collection service.

## Investment Advice

National Fuel Gas has a good track record of dividend growth and favorable total-return prospects. The stock is not likely to match its strong performance of the decade ending in 1995. Still, these shares should provide decent returns for patient investors.

National Westminster Bank PLC

**NatWest Group**    NYSE: NW

c/o Morgan Guaranty Trust Co., PO Box 9073
Boston, MA 02205
(800) 749-1687 • (800) 774-4117

> **Performance Rating:** * * * *

## Performance History: Not available. ——————

## Plan Specifics ——————————————

- Initial purchase is available to investors in all states except North Dakota, Oregon, and Texas ( $250 minimum initial investment).
- Partial dividend reinvestment is available.
- No discount.
- OCP: $50 to $100,000 per year.
- OCP is invested weekly.
- Automatic investment services are available.
- Annual administration fee of $15 must accompany initial stock purchase and may be paid with a credit card.
- Purchasing and selling fees include a transaction fee of $5, plus brokerage commissions of approximately 12 cents per share.
- Investors will be assessed a brokerage commission of approximately 12 cents per share to reinvest dividends.
- Shares may be sold via the telephone.
- Plan Administrator: Morgan Guaranty Trust Co. (800) 749-1687.
- Dividends are paid May and October.

## Corporate Profile ——————————————

National Westminster Bank is a London-based banking organization. The firm sold its NatWest U.S. operations in early 1996. The firm has been expanding its money management services.

## Investment Advice ——————————————

National Westminster has a decent growth record, and long-term prospects are above average. While my favorite banking stock among no-load stock plans is Regions Financial, National Westminster should move at least in line with the overall market.

Nevada Power Co.
NYSE: NVP
PO Box 98669
Las Vegas, NV 89193-8669
(800) 344-9239 • (800) 774-4117

> **Performance Rating: * * ***

## Performance History

- $1,000 invested on 12/31/85 was worth $2,653 on 12/31/95 — a 165 percent increase in 10 years.

## Plan Specifics

- Initial purchase is available to customers of the company ($25 minimum initial investment).
- Partial dividend reinvestment is available only on stock certificates.
- No discount.
- OCP: $25 to $25,000 per quarter.
- OCP is invested twice monthly.
- There are no purchasing fees. Selling fees include brokerage commissions.
- Automatic investment services are available.
- Preferred dividends may be reinvested for additional common shares.
- Dividends are paid February, May, August, and November.

## Corporate Profile

Nevada Power provides electricity services to the Las Vegas area and southeastern Nevada. Residential customers comprise more than 40 percent of total revenue. The hotel-gaming industry is the largest customer. One positive is the attractive growth potential of the service region.

## Investment Advice

While Nevada Power's growth prospects are a plus, the company's overall investment merit is limited. Poor dividend-growth prospects will likely hinder total returns.

New Jersey Resources Corp.

*D*NJRESOURCES     NYSE: NJR
1415 Wyckoff Rd.
Wall, NJ 07719
(908) 938-1230 • (800) 817-3955

| Performance Rating: * * * * |

## Performance History

■ $1,000 invested on 12/31/85 was worth $4,526 on 12/31/95 — a 353 percent increase in 10 years.

## Plan Specifics

■ Initial purchase is available to customers of the utility ($25 minimum initial investment).
■ Partial dividend reinvestment is not available.
■ No discount.
■ OCP: $25 to $60,000 per year.
■ OCP is invested twice per month.
■ There are no purchasing fees. Selling fees include brokerage commissions.
■ Automatic investment services are available.
■ Plan Administrator: Bank of Boston (800) 817-3955.
■ Dividends are paid January, April, July, and October.

## Corporate Profile

New Jersey Resources is a holding company engaged in natural-gas distribution. The firm serves more than 345,000 customers in Monmouth and Ocean counties and parts of Morris and Middlesex counties.

## Investment Advice

New Jersey Resources is a decent holding. Moderate dividend growth is expected. The stock has some appeal as an income investment.

Nippon Telegraph and Telephone Corp.
   NYSE: NTT
c/o Morgan Guaranty Trust Co., PO Box 9073
Boston, MA 02205

**NTT**    (800) 749-1687 • (800) 774-4117

Performance Rating: * * *

## Performance History: Not available.

## Plan Specifics

- Initial purchase is available to investors in all states except North Dakota, Oregon, and Texas ($250 minimum initial investment).
- Partial dividend reinvestment is available.
- No discount.
- OCP: $50 to $100,000 per year.
- OCP is invested weekly.
- Automatic investment services are available.
- Annual administration fee of $15 must accompany initial stock purchase and may be paid with a credit card.
- Purchasing and selling costs include a transaction fee of $5, plus brokerage commissions of approximately 12 cents per share.
- Investors will be assessed a brokerage commission of approximately 12 cents per share to reinvest dividends.
- Shares may be sold via the telephone.
- Plan Administrator: Morgan Guaranty Trust Co. (800) 749-1687.
- Dividends are paid July and December.

## Corporate Profile

Nippon Telegraph, Japan's largest provider of telecommunications services, provides local and long-distance services, data communications, telegraph services, and terminal equipment sales.

## Investment Advice

Due to Nippon's limited trading history — the stock has been listed on the New York Stock Exchange only since 1994 — it is difficult to give these shares more than three stars. However, given the global opportunities in the telecommunications markets, these shares have above-average long-term appeal.

**NorAm** *ENERGY CORP.*
NorAm Energy Corp.
NYSE: NAE
PO Box 2628, 1600 Smith St.
Houston, TX 77002
(800) 843-3445 • (713) 654-7502 • (800) 316-6726

| Performance Rating: * * |
| --- |

## Performance History

- $1,000 invested on 12/31/85 was worth $840 on 12/31/95 — a 16 percent decrease in 10 years.

## Plan Specifics

- Initial purchase is available to investors in all 50 states ($200 minimum initial investment).
- Partial dividend reinvestment is available.
- 3 percent discount on reinvested dividends.
- OCP: $25 to $120,000 per year.
- OCP is invested at least weekly.
- There are no purchasing fees. Selling costs include brokerage commissions.
- Automatic investment services are available.
- Shares may be sold via the telephone.
- Plan Administrator: First Chicago Trust-NY (800) 316-6726.
- Dividends are paid March, June, September, and December.

## Corporate Profile

NorAm Energy, formerly Arkla, provides natural-gas distribution and gathering services. Natural-gas sales account for more than 90 percent of total sales. The firm has received a takeover offer from Houston Industries. The company's track record over the last several years has been rather inconsistent.

## Investment Advice

NorAm has not been a stellar performer over the last decade in terms of price appreciation and dividend growth. Given the uninspiring track record and pending takeover by Houston Industries, investors should look elsewhere.

Norsk Hydro A.S.
NYSE: NHY
c/o Morgan Guaranty Trust Co., PO Box 9073
Boston, MA 02205
(800) 749-1687 • (800) 774-4117

> **Performance Rating: * * * ***

## Performance History: Not available.

## Plan Specifics

- Initial purchase is available to investors in all states except North Dakota, Oregon, Texas ($250 minimum initial investment).
- Partial dividend reinvestment is available.
- No discount.
- OCP: $50 to $100,000 per year.
- OCP is invested weekly.
- Automatic investment services are available.
- Annual administration fee of $15 must accompany initial stock purchase and may be paid with a credit card.
- Purchasing and selling costs include a transaction fee of $5, plus brokerage commissions of approximately 12 cents per share.
- Investors will be assessed a brokerage commission of approximately 12 cents per share to reinvest dividends.
- Shares may be sold via the telephone.
- Plan Administrator: Morgan Guaranty Trust Co. (800) 749-1687.
- Dividends are paid in June.

## Corporate Profile

Norsk Hydro has interests in a variety of industries — metals, petrochemicals, fertilizers, oil, and natural gas. The firm, based in Norway, is 51 percent owned by the Norwegian government.

## Investment Advice

Norsk Hydro provides an interesting way to give your portfolio overseas exposure and exposure to various natural resources. The firm's fertilizer business, in particular, has interesting appeal given the expected growth in global demand for fertilizers. The stock is one of the better foreign stocks offering a no-load stock plan.

NORTHERN STATES
POWER COMPANY

Northern States Power Co.
NYSE: NSP
414 Nicollet Mall
Minneapolis, MN 55401
(612) 330-5560

Performance Rating: * * * * *

## Performance History

- $1,000 invested on 12/31/85 was worth $3,284 on 12/31/95 — a 228 percent increase in 10 years.

## Plan Specifics

- Initial purchase is available to residents of Minnesota, North Dakota, South Dakota, Wisconsin, and Michigan ($100 minimum initial investment).
- Partial dividend reinvestment is available.
- No discount.
- OCP: $25 to $10,000 per quarter.
- OCP is invested monthly.
- There are no purchasing or selling fees. Participants may sell up to 25 shares through the plan.
- Preferred dividends may be reinvested for additional common shares.
- Dividends are paid January, April, July, and October.

## Corporate Profile

Northern States Power distributes electricity in Minnesota, Wisconsin, North Dakota, South Dakota, and Michigan. Coal, nuclear, and purchased power are the primary fuel sources. The company is merging with Wisconsin Energy.

## Investment Advice

Investors who have the opportunity to take advantage of the firm's no-load stock program should do so. Strong finances, dividend growth at least in line with the industry average, and competitive rates put the company in a good position to outperform the industry over the long term. The merger with Wisconsin Energy, another leading electric utility, should result in one of the best electric utilities in the country.

Northwestern Public Service Co.
NYSE: NPS
33 Third St. SE, PO Box 1318
Huron, SD 57350-1318
(605) 352-8411 • (800) 245-6977

> **Performance Rating: * * * ***

## Performance History

- $1,000 invested on 12/31/85 was worth $4,276 on 12/31/95 — a 328 percent increase in 10 years.

## Plan Specifics

- Initial purchase is available to customers of the utility ($10 minimum initial investment).
- Partial dividend reinvestment is available.
- No discount.
- OCP: $10 to $2,000 per month.
- OCP is invested monthly.
- There are no purchasing fees. Selling costs are brokerage commissions and other fees.
- Dividends are paid March, June, September, and December.

## Corporate Profile

Northwestern Public Service provides electric and natural-gas services in South Dakota and gas service in Nebraska. Residential customers account for more than 50 percent of total sales. Coal generates virtually all its electricity. Dividends have increased annually for the last decade. The company has moved aggressively into propane gas distribution via the acquisition of Synergy Group.

## Investment Advice

Northwestern Public Service has decent finances, reasonable dividend-growth prospects, and appreciation potential that should at least match the industry average. The stock is a worthwhile holding.

Norwest Corp.
NYSE: NOB
Norwest Center, Sixth and Marquette
Minneapolis, MN 55479
(612) 667-1234 • (888) 291-3713 • (800) 813-3324

> **Performance Rating:** * * * *

## Performance History

- $1,000 invested on 12/31/85 was worth $8,951 on 12/31/95 — a 795 percent increase in 10 years.

## Plan Specifics

- Initial purchase is available to investors in all 50 states ($250 minimum initial investment or automatic monthly cash investments of at least $25). There is a one-time account set-up fee of $10.
- Partial dividend reinvestment is available.
- No discount.
- OCP: $25 to $10,000 per month.
- OCP is invested weekly.
- Purchase fees include 3 cents per share brokerage commission and a service fee of $3 per OCP and 4 percent (maximum $4) per dividend reinvestment. Selling costs are $10 service fee and 3 cents per share brokerage commission.
- Automatic investment services are available ($1 charge per transaction).
- Shares may be sold via the telephone.
- Plan Administrator: Norwest Shareowner Services (888) 291-3713.
- Dividends are paid March, June, September, and December.

## Corporate Profile

Norwest is a bank holding company with operations in 16 states. The company has a sizable mortgage banking business. Earnings have trended higher in recent years, and the upward trend should continue.

## Investment Advice

Norwest has a solid position as a regional banking power. The stock has done extremely well over the last decade. While unlikely to duplicate that performance over the next decade, these shares should still outperform the market.

Novo-Nordisk A/S
  NYSE: NVO
c/o Morgan Guaranty Trust Co., PO Box 9073
Boston, MA 02205
(800) 749-1687 • (800) 774-4117

Novo Nordisk

| Performance Rating: * * * * * |

## Performance History

- $1,000 invested on 12/31/85 was worth $5,102 on 12/31/95 — a 410 percent increase in 10 years.

## Plan Specifics

- Initial purchase is available to investors in all states except North Dakota, Oregon, and Texas ($250 minimum initial investment).
- Partial dividend reinvestment is available.
- No discount.
- OCP: $50 to $100,000 per year.
- OCP is invested weekly.
- Automatic investment services are available.
- Annual administration fee of $15 must accompany initial stock purchase and may be paid with a credit card.
- Purchasing and selling costs include a transaction fee of $5, plus brokerage commissions of approximately 12 cents per share.
- Investors will be assessed a brokerage commission of approximately 12 cents per share to reinvest dividends.
- Shares may be sold via the telephone.
- Plan Administrator: Morgan Guaranty Trust Co. (800) 749-1687.
- Dividends are paid in May.

## Corporate Profile

Novo-Nordisk, a Danish company, is the world's leading producer of insulin used in the treatment of diabetes. The company also manufactures industrial enzymes used in detergents, food and paper products, and biochemicals. Revenues are distributed fairly evenly throughout the world.

## Investment Advice

Novo-Nordisk has ample appeal. The stock provides an excellent way to add foreign exposure to a no-load stock portfolio. Its position in good growth markets is a plus.

NUI Corp.
NYSE: NUI
550 Route 202-206, PO Box 760
Bedminster, NJ 07921-0760
(908) 781-0500 • (800) 374-5775

> **Performance Rating: * * ***

## Performance History

- $1,000 invested on 12/31/85 was worth $1,557 on 12/31/95 — a 56 percent increase in 10 years.

## Plan Specifics

- Initial purchase is available to residents of Florida, Maryland, New Jersey, New York, North Carolina, and Pennsylvania ($125 minimum initial investment).
- Partial dividend reinvestment is available.
- No discount.
- OCP: $25 to $60,000 per year.
- OCP is invested monthly.
- There are no purchasing fees. Selling fees include brokerage commissions, service charges, and an administrative fee.
- Automatic investment services are available.
- Plan Administrator: First Chicago Trust-NY (800) 374-5775.
- Dividends are paid March, June, September, and December.

## Corporate Profile

NUI is a geographically diversified provider of natural-gas services. The firm provides services primarily in New Jersey and Florida. The company expanded its operations with the 1994 acquisition of Pennsylvania & Southern Gas.

## Investment Advice

NUI has some appeal, especially as the dividend rebounds following the cut in late 1994. Still, these shares are suited primarily for more aggressive investors.

**OG&E**

Oklahoma Gas & Electric Co.
NYSE: OGE
PO Box 321
Oklahoma City, OK 73101-0321
(405) 553-3211 • (800) 395-2662 • (800) 774-4117

| Performance Rating: * * * |

## Performance History

- $1,000 invested on 12/31/85 was worth $3,032 on 12/31/95 — a 203 percent increase in 10 years.

## Plan Specifics

- Initial purchase is available to residential customers of the company ($250 minimum initial investment).
- Partial dividend reinvestment is available.
- No discount.
- OCP: $25 to $100,000 per year.
- OCP is invested twice monthly.
- There are no purchasing or selling fees.
- Automatic investment services are available.
- IRA option is available.
- Preferred dividends and interest on mortgage bonds may be reinvested for additional common shares.
- Plan Administrator: Liberty Bank & Trust Co. (800) 395-2662.
- Dividends are paid January, April, July, and October.

## Corporate Profile

Oklahoma Gas & Electric provides electric service to customers in Oklahoma and western Arkansas. The firm's natural-gas activity is conducted through Enogex, a wholly owned gas transportation subsidiary. Residential customers account for roughly one-third of total revenues.

## Investment Advice

Little or no dividend growth makes these shares relatively unappealing. On the plus side, the firm's no-load stock plan includes an IRA option and no charges when selling shares from the plan. Still, investors should preference other utilities for the income portion of their no-load stock portfolio.

Oneok, Inc.

**ONEOK** *Inc.*   NYSE: OKE
PO Box 871
Tulsa, OK 74102-0871
(918) 588-7000 • (800) 395-2662

| Performance Rating: * * * |

## Performance History

- $1,000 invested on 12/31/85 was worth $2,630 on 12/31/95 — a 163 percent increase in 10 years.

## Plan Specifics

- Initial purchase is available to investors in all 50 states ($100 minimum initial investment).
- Partial dividend reinvestment is available.
- 3 percent discount on reinvested dividends.
- OCP: $25 to $100,000 per year.
- OCP is invested twice monthly.
- There are no purchasing fees. Selling costs are brokerage commissions.
- Automatic investment services are available.
- IRA option is available.
- Preferred dividends may be reinvested for additional common shares.
- Plan Administrator: Liberty Bank and Trust Co. (800) 395-2662.
- Dividends are paid February, May, August, and November.

## Corporate Profile

Oneok provides natural-gas services in Oklahoma. The firm also has operations in gas marketing and oil and gas exploration. Oneok cut its dividend in 1988. However, the firm has been expanding the dividend in recent years, and growth in the payout should be above average for the group.

## Investment Advice

Oneok's solid dividend-growth potential gives these shares an advantage over other utility stocks. Still, finances are only average for the group. I would not want to have a large exposure to these shares.

Owens Corning
NYSE: OWC
Fiberglas Tower
Toledo, OH 43659
(419) 248-8000 • (800) 472-2210 • (800) 438-7465

| Performance Rating: * * * |
| --- |

## Performance History: Not available.

## Plan Specifics

- Initial purchase is available to investors in all 50 states ($1,000 minimum initial investment or $100 minimum automatic monthly investment).
- Partial dividend reinvestment is available.
- No discount.
- OCP: $100 to $120,000 per year.
- OCP is invested weekly.
- Must own 25 shares to reinvest dividends.
- No purchasing fees. Selling costs are $15 plus 12 cents per share.
- Automatic investment services are available.
- Plan Administrator: ChaseMellon Shareholder Investment Service (800) 472-2210.
- Dividends are paid January, April, July, and October.

## Corporate Profile

Owens Corning produces high-performance glass composites used in insulation and other building materials. Earnings have been choppy over the years due to the cyclical nature of the industry. However, the firm is taking a number of measures to improve its long-term position. A quarterly dividend was recently instated.

## Investment Advice

I like Owens Corning's future better than its past. These shares have reasonable upside potential, although the firm's spotty track record merits only a three-star performance rating.

Pacific Dunlop Limited
**PACIFIC DUNLOP**   NASDAQ: PDLPY
c/o Morgan Guaranty Trust Co., PO Box 9073
Boston, MA 02205
(800) 749-1687 • (800) 774-4117

Performance Rating: * * *

## Performance History: Not available.

## Plan Specifics

- Initial purchase is available to investors in all states except North Dakota, Oregon, and Texas ($250 minimum initial investment).
- Partial dividend reinvestment is available.
- No discount.
- OCP: $50 to $100,000 per year.
- OCP is invested weekly.
- Automatic investment services are available.
- Annual administration fee of $15 must accompany initial stock purchase and may be paid with a credit card.
- Purchasing and selling costs include a transaction fee of $5, plus brokerage commissions of approximately 12 cents per share.
- Investors will be assessed a brokerage commission of approximately 12 cents per share to reinvest dividends.
- Shares may be sold via the telephone.
- Plan Administrator: Morgan Guaranty Trust Co. (800) 749-1687.
- Dividends are paid July and November.

## Corporate Profile

Pacific Dunlop, based in Australia, is a diversified manufacturing concern. The firm has positions in automotive, distribution, health care, and building and construction markets. Roughly two-thirds of revenues and profits come from Australia.

## Investment Advice

A pared-down Pacific Dunlop has some interesting appeal for its turnaround potential. However, it is unlikely that Wall Street will get behind these shares in full force until more evidence of a sustained turnaround in the bottom line is seen.

Peoples Energy Corp.
NYSE: PGL
Shareholder Services
PO Box 2000
Chicago, IL 60609-2000
(800) 901-8878 • (800) 774-4117

| Performance Rating: * * * |

## Performance History

- $1,000 invested on 12/31/85 was worth $3,071 on 12/31/95 — a 207 percent increase in 10 years.

## Plan Specifics

- Initial purchase is available to investors in all 50 states ($250 minimum initial investment).
- Partial dividend reinvestment is available.
- No discount.
- OCP: $25 to $100,000 per year.
- OCP is invested twice monthly.
- There are no purchasing fees. Selling costs are approximately 8 cents per share.
- Automatic investment services are available.
- Dividends are paid January, April, July, and October.

## Corporate Profile

Peoples Energy provides natural-gas services to Chicago and parts of Illinois. Dividends have generally trended higher over the years, although dividend growth will likely be on the moderate side going forward. The company's service region is fairly mature, which will hinder growth prospects.

## Investment Advice

Peoples Energy is an acceptable holding among natural gas issues. The stock will likely be an average performer in the group.

Pharmacia & Upjohn

Pharmacia & Upjohn, Inc.
  NYSE: PNU
c/o Harris Trust and Savings Bank
PO Box A3309
Chicago, IL 60690
(800) 323-1849 • (800) 286-9178 • (800) 774-4117

> **Performance Rating: * * ***

## Performance History: Not available. ——————

## Plan Specifics ————————————

- Initial purchase is available to investors in all 50 states ($250 minimum initial investment).
- Partial dividend reinvestment is available.
- No discount.
- OCP: $50 to $100,000 per year.
- OCP is invested weekly.
- Purchasing fees include a transaction fee of $3 plus 8 cents per share. Selling costs include a transaction fee of $10 plus 8 cents per share.
- Investors will be assessed a 5 percent (maximum $2.50) fee plus brokerage commissions to reinvest dividends.
- Automatic investment services are available ($1.50 processing fee per transaction plus 8 cents per share).
- Plan Administrator: Harris Trust and Savings Bank (800) 323-1849.
- Dividends are paid February, May, August, and November.

## Corporate Profile ————————————

   Pharmacia & Upjohn is the result of the 1995 merger of Upjohn and Swedish-based Pharmacia AB. Economies of scale from the merger should help lower costs. The ability for each of the firms to leverage off its market position in its respective country is a plus going forward.

## Investment Advice ————————————

   The fact that Pharmacia & Upjohn has lagged during a time when many health-care stocks have done well points to Wall Street's wariness over these shares. My preference among health-care no-load stocks is Novo-Nordisk.

Philadelphia Suburban Corp.
NYSE: PSC
762 Lancaster Ave.
Bryn Mawr, PA 19010-3489
(610) 645-1013 • (800) 205-8314 • (800) 774-4117

Performance Rating: * * * *

## Performance History

- $1,000 invested on 12/31/85 was worth $2,734 on 12/31/95 — a 173 percent increase in 10 years.

## Plan Specifics

- Initial purchase is available to investors in all 50 states ($500 minimum initial investment).
- Partial dividend reinvestment is available.
- 5 percent discount on reinvested dividends.
- OCP: $25 to $10,000 per year.
- OCP is invested 4 times a year.
- There are no purchasing fees. Selling fees include brokerage commissions and taxes.
- IRA option is available.
- Plan Administrator: ChaseMellon Shareholder Investment Service (800) 205-8314.
- Dividends are paid March, June, September, and December.

## Corporate Profile

Philadelphia Suburban is a water utility servicing parts of southeastern Pennsylvania. Residential customers account for approximately two-thirds of total sales. Philadelphia Suburban has been focusing on expanding its water utility business while divesting its nonwater-related subsidiaries in recent years.

## Investment Advice

Philadelphia Suburban is a well-managed water utility that would be an acceptable holding in any no-load stock portfolio. Dividend growth should be above average for its industry. The company's no-fee IRA option is especially attractive.

Piedmont Natural Gas Co.
  NYSE: PNY
PO Box 33068
Charlotte, NC 28233
(800) 438-8410 • (800) 633-4236 • (800) 774-4117

| Performance Rating: * * * * |

## Performance History

- $1,000 invested on 12/31/85 was worth $4,309 on 12/31/95 — a 331 percent increase in 10 years.

## Plan Specifics

- Initial purchase is available to investors in all 50 states ($250 minimum initial investment).
- Partial dividend reinvestment is available.
- 5 percent discount on reinvested dividends.
- OCP: $25 to $3,000 per month.
- OCP is invested monthly.
- There are no purchasing fees. Selling costs are brokerage commissions and any transfer tax.
- Automatic investment services are available.
- Plan Administrator: Wachovia Bank (800) 633-4236.
- Dividends are paid January, April, July, and October.

## Corporate Profile

Piedmont Natural Gas provides natural-gas services in parts of North Carolina, South Carolina, and Tennessee. Presence in a high growth area of the country is a plus. Dividend growth has been well above the industry average and should continue at a steady rate.

## Investment Advice

Piedmont offers a high-quality selection in the natural-gas group. Dividend growth should be impressive. Furthermore, the bottom line should benefit from meter additions as a result of continued population increases.

Pinnacle West Capital Corp.
NYSE: PNW
PO Box 52133
Phoenix, AZ 85072-2133
(800) 457-2983 • (800) 774-4117

Performance Rating: * * *

## Performance History: Not available.

## Plan Specifics

- Initial purchase is available to investors in all 50 states ($50 minimum initial investment).
- Partial dividend reinvestment is available.
- No discount.
- OCP: up to $60,000 per year.
- OCP is invested monthly.
- Purchasing and selling fees may include brokerage commissions and related service charges.
- Automatic investment services are available.
- Preferred dividends may be reinvested for additional common shares.
- Dividends are paid March, June, September, and December.

## Corporate Profile

Pinnacle West Capital is the holding company for Arizona Public Service, the state's largest electric utility. Primary sources of fuel generation are coal and nuclear. The largest industrial customer is the mining industry.

## Investment Advice

Pinnacle West is a utility on the mend. Dividend growth should be decent in upcoming years. However, competition could be a problem for the company down the road. Thus, while these shares have some appeal, they are geared more for aggressive investors.

Portland General Corp.
NYSE: PGN
121 SW Salmon St.
Portland, OR 97204
(503) 464-8599 • (800) 446-2617

---

| Performance Rating: * * * |
| :---: |

## Performance History

- $1,000 invested on 12/31/85 was worth $2,623 on 12/31/95 — a 162 percent increase in 10 years.

## Plan Specifics

- Initial purchase is available to investors in all 50 states ($250 minimum initial investment).
- Partial dividend reinvestment is available.
- No discount.
- OCP: $25 to $75,000 per year.
- OCP is invested weekly.
- Purchasing and selling costs are brokerage commissions.
- Automatic investment services are available.
- IRA option is available.
- Plan Administrator: First Chicago Trust-NY (800) 446-2617.
- Dividends are paid January, April, July, and October.

## Corporate Profile

Portland General provides electricity services to parts of Oregon. Following several years of no dividend growth, the dividend was boosted in the second quarter of 1996. Given a still moderate payout ratio (dividends divided by 12-month earnings per share), Portland General has ample room to expand the dividend further. Net income should show reasonably healthy gains going forward.

## Investment Advice

Portland General, given its dividend-growth prospects and above-average earnings growth for the industry, offers decent total-return potential within the utility group. The stock is an acceptable holding in a portfolio.

Procter & Gamble Co.
NYSE: PG
PO Box 5572
Cincinnati, OH 45201-5572
(800) 742-6253 • (800) 764-7483

> **Performance Rating: * * * * ***

## Performance History

- $1,000 invested on 12/31/85 was worth $6,065 on 12/31/95 — a 507 percent increase in 10 years.

## Plan Specifics

- Initial purchase is available to investors in all 50 states ($250 minimum initial investment). There is a one-time enrollment fee of $5 for new investors.
- Partial dividend reinvestment is available.
- No discount.
- OCP: $100 to $120,000 per year.
- OCP is invested weekly.
- Purchasing fees are $2.50 plus nominal brokerage fees. The firm also charges up to $1 per reinvested dividend. Selling costs are brokerage fees.
- Automatic investment services are available ($1 charge per transaction).
- Dividends are paid February, May, August, and November.

## Corporate Profile

Procter & Gamble is one of the world's leading consumer-products companies. Popular brand names include Tide, Pampers, Folgers, Cover Girl, and Charmin. International sales contribute roughly 50 percent of sales. The company's bottom line and dividend stream have shown steady growth over the years, and further gains are likely.

## Investment Advice

I'm a shareholder of Procter & Gamble and recommend these shares for any portfolio. The company's strong performance over the years leaves it vulnerable during market corrections. However, for investors with a long-term investment horizon, the stock should show superior gains.

Public Service of New Mexico
     NYSE: PNM
PO Box 1047
Albuquerque, NM 87103-9937
(800) 545-4425

| Performance Rating: * * * |

## Performance History: Not available.

## Plan Specifics

- Initial purchase is available to investors in all 50 states ($50 minimum initial investment).
- Partial dividend reinvestment is available.
- No discount.
- OCP: $50 to $60,000 per year.
- OCP is invested monthly.
- Purchase fees include brokerage commissions for shares purchased on the open market. Selling costs include brokerage commissions, service charge, and any applicable taxes.
- Dividends are paid February, May, August, and November.

## Corporate Profile

Public Service of New Mexico provides electricity and gas service in north central New Mexico. The firm had problems in the late '80s and early '90s when it was forced to eliminate its dividend. The dividend was reinstated in 1996 and has the potential to show decent growth from its rather modest base. Still, finances are a cut below most utilities.

## Investment Advice

Although the dividend growth should be above the industry average, unimpressive finances and lackluster long-term growth prospects make these shares among the more aggressive holdings in the group.

Puget Sound Power & Light Co.
NYSE: PSD
PO Box 96010
Bellevue, WA 98009-9610
(206) 462-3719 • (800) 997-8438

> **Performance Rating: * ***

## Performance History

- $1,000 invested on 12/31/85 was worth $2,768 on 12/31/95 — a 177 percent increase in 10 years.

## Plan Specifics

- Initial purchase is available to residents of Washington ($25 minimum initial investment).
- Partial dividend reinvestment is not available.
- No discount.
- OCP: $25 to $100,000 per year.
- OCP is invested twice per month.
- Purchasing and selling fees are brokerage commissions of approximately 5 cents per share.
- Preferred dividends may be reinvested for additional common shares.
- Dividends are paid February, May, August, and November.

## Corporate Profile

Puget Sound Power & Light provides electricity in Washington state. Hydroelectric, coal, and purchased power make up the primary fuel sources. Residential customers account for approximately 45 percent of total revenue. Largest industries serviced are oil refining and aircraft. The company is proposing to merge with Washington Energy.

## Investment Advice

While the merger provides some appeal, these shares are likely to lag the group over time. Total-return prospects appear to be limited. The stock is a below-average holding in the utility group.

Rank Group PLC
   NASDAQ: RANKY
c/o Morgan Guaranty Trust Co., PO Box 9073
Boston, MA 02205
(800) 749-1687 • (800) 774-4117

The Rank Group Plc

> **Performance Rating: * * ***

## Performance History: Not available.

## Plan Specifics

- Initial purchase is available to investors in all states except North Dakota, Oregon, and Texas ($250 minimum initial investment).
- Partial dividend reinvestment is available.
- No discount.
- OCP: $50 to $100,000 per year.
- OCP is invested weekly.
- Automatic investment services are available.
- Annual administration fee of $15 must accompany initial stock purchase and may be paid with a credit card.
- Purchasing and selling costs include a transaction fee of $5, plus brokerage commissions of approximately 12 cents per share.
- Investors will be assessed a brokerage commission of approximately 12 cents per share to reinvest dividends.
- Shares may be sold via the telephone.
- Plan Administrator: Morgan Guaranty Trust Co. (800) 749-1687.
- Dividends are paid April and October.

## Corporate Profile

Rank Group PLC, based in the United Kingdom, has operations in film and television, recreation, leisure, and vacation spots. The company, with MCA, plans to build a resort in Orlando, Florida.

## Investment Advice

Because of its spotty track record, Rank can be rated only as an average performer. However, assets sales or restructuring moves give these shares some speculative appeal.

Reader's Digest Association, Inc.
NYSE: RDA
Pleasantville, NY 10570
(914) 238-1000 • (800) 230-2771 • (800) 242-4653

Performance Rating: * * * *

## Performance History: Not available.

## Plan Specifics

- Initial purchase is available to investors in all 50 states ($1,000 minimum initial investment).
- Partial dividend reinvestment is available.
- Investors must have at least 10 shares in the plan in order to reinvest dividends.
- No discount.
- OCP: $100 to $10,000 per month.
- OCP is invested weekly.
- Purchasing costs are $5 plus 12 cents per share. Selling costs are $15 plus 12 cents per share.
- Automatic investment services are available.
- Plan Administrator: Chemical Bank (800) 230-2771.
- Dividends are paid February, May, August, and November.

## Corporate Profile

Reader's Digest Association is a leading publisher and direct marketer of books, videos, and recorded music. Profits have traditionally shown good growth. However, a restructuring charge and higher paper prices hurt 1996 results.

## Investment Advice

Reader's Digest has a strong product franchise. The restructuring by the company should pay dividends over time. One could argue that perhaps these shares have seen better days due to the difficulty of growing its markets. However, I remain a believer in this issue and would hold the stock in a portfolio.

**Regions**
Financial Corp.

Regions Financial Corp.
NASDAQ: RGBK
417 N. 20th St.
Birmingham, AL 35203
(800) 922-3468 • (800) 446-2617

| Performance Rating: * * * * * |

## Performance History

- $1,000 invested on 12/31/85 was worth $4,268 on 12/31/95 — a 327 percent increase in 10 years.

## Plan Specifics

- Initial purchase is available to investors in all 50 states ($500 minimum initial investment).
- Partial dividend reinvestment is available.
- No discount.
- OCP: $25 to $120,000 per year.
- OCP is invested monthly.
- There are no purchasing fees. Selling fees include brokerage commissions.
- Shares may be sold via the telephone.
- Automatic investment services are available ($1 transaction fee).
- Plan Administrator: First Chicago Trust-NY (800) 922-3468.
- Dividends are paid January, April, July, and October.

## Corporate Profile

Regions Financial, formerly First Alabama Bancshares, operates banks in Alabama, Florida, Georgia, Louisiana, and Tennessee. The company has been extremely active on the acquisition front. Net income has risen each year for more than two decades.

## Investment Advice

Regions Financial is a top no-load stock. Strong profit and dividend growth, solid finances, a growing geographic region, and favorable expansion prospects point to solid gains over the long term. With take-over activity in the banking group likely to remain steady, Regions has appeal as a takeover candidate. I'm a shareholder of Regions Financial, and you should be, too.

REUTERS

Reuters Holdings PLC
  NASDAQ: RTRSY
c/o Morgan Guaranty Trust Co., PO Box 9073
Boston, MA 02205
(800) 749-1687 • (800) 774-4117

Performance Rating: * * * * *

## Performance History: Not available.

## Plan Specifics

- Initial purchase is available to investors in all states except North Dakota, Oregon, and Texas ($250 minimum initial investment).
- Partial dividend reinvestment is available.
- No discount.
- OCP: $50 to $100,000 per year.
- OCP is invested weekly.
- Annual administrative fee of $15 must accompany initial stock purchase and may be paid with a credit card.
- Purchasing and selling costs include a transaction fee of $5 plus brokerage commissions of approximately 12 cents per share.
- Investors will be assessed a brokerage commission of approximately 12 cents per share to reinvest dividends.
- Automatic investment services are available.
- Shares may be sold via the telephone.
- Plan Administrator: Morgan Guaranty Trust Co. (800) 749-1687.
- Dividends are paid May and September.

## Corporate Profile

Reuters Holdings is a world leader in electronic publishing and information services. Based in the United Kingdom, the company has a strong niche in financial information. Per-share profits have grown at a rapid rate since 1992.

## Investment Advice

Among foreign-based companies offering no-load stock plans, Reuters Holdings is one of my favorites. I like information-services firms for their ability to repackage information to churn out new products. These shares are rarely cheap. However, growth investors should find the stock especially appealing.

**SCANA** ~~~~~

SCANA Corp.
   NYSE: SCG
Shareholder Services 054
Columbia, SC 29218
(803) 733-6817 • (800) 763-5891 • (800) 774-4117

Performance Rating: * * * *

## Performance History

■ $1,000 invested on 12/31/85 was worth $3,861 on 12/31/95 — a 286 percent increase in 10 years.

## Plan Specifics

■ Initial purchase is available to investors in all 50 states ($250 minimum initial investment).
■ Partial dividend reinvestment is available.
■ No discount.
■ OCP: $25 to $100,000 per year.
■ OCP is invested twice monthly.
■ There are no purchasing fees. Selling fees include brokerage commissions and transfer taxes.
■ Automatic investment services are available.
■ Preferred dividends may be reinvested for additional common shares.
■ Dividends are paid January, April, July, and October.

## Corporate Profile

SCANA is a utility holding company. The firm's service area includes Columbia, the state capital, and Charleston. Textile and chemical companies are major industrial customers. Coal and nuclear comprise the bulk of generating fuel.

## Investment Advice

SCANA is a solid utility. Strong dividend-growth prospects enhance total-return potential. Of course, the stock's performance will correlate closely with the performance of utility stocks in general. Still, investors who want exposure to this group should give these shares high priority.

**SEARS**

Sears, Roebuck & Co.
NYSE: S
3333 Beverly Rd.
Hoffman Estates, IL 60179
(847) 286-2500 • (888) 732-7788

| Performance Rating: * * * * |
| --- |

## Performance History

- $1,000 invested on 12/31/85 was worth $1,601 on 12/31/95 — a 60 percent increase in 10 years.

## Plan Specifics

- Initial purchase is available to investors in all 50 states ($500 minimum initial investment or automatic monthly investments of at least $100). Initial purchase fees are $10 plus 3 cents per share.
- Partial dividend reinvestment is available.
- No discount.
- OCP: $50 to $150,000 per year.
- OCP is invested weekly.
- Purchasing fees are 5 percent of the amount invested (maximum $7.50 on OCPs and $3 on reinvested dividends) plus 3 cents per share. Selling costs are $15 plus 12 cents per share.
- IRA option is available.
- Automatic investment services are available ($1 per transaction).
- Shares may be sold via the telephone.
- Plan Administrator: First Chicago Trust-NY (888) 732-7788.
- Dividends are paid January, April, July, and October.

## Corporate Profile

Sears is a leading retailing concern. The firm underwent a restructuring in 1993, shedding certain assets and refocusing on its retailing sector. Sears has been able to reinvigorate its retail operations.

## Investment Advice

Sears seems to have done a good job convincing investors that it can produce higher profits on a regular basis. While I still would preference Home Depot and Wal-Mart Stores among retailers offering no-load stock plans, Sears has above-average appreciation potential.

Sierra Pacific Resources
   NYSE: SRP
Shareholder Relations
PO Box 30150
Reno, NV 89520-3150
(702) 689-3610 • (800) 662-7575

| Performance Rating: * * * |
| --- |

## Performance History

- $1,000 invested on 12/31/85 was worth $2,261 on 12/31/95 — a 126 percent increase in 10 years.

## Plan Specifics

- Initial purchase is available to investors in all 50 states ($50 minimum initial investment).
- Partial dividend reinvestment is available.
- No discount.
- OCP: $50 to $100,000 per year.
- OCP is invested monthly.
- There are no purchase fees. Selling costs are 6 cents per share.
- Dividends are paid February, May, August, and November.

## Corporate Profile

Sierra Pacific Resources provides electricity services in part of Nevada and California. The firm's merger plans with Washington Water Power have been terminated. Dividend growth is likely to be on the moderate side. Finances are acceptable.

## Investment Advice

Sierra Pacific should do about as well as the average electric utility. These shares are an acceptable portfolio holding, although there are more attractive utilities among the ranks of no-load stocks.

**SONY**

Sony Corp.
NYSE: SNE
c/o Morgan Guaranty Trust Co., PO Box 9073
Boston, MA 02205
(800) 749-1687 • (800) 774-4117

> Performance Rating: * * * *

## Performance History: Not available. ——————

## Plan Specifics ——————

- Initial purchase is available to investors in all states except North Dakota, Oregon, and Texas ($250 minimum initial investment).
- Partial dividend reinvestment is available.
- No discount.
- OCP: $50 to $100,000 per year.
- OCP is invested weekly.
- Annual administrative fee of $15 must accompany initial stock purchase and may be paid with a credit card.
- Purchasing and selling costs include a transaction fee of $5 plus brokerage commissions of approximately 12 cents per share.
- Investors will be assessed a brokerage commission of approximately 12 cents per share to reinvest dividends.
- Automatic investment services are available.
- Shares may be sold via the telephone.
- Plan Administrator: Morgan Guaranty Trust Co. (800) 749-1687.
- Dividends are paid July and December.

## Corporate Profile ——————

Sony is a world leader in consumer electronics. The firm also has operations in the movie business via Columbia Pictures Entertainment. The U.S. accounts for nearly 30 percent of total sales; Japan, roughly 28 percent; and Europe, 23 percent.

## Investment Advice ——————

Sony should continue to do well for investors. The stock will show above-average volatility. Nevertheless, for investors who are willing to ride through the ups and downs, these shares should be rewarding.

Southern Union Company

## Southern Union Company
### NYSE: SUG
Investor Relations, 504 Lavaca, Ste. 800
Austin, TX 78701
(512) 370-8302 • (800) 793-8938 • (800) 736-3001

> **Performance Rating: * * ***

## Performance History: Not available. ——————————

## Plan Specifics ——————————————————————

- Initial purchase is available to investors in all 50 states ($250 minimum initial investment). There is a one-time enrollment fee of $5.
- No discount.
- OCP: $50 to $100,000 per year.
- OCP is invested twice monthly.
- Purchase fees include $2.50 transaction fee plus 15 cents per share. Selling costs are $10 plus 15 cents per share.
- Automatic investment services are available.
- Plan Administrator: First National Bank of Boston (800) 736-3001.
- The firm does not currently pay a cash dividend.

## Corporate Profile ——————————————————————

Southern Union distributes natural gas to portions of Texas, Missouri, and Oklahoma. Per-share earnings have advanced nicely in recent years. The company does not pay a cash dividend. Rather, dividends are paid in the form of stock.

## Investment Advice ——————————————————————

Southern Union has decent growth potential relative to other natural gas concerns. The stock is an acceptable holding in the group.

**SOUTHWEST GAS CORPORATION**

Southwest Gas Corp.
NYSE: SWX
PO Box 98510
Las Vegas, NV 89193-8510
(702) 876-7280 • (800) 331-1119

> **Performance Rating: * ***

## Performance History

- $1,000 invested on 12/31/85 was worth $1,917 on 12/31/95 — a 92 percent increase in 10 years.

## Plan Specifics

- Initial purchase is available to customers of the company ($100 minimum initial investment).
- Partial dividend reinvestment is available at 50 percent if account has at least 250 shares.
- No discount.
- OCP: $25 to $50,000 per year.
- OCP is invested twice monthly.
- There are no purchasing fees. Selling fees are approximately 5 cents per share.
- Dividends are paid March, June, September, and December.

## Corporate Profile

Southwest Gas provides natural-gas service to roughly one million customers in Arizona, Nevada, and California. The company's Paiute Pipeline company provides transportation service of natural gas to Southwest.

## Investment Advice

Southwest Gas is not an investment-caliber utility. While the firm's service region has ample growth prospects, the company's inability to sustain earnings and dividend growth over the years is a negative.

TDK Corp.
  NYSE: TDK
c/o Morgan Guaranty Trust Co., PO Box 9073
Boston, MA 02205
(800) 749-1687 • (800) 774-4117

| Performance Rating: * * * * |

## Performance History: Not available.

## Plan Specifics

- Initial purchase is available to investors in all states except North Dakota, Oregon, and Texas ($250 minimum initial investment).
- Partial dividend reinvestment is available.
- No discount.
- OCP: $50 to $100,000 per year.
- OCP is invested weekly.
- Annual administrative fee of $15 must accompany initial stock purchase and may be paid with a credit card.
- Purchasing and selling costs include a transaction fee of $5, plus brokerage commissions of approximately 12 cents per share.
- Investors will be assessed a brokerage commission of approximately 12 cents per share to reinvest dividends.
- Automatic investment services are available.
- Shares may be sold via the telephone.
- Plan Administrator: Morgan Guaranty Trust Co. (800) 749-1687.
- Dividends are paid July and December.

## Corporate Profile

TDK is a Japanese-based producer of electronic materials and components. Products include magnetic recording media, such as audio tapes, videotapes, and optical disks. Japan accounts for more than 40 percent of sales. Profits have picked up nicely in recent years, and growth should continue in 1997.

## Investment Advice

TDK has been a good performer in recent years, and higher profits should fuel further price gains. The stock will be volatile due to currency fluctuations. However, the issue has ample upside potential.

Telefonos de Mexico S.A. de C.V. Series L
   NYSE: TMX
c/o Morgan Guaranty Trust Co., PO Box 9073
Boston, MA 02205
(800) 749-1687 • (800) 774-4117

| Performance Rating: * * * |

## Performance History: Not available.

## Plan Specifics

- Initial purchase is available to investors in all states except North Dakota, Oregon, and Texas  ($250 minimum initial investment).
- Partial dividend reinvestment is available.
- No discount.
- OCP: $50 to $100,000 per year.
- OCP is invested weekly.
- Annual administrative fee of $15 must accompany initial stock purchase and may be paid with a credit card.
- Purchasing and selling costs include a transaction fee of $5 plus brokerage commissions of approximately 12 cents per share.
- Investors will be assessed a brokerage commission of approximately 12 cents per share to reinvest dividends.
- Automatic monthly investment services are available.
- Shares may be sold via the telephone.
- Plan Administrator: Morgan Guaranty Trust Co. (800) 749-1687.
- Dividends are paid June and December.

## Corporate Profile

Telefonos de Mexico is a major provider of long-distance and local telephone services in Mexico. Peso devaluation and economic upheaval in Mexico took its toll on these shares in 1994 and 1995. On the plus side, Mexico offers ample growth potential, especially with an improvement in the economy.

## Investment Advice

The political and economic instability of Mexico over the years makes it difficult to give Telefonos de Mexico a rating higher than three stars. However, over time, especially with a growing middle class in Mexico and heightened demands for quality telephone services, this company could generate impressive growth.

Tenneco, Inc.
  NYSE: TEN
127 King St.
Greenwich, CT 06831
(203) 863-1000 • (800) 446-2617

> **Performance Rating: * * ***

## Performance History ──────────────────────────

- $1,000 invested on 12/31/85 was worth $2,152 on 12/31/95 — a 115 percent increase in 10 years.

## Plan Specifics ──────────────────────────

- Initial purchase is available to investors in all 50 states ($500 minimum initial investment).
- Partial dividend reinvestment is available.
- No discount.
- OCP: $50 to $60,000 per year.
- OCP is invested weekly.
- Purchasing fees are brokerage commissions and a service charge of 5 percent of the amount invested ($3 maximum). Selling costs are brokerage commissions and service fee.
- Automatic investment services are available ($1 per transaction).
- Preferred dividends may be reinvested for additional common shares.
- Stock may be sold via the telephone.
- Plan Administrator: First Chicago Trust-NY (800) 446-2617.
- Dividends are paid March, June, September, and December.

## Corporate Profile ──────────────────────────

Tenneco is a diversified company with interests in natural-gas pipelines, packaging material, and automotive parts. The firm has aggressively restructured its operations in recent years. Per-share profits have picked up in recent years.

## Investment Advice ──────────────────────────

Tenneco's restructuring program enhances the long-term appeal of these shares. However, the stock's performance will likely be only average until Wall Street sees sustained earnings growth.

**TEXACO**

Texaco, Inc.
NYSE: TX
Investor Services Plan
2000 Westchester Ave.
White Plains, NY 10650
(800) 283-9785 • (800) 774-4117

> **Performance Rating: * * * ***

## Performance History

- $1,000 invested on 12/31/85 was worth $4,740 on 12/31/95 — a 374 percent increase in 10 years.

## Plan Specifics

- Initial purchase is available to investors in all 50 states ($250 minimum initial investment).
- Partial dividend reinvestment is not available.
- No discount.
- OCP: $50 to $120,000 per year.
- OCP is invested every 10 days.
- Commission of 5 cents per share for both purchasing and selling.
- Automatic investment services are available.
- Dividends are paid March, June, September, and December.

## Corporate Profile

Texaco is a leading integrated oil company. Operations are evenly divided between U.S. and international exploration and marketing. Texaco has been making strides in improving its cost position. The company has also been diligent in broadening its overseas exposure.

## Investment Advice

I like the oil stocks going forward and expect Texaco to perform well over the next few years. The yield, combined with capital gains, should produce total returns at least in line with the market. While I prefer Exxon among no-load oil stocks, Texaco would be a worthwhile holding as well.

Tyson Foods, Inc.
  NASDAQ: TYSNA
2210 W. Oaklawn Dr.
Springdale, AR 72764
(800) 446-2617 • (800) 822-7096 • (800) 317-4445

> **Performance Rating: * * ***

## Performance History: Not available. ───────────

## Plan Specifics ────────────────────────────

- Initial purchase is available to investors in all 50 states ($250 minimum initial investment). Initial investments will be charged a $7.50 fee plus brokerage commissions.
- Partial dividend reinvestment is not available.
- No discount.
- OCP: $50 minimum to no maximum.
- OCP is invested at least weekly.
- There are no purchasing fees after the initial investment. Selling fees are $15 plus brokerage commissions.
- Automatic investment services are available. Minimum investment with automatic monthly investments is $25 ($1 per transaction).
- Shares may be sold via the telephone.
- Plan Administrator: First Chicago Trust-NY (800) 446-2617.
- Dividends are paid March, June, September, and December.

## Corporate Profile ──────────────────────────

Tyson Foods is a leading producer of fresh and processed poultry products. Per-share profits have been erratic over the years partly due to the volatility of feed prices. Increasing demand for chicken, especially abroad, should help profits over time.

## Investment Advice ──────────────────────────

Tyson's stock has marked time for the last several years, indicative of the firm's inability to generate sustained earnings growth. While these shares have appeal as a trading vehicle, I cannot get too excited about them for their long-term return potential.

Unilever

Unilever NV
  NYSE: UN
c/o Morgan Guaranty Trust Co., PO Box 9073
Boston, MA 02205
(800) 749-1687 • (800) 774-4117

Performance Rating: * * * *

## Performance History: Not available.

## Plan Specifics

- Initial investment is available to investors in all states except North Dakota, Oregon, and Texas ($250 minimum initial investment).
- Partial dividend reinvestment is available.
- No discount.
- OCP: $50 to $100,000 per year.
- OCP is invested weekly.
- Annual administration fee of $15 must accompany initial stock purchase and may be paid with a credit card.
- Purchasing and selling fees include a transaction fee of $5 plus brokerage commissions of approximately 12 cents per share.
- Investors will be assessed a brokerage commission of 12 cents per share to reinvest dividends.
- Automatic investment services are available.
- Shares may be sold via the telephone.
- Plan Administrator: Morgan Guaranty Trust Co. (800) 749-1687.
- Dividends are paid June and December.

## Corporate Profile

Unilever NV, together with Unilever PLC, comprise the Unilever Group. The two companies act as one company, although investors may own shares in each of the entities. Unilever NV is the Dutch unit. The company is one of the largest consumer-products concerns in the world. Sales to Europe account for approximately 50 percent of total revenues.

## Investment Advice

While Procter & Gamble is my preference among consumer-products companies offering no-load stock plans, Unilever should be a solid performer over the next 3-5 years.

Union Electric Co.
NYSE: UEP
Investor Services
1901 Chouteau
St. Louis, MO 63103
(800) 255-2237 • (800) 774-4117

---
**Performance Rating: * * * ***
---

## Performance History

- $1,000 invested on 12/31/85 was worth $3,753 on 12/31/95 — a 275 percent increase in 10 years.

## Plan Specifics

- Initial purchase is available to customers of the company ($10 minimum initial investment).
- Partial dividend reinvestment is available.
- No discount.
- OCP: $10 to $60,000 per year.
- OCP is invested monthly.
- There are no purchasing fees. Selling fees include brokerage commissions.
- Automatic investment services are available.
- Preferred dividends may be reinvested for additional common shares.
- Dividends are paid March, June, September, and December.

## Corporate Profile

Union Electric is the largest electric utility in Missouri. The service area covers about 24,500 square miles. Residential customers account for more than 40 percent of total sales. Primary fuel sources are coal and nuclear. The company is merging with CIPSCO, an Illinois-based utility.

## Investment Advice

Union Electric combines a good yield with worthwhile upside potential relative to most utilities. Fairly low rates are a plus, and the merger should boost economies of scale.

United Water Resources, Inc.
NYSE: UWR
200 Old Hook Rd.
Harrington Park, NJ 07640
(201) 767-2811 • (800) 522-6645

> **Performance Rating: * * ***

## Performance History

- $1,000 invested on 12/31/85 was worth $1,796 on 12/31/95 — an 80 percent increase in 10 years.

## Plan Specifics

- Initial purchase is available to customers of certain company subsidiaries ($25 minimum investment).
- Partial dividend reinvestment is available.
- No discount.
- OCP: $25 to $3,000 per quarter.
- OCP is invested monthly.
- There are no purchasing fees. Selling fees include brokerage commissions.
- Plan Administrator: ChaseMellon Shareholder Investment Service (800) 522-6645.
- Dividends are paid March, June, September, and December.

## Corporate Profile

United Water Resources is one of the largest investor-owned water utilities in the country. The company provides services to over 2 million customers in 14 states. The geographical diversification provides benefits in the way of reducing weather fluctuations and regulatory problems that can affect one service area.

## Investment Advice

United Water Resources has average prospects. Dividend growth is likely to be modest or nonexistent. Among water utilities offering open enrollment for investors in all 50 states, my preference is Philadelphia Suburban.

Urban Shopping Centers, Inc.
  NYSE: URB
900 N. Michigan Ave.
Chicago, IL 60611
(312) 915-2000 • (800) 992-4566 • (800) 774-4117

<hr />

| Performance Rating: * * * |

## Performance History: Not available. ——————————

## Plan Specifics ————————————————————————————

- Initial purchase is available to investors in all 50 states ($500 minimum initial investment). Initial transaction fee is $7.50 plus brokerage commissions.
- Partial dividend reinvestment is available.
- No discount.
- OCP: $50 minimum to no maximum.
- OCP is invested at least weekly.
- Purchasing costs are 5 percent of investment ($3 maximum) plus brokerage fees. Selling costs are $10 plus brokerage commissions.
- Stock may be sold via the telephone.
- Automatic investment services are available ($1 charge).
- Plan Administrator: First Chicago Trust-NY (800) 446-2617.
- Dividends are paid March, June, September, and December.

## Corporate Profile ——————————————————————————

Urban Shopping Centers is a real estate investment trust that manages and develops super-regional malls. Properties include Chicago's Water Tower Place mall; Oakbrook Center in Oak Brook, Illinois; and MainPlace in Orange County, California. Per-share profits and the dividend have edged higher over the years. The upscale nature of its malls, with its strong anchor stores, has been a plus.

## Investment Advice ——————————————————————————

Although Urban Shopping Centers will be volatile due to interest-rate movements, the firm is an above-average holding in the real estate investment trust sector.

U S West Communications Group
NYSE: USW
7800 E. Orchard Rd.
Englewood, CO 80111
(800) 537-0222 • (303) 793-6500

> **Performance Rating: \* \* \* \***

## Performance History

■ $1,000 invested on 12/31/85 was worth $2,738 on 12/31/95 — a 174 percent increase in 10 years.

## Plan Specifics

■ Initial purchase is available to investors in all 50 states ($300 minimum initial investment).
■ Partial dividend reinvestment is available.
■ No discount.
■ OCP: $25 to $100,000 per year.
■ OCP is invested weekly.
■ There are no purchasing fees. Selling fees are approximately 6 cents per share. Administrative fees are $4 per year.
■ Participants owning 100 shares or fewer may sell their shares via the telephone.
■ Automatic investment services are available.
■ Participants may reinvest dividends to purchase shares of either U S West Communications or U S West Media Group.
■ Plan Administrator: State Street Bank & Trust Co. (800) 537-0222.
■ Dividends are paid February, May, August, and November.

## Corporate Profile

U S West Communications is one of the seven regional telephone companies resulting from the AT&T breakup. The firm provides local telephone service in Arizona, Colorado, Idaho, Iowa, Minnesota, Montana, Nebraska, New Mexico, North Dakota, Oregon, South Dakota, Utah, Washington, and Wyoming.

## Investment Advice

As an income vehicle, U S West Communications has some merit. However, the stock's appreciation potential is limited. Furthermore, the changing telecommunications industry increases the uncertainties surrounding these shares.

**USWEST**

U S West Media Group
NYSE: UMG
7800 E. Orchard Rd.
Englewood, CO 80111
(303) 793-6500 • (800) 537-0222

| Performance Rating: * * * * |
| --- |

## Performance History: Not available. ──────────

## Plan Specifics ──────────────────────

- Initial purchase is available to investors in all 50 states ($300 minimum initial purchase).
- No discount.
- OCP: $25 to $100,000 per year.
- OCP is invested weekly.
- Purchasing costs are $1 per OCP investment. Selling costs are approximately 6 cents per share.
- Participants owning 100 shares or fewer may sell their shares via the telephone.
- Automatic investment services are available.
- Plan Administrator: State Street Bank & Trust Co. (800) 537-0222.
- Company is currently not paying a dividend.

## Corporate Profile ───────────────────

U S West Media has operations in the cellular telephone, cable television, and directory and information services markets. The shares began trading near the end of 1995. The issue is a "target" stock; that is, U S West Media is still under the corporate umbrella of U S West. The shares are linked to the performance of these three units. Profit growth should be impressive over the long term, although earnings will be erratic on a quarterly basis.

## Investment Advice ───────────────────

U S West Media will be volatile. However, I like the long-term growth potential of the stock. These shares are well suited for the growth portion of a no-load stock portfolio.

UtiliCorp United, Inc.
NYSE: UCU
Shareholder Relations
911 Main, Suite 3000
Kansas City, MO 64105
(816) 421-6600 • (800) 487-6661 • (800) 884-5426

Performance Rating: * * * *

## Performance History

- $1,000 invested on 12/31/85 was worth $3,979 on 12/31/95 — a 298 percent increase in 10 years.

## Plan Specifics

- Initial purchase is available to investors in all 50 states ($250 minimum initial investment).
- Partial dividend reinvestment is available.
- 5 percent discount on reinvested dividends.
- OCP: $50 to $10,000 per month. Company may waive maximum OCP. Call (800) 487-6661 for a waiver.
- OCP is invested monthly.
- There are no purchasing fees. Selling costs are approximately $20 plus 12 cents per share.
- IRA option is available.
- Automatic investment services are available.
- Shares may be sold via the telephone.
- Plan Administrator: First Chicago Trust-NY (800) 884-5426.
- Dividends are paid March, June, September, and December.

## Corporate Profile

UtiliCorp United provides electric and gas services in eight states. The firm also has operations in Canada, the United Kingdom, New Zealand, and Australia. Coal, oil, and hydro are the primary fuel sources.

## Investment Advice

UtiliCorp has appeal on several fronts. Overseas expansion is a plus and should generate better-than-average growth. Dividends should rise at least in line with the industry average. The firm has demonstrated the type of decisive action and expansion plans needed to compete successfully in the utility markets of tomorrow.

# VĮAD

Viad Corp.
NYSE: VVI
Dial Tower
Phoenix, AZ 85077
(800) 453-2235 • (602) 207-2010

---

> **Performance Rating: \* \* \***

## Performance History: Not available. —————

## Plan Specifics —————————————————————

- Initial purchase is available to investors in all 50 states ($100 minimum initial investment).
- Partial dividend reinvestment is available.
- No discount.
- OCP: $10 to $5,000 per month.
- OCP is invested monthly.
- No fees for buying or selling shares.
- Shares may be sold via the telephone.
- Dividends are paid January, April, July, and October.

## Corporate Profile —————————————————————

Viad represents the services businesses of the former Dial Corporation. Operations include Dobbs airline catering business, Premier cruise lines, and convention services. The former Dial's consumer-products business is now operated by the "new" Dial.

## Investment Advice —————————————————————

Viad has some interesting potential, although the appeal of the "old" Dial was its exposure to the consumer-products markets. Viad has the potential to generate investor interest via asset sales and restructuring moves. However, the stock is likely to be only an average performer over the long term.

**WAL★MART**

Wal-Mart Stores, Inc.
NYSE: WMT
702 Southwest 8th St., PO Box 116
Bentonville, AR 72716
(501) 273-4000 • (800) 438-6278

> Performance Rating: * * * * *

## Performance History

■ $1,000 invested on 12/31/85 was worth $5,867 on 12/31/95 — a 487 percent increase in 10 years.

## Plan Specifics

■ Initial purchase is available to investors in all 50 states ($250 minimum initial investment or automatic monthly withdrawals of at least $25). Initial cash investments will incur a fee of $20 plus 10 cents per share.

■ Partial dividend reinvestment is available.

■ No discount.

■ OCP: $50 to $150,000 per year.

■ OCP is invested at least weekly.

■ Optional cash investments will incur a $5 charge plus 10 cents per share. Shares purchased with automatic withdrawals will incur a charge of $2 plus 10 cents per share. Selling costs are $20 plus 10 cents per share.

■ Shares may be sold via the telephone.

■ Plan Administrator: First Chicago Trust-NY (800) 438-6278.

■ Dividends are paid January, April, July, and October.

## Corporate Profile

Wal-Mart is the largest retailer in the country, with annual sales exceeding $100 billion. Wal-Mart has been a huge gainer for long-term shareholders. While profit growth has slowed from the heady days of the 1980s and early 1990s, Wal-Mart should still be able to post healthy gains on an annual basis.

## Investment Advice

Wal-Mart stock has been trading sideways in recent years. However, the stock should do better than the average equity over the next 10 years.

Western Resources, Inc.

NYSE: WR
PO Box 750320
Topeka, KS 66675-0320
(800) 527-2495 • (800) 774-4117

Performance Rating: * * * *

## Performance History

- $1,000 invested on 12/31/85 was worth $3,226 on 12/31/95 — a 223 percent increase in 10 years.

## Plan Specifics

- Initial purchase is available to investors in all 50 states ($250 minimum initial investment).
- Partial dividend reinvestment is available.
- No discount.
- OCP: $20 to $60,000 per year.
- OCP is invested twice monthly.
- Purchasing fees include brokerage commissions and any other fees.
- Selling costs are brokerage commissions and transfer tax.
- Automatic investment services are available.
- Dividends are paid January, April, July, and October.

## Corporate Profile

Western Resources provides utility services to customers in Kansas and Oklahoma. Residential customers provide approximately 35 percent of total revenues. The company has an equity stake in ADT, a leading home-security services provider.

## Investment Advice

Western Resources should at least match the performance of the utility industry overall. Positions in growing nonutility areas enhance prospects.

Whitman Corp.
  NYSE: WH
3501 Algonquin Rd.
Rolling Meadows, IL 60008
(847) 818-5000 • (800) 660-4187 • (800) 446-2617

Performance Rating: * * *

## Performance History

- $1,000 invested on 12/31/85 was worth $1,617 on 12/31/95 — a 62 percent increase in 10 years.

## Plan Specifics

- Initial purchase is available to investors in all 50 states ($250 minimum initial investment). Initial investments will entail a transaction fee of $10 plus brokerage fees of 3 cents per share.
- Partial dividend reinvestment is available.
- No discount.
- OCP: $50 to $150,000 per year.
- OCP is invested at least weekly.
- Purchase fees are 5 percent of the amount invested (maximum $7.50 on OCPs and maximum $3 on reinvested dividends) plus brokerage commissions. Selling costs are $15 plus 12 cents per share.
- Automatic investment services are available ($2 transaction fee).
- Shares may be sold via the telephone.
- Plan Administrator: First Chicago Trust-NY (800) 446-2617.
- Dividends are paid January, April, July, and October.

## Corporate Profile

Whitman is the largest independent bottler of PepsiCo products. The firm operates the Midas International auto-services center and owns Hussmann Corp., a producer of commercial refrigeration equipment.

## Investment Advice

Whitman's stock has trended higher in recent years. However, long-term prospects are limited by the uninspiring growth potential of its operations. One factor that could increase investor support is a spin-off of one or more of its units.

WICOR, Inc.
 NYSE: WIC
626 E. Wisconsin Ave., PO Box 334
Milwaukee, WI 53201
(414) 291-7026 • (800) 236-3453 • (800) 621-9609

> **Performance Rating: * * * * ***

## Performance History

- $1,000 invested on 12/31/85 was worth $3,730 on 12/31/95 — a 273 percent increase in 10 years.

## Plan Specifics

- Initial purchase is available to residents of Wisconsin ($100 minimum initial investment).
- Partial dividend reinvestment is not available.
- No discount.
- OCP: $100 to $10,000 per month.
- OCP is invested monthly.
- There are no purchasing fees. Selling costs are $10 service fee plus brokerage commissions.
- Plan Administrator: ChaseMellon Shareholder Investment Service (800) 621-9609.
- Dividends are paid February, May, August, and November.

## Corporate Profile

WICOR is a holding company for Wisconsin Gas, the state's largest natural-gas utility. The company also has nonutility operations under its Sta-Rite Industries and Shurflo Pump Manufacturing units. Sta-Rite makes pumps and water-processing equipment. Shurflo makes pumps and fluid-handling equipment for the beverage, marine, and water-purification markets.

## Investment Advice

WICOR is an attractive holding in the natural-gas field. Growing nonutility businesses provide a kicker to this utility and should help earnings and dividend growth. Investors who are eligible to make initial purchases directly should take advantage of the firm's no-load stock program.

Wisconsin Energy Corp.
NYSE: WEC
231 W. Michigan St., PO Box 2949
Milwaukee, WI 53201
(414) 221-2345 • (800) 558-9663

Performance Rating: * * * * *

## Performance History

- $1,000 invested on 12/31/85 was worth $3,837 on 12/31/95 — a 284 percent increase in 10 years.

## Plan Specifics

- Initial purchase is available to investors in all 50 states ($50 minimum initial investment).
- Partial dividend reinvestment is available.
- No discount.
- OCP: $25 to $50,000 per quarter.
- OCP is invested twice monthly.
- There are no purchasing or selling fees.
- Preferred dividends may be reinvested for additional common shares.
- Shares may be sold via the telephone.
- Plan Administrator: First National Bank of Boston (800) 558-9663.
- Dividends are paid March, June, September, and December.

## Corporate Profile

Wisconsin Energy provides utility services in parts of Wisconsin and Michigan. Commercial and industrial users account for nearly 60 percent of total revenues. Coal and nuclear energy are the primary fuel sources. The firm is merging with Northern States Power.

## Investment Advice

Wisconsin Energy is one of the best utilities in the market. The merger with Northern States Power should create a utility powerhouse. The stock is a top choice for no-load stock investors who desire a utility.

WPS Resources Corp.
  NYSE: WPS
700 N. Adams St., PO Box 19001
Green Bay, WI 54307
(414) 433-1050 • (800) 236-1551

> **Performance Rating: * * * * ***

## Performance History: Not available. ——————————

## Plan Specifics ——————————————————

- Initial purchase is available to investors in all 50 states ($100 minimum initial investment).
- Partial dividend reinvestment is available.
- No discount.
- OCP: $25 to $100,000 per year.
- OCP is invested monthly.
- There are no purchasing fees. Selling costs are brokerage commissions.
- Dividends are paid March, June, September, and December.

## Corporate Profile ——————————————

WPS Resources provides electricity and natural gas to parts of Wisconsin and Michigan. Residential customers account for around one-third of total revenues. Coal, nuclear, and purchased power are the primary fuel sources. Finances are solid, and dividends have been raised for nearly four decades straight. The regulatory environment of Wisconsin has generally been accommodating, which is a plus.

## Investment Advice ——————————————

WPS Resources is a top-flight electric utility. With so many quality utilities located in the state of Wisconsin, it will be interesting to see how WPS Resources will fare over time should "open" utility markets develop in the state. I suspect the company and stock will do fine.

York International Corp.
NYSE: YRK
631 S. Richland Ave.
York, PA 17403
(717) 771-7890 • (800) 437-6726 • (800) 774-4117

Performance Rating: * * * *

## Performance History: Not available.

## Plan Specifics

- Initial purchase is available to investors in all 50 states ($1,000 minimum initial investment or automatic monthly withdrawals of at least $100).
- Partial dividend reinvestment is available.
- No discount.
- Investors need to have at least 100 shares in the plan in order to reinvest dividends.
- OCP: $100 to $10,000 per month.
- OCP is invested at least weekly.
- There are no purchasing fees. Selling fees are $15 plus 12 cents per share.
- Automatic investment services are available.
- Plan Administrator: Chemical Bank (800) 230-2574.
- Dividends are paid March, June, September, and December.

## Corporate Profile

York International is a major provider of heating, ventilating, and air conditioning and refrigeration products. Foreign operations account for about one-third of total sales. Despite the cyclical nature of its markets, profits have trended higher in recent years. Plentiful overseas opportunities for the company's heating and cooling equipment should provide a boost to the bottom line. Also, replacement equipment for systems using chlorofluorocarbons will help profits.

## Investment Advice

York International offers an interesting choice for investors who want to include some economically sensitive stocks in their portfolio. Decent finances, a good track record of earnings growth, and favorable growth prospects abroad should keep these shares ahead of the overall market over the next 3-5 years.

# Bibliography

## Chapter 1

*Bloomberg*, May 1994.
*Business Week*, December 21, 1992.
*Business Week*, June 6, 1994.
*No Cost/Low Cost Investing* (Franklin Watts, 1987), by Chet Currier and David Smyth.
*Shareholder and Direct Purchase Program IRAs Market Research Evaluation*, prepared by First Trust Corporation, 1994.
*SmartMoney*, June 1993.
*The Wall Street Journal*, July 23, 1993.
*The Wall Street Journal*, August 30, 1993.
*The Wall Street Journal*, November 22, 1993.
*The Wall Street Journal*, February 11, 1994.

## Chapter 2

*Barron's*, April 11, 1993.
Bureau of the Public Debt reports.
*Business Week*, December 21, 1992.
*The Economic Effects of Federal Regulation of the Market for New Security Issues*, by Gregg A. Jarrell.
*Financial Analysts Journal*, January–February 1994.
*Forbes*, October 26, 1992.
*FW*, March 16, 1993.
*FW*, February 1, 1994.
*FW*, February 15, 1994.
*Individual Investor*, March 1994.
*Investor's Business Daily*, July 30, 1992.
*Investor's Business Daily*, January 28, 1994.
*Investor's Business Daily*, May 25, 1994.
*Investor's Business Daily*, June 9, 1994.
*Investor's Business Daily*, March 26, 1996.
*Kiplinger's Personal Finance Magazine*, July 1994.
*Management Accounting*, September 1993.

*Market 2000:* An Examination of Current Equity Market Developments, prepared by the Division of Market Regulation of the United States Securities and Exchange Commission, January 1994.

*Newsweek,* April 8, 1996.

Press release from Uniform Capital Access Network, Inc., June 2, 1994.

*Redemption Digest and Securities Industry Daily,* May 17, 1994.

*Redemption Digest and Securities Industry Daily,* June 9, 1994.

*Redemption Digest and Securities Industry Daily,* June 10, 1994.

*Redemption Digest and Securities Industry Daily,* March 4, 1996.

*Redemption Digest and Securities Industry Daily,* March 21, 1996.

*The Wall Street Journal,* February 26, 1992.

*The Wall Street Journal,* March 6, 1992.

*The Wall Street Journal,* May 14, 1992.

*The Wall Street Journal,* September 8, 1992.

*The Wall Street Journal,* September 26, 1992.

*The Wall Street Journal,* October 2, 1992.

*The Wall Street Journal,* October 26, 1992.

*The Wall Street Journal,* January 14, 1993.

*The Wall Street Journal,* April 28, 1993.

*The Wall Street Journal,* May 18, 1993.

*The Wall Street Journal,* June 18, 1993.

*The Wall Street Journal,* September 1, 1993.

*The Wall Street Journal,* September 15, 1993.

*The Wall Street Journal,* December 23, 1993.

*The Wall Street Journal,* January 28, 1994.

*The Wall Street Journal,* January 31, 1994.

*The Wall Street Journal,* February 24, 1994.

*The Wall Street Journal,* March 15, 1994.

*The Wall Street Journal,* March 17, 1994.

*The Wall Street Journal,* April 26, 1994.

*The Wall Street Journal,* May 5, 1994.

*The Wall Street Journal,* May 6, 1994.

*The Wall Street Journal,* May 11, 1994.

*The Wall Street Journal,* May 16, 1994.

*The Wall Street Journal,* May 25, 1994.

*The Wall Street Journal,* May 27, 1994.

*The Wall Street Journal,* June 2, 1994.

*A White Paper for the Individual Investor: A Four-Part Report Concerning the Individual Investor,* prepared by the National Association of Investors Corporation, 1994.

*Worth,* March 1994.

## Chapter 3

*AAII Journal,* August 1991.

*Barron's,* April 18, 1994.

*Dick Davis Digest,* May 23, 1994.

*Directory of Dividend Reinvestment Plans* (1994 edition), prepared by Standard & Poor.

*Investment: Concepts, Analysis, and Strategy* (2nd ed; Scott, Foresman and Co., 1987), by Robert C. Radcliffe.

*Investor's Business Daily,* June 5, 1992.

*Investor's Business Daily,* April 26, 1994.

*Mutual Fund News Service,* May 18, 1994.

*The Stock Market: Theories and Evidence,* (2nd ed; Dow Jones-Irwin, 1985), by James H. Lorie, Peter Dodd, and Mary Hamilton Kimpton.

*The Wall Street Journal,* April 20, 1994.

# Chapter 4

*Barron's,* April 12, 1993.

*Barron's,* January 10, 1994.

*Bill Staton's Money Advisory,* May 12, 1993.

*Bogle on Mutual Funds: New Perspectives for the Intelligent Investor* (Irwin, 1994), by John C. Bogle.

*Business Week,* January 31, 1994.

*Business Week,* February 14, 1994.

*Business Week,* April 4, 1994.

*Business Week,* May 23, 1994.

*Chicago Tribune,* March 23, 1993.

*Chicago Tribune,* May 19, 1993.

*Chicago Tribune,* March 6, 1994.

*Chicago Tribune,* April 6, 1994.

*Chicago Tribune,* May 11, 1994.

*Daily Herald,* March 31, 1992.

*Donoghue's MONEYLETTER,* May 1993.

*5 Star Investor,* December 1993.

*5 Star Investor,* March 1994.

*Forbes,* January 18, 1993.

*Forbes,* February 15, 1993.

*Fortune,* December 27, 1993.

*FW,* May 10, 1994.

*In the Vanguard,* Winter 1994.

*Individual Investor,* June 1993.

*Individual Investor,* March 1994.

Investment Company Institute, 1992 Annual Report.

*Investor's Business Daily,* May 1, 1992.

*Investor's Business Daily,* March 4, 1993.

*Investor's Business Daily,* May 28, 1993.

*Investor's Business Daily,* August 6, 1993.

*Investor's Business Daily,* December 14, 1993.

*Investor's Business Daily,* December 21, 1993.

*Investor's Business Daily*, March 4, 1994.
*Investor's Business Daily*, April 8, 1994.
*Investor's Business Daily*, April 21, 1994.
*Investor's Business Daily*, May 27, 1994.
*Investor's Business Daily*, June 10, 1994.
*Investor's Business Daily*, June 16, 1994.
*Investor's Business Daily*, June 20, 1994.
*Kiplinger's Personal Finance Magazine*, May 1994.
*Money*, September 1993.
*Money*, May 1994.
*Mutual Fund News Service*, October 4, 1989.
*Mutual Fund News Service*, September 2, 1993.
*Mutual Fund News Service*, February 10, 1994.
*The New York Times*, March 27, 1993.
*The New York Times*, January 22, 1994.
Press release from Investment Company Institute, February 16, 1994.
Press release from Investment Company Institute, March 8, 1994.
*SmartMoney*, February 1994.
*SmartMoney*, March 1994.
*SmartMoney*, April 1994.
*Tax Wise Money*, May 1994.
*The Wall Street Journal*, March 5, 1992.
*The Wall Street Journal*, March 19, 1993.
*The Wall Street Journal*, April 20, 1993.
*The Wall Street Journal*, August 16, 1993.
*The Wall Street Journal*, September 27, 1993.
*The Wall Street Journal*, November 10, 1993.
*The Wall Street Journal*, December 17, 1993.
*The Wall Street Journal*, January 17, 1994.
*The Wall Street Journal*, January 20, 1994.
*The Wall Street Journal*, January 21, 1994.
*The Wall Street Journal*, January 25, 1994.
*The Wall Street Journal*, January 28, 1994.
*The Wall Street Journal*, February 1, 1994.
*The Wall Street Journal*, February 11, 1994.
*The Wall Street Journal*, February 15, 1994.
*The Wall Street Journal*, February 17, 1994.
*The Wall Street Journal*, February 28, 1994.
*The Wall Street Journal*, March 2, 1994.
*The Wall Street Journal*, April 7, 1994.
*The Wall Street Journal*, May 17, 1994.
*The Wall Street Journal*, June 10, 1994.
*The Wall Street Journal*, June 23, 1994.
*The Wall Street Journal*, June 27, 1994.
*Worth*, July–August 1993.
*Worth*, October 1993.
*Worth*, March 1994.

# Chapter 5

*Barron's,* June 21, 1993.

*Barron's,* April 11, 1994.

*Business Week,* Reinventing America 1992.

*Companies With a Conscience: Intimate Portraits of Twelve Firms That Make a Difference* (Carol Publishing Group, 1992), by Mary Scott and Howard Rothman.

*Daily Local News* (West Chester, PA), July 8, 1992.

*Delaware County Daily Times,* August 21, 1992.

*Delaware County Daily Times,* August 27, 1992.

*Discussion Document on Providing Alternatives to Certificates for the Retail Investor,* prepared by the U.S. Working Committee-Group of Thirty Clearance and Settlement Project, July 1991.

*The Hidden Market: A Survey of Corporate Attitudes Toward Marketing to Shareholders,* prepared for ADP by Capital Analytics Inc., 1993.

*Investor Relations Update,* April 1992.

*Investor's Business Daily,* September 30, 1992.

*Investor's Business Daily,* December 31, 1992.

*Investor's Business Daily,* March 24, 1993.

*Investor's Business Daily,* April 12, 1994.

*Kiplinger's Personal Finance Magazine,* June 1992.

*Main Line Times,* September 3, 1992.

*Management Accounting,* September 1990.

*Management Accounting,* September 1993.

*The New York Times,* July 31, 1993.

*The New York Times,* August 7, 1993.

*The News & Observer,* June 18, 1994.

*The Output,* January 1, 1994.

*The Output,* February 1, 1994.

*The Philadelphia Inquirer,* August 17, 1992.

*The Philadelphia Inquirer,* August 25, 1992.

*The Philadelphia Inquirer,* August 28, 1992.

*The Philadelphia Inquirer,* September 30, 1992.

*Redemption Digest and Securities Industry Daily,* April 18, 1994.

*Redemption Digest and Securities Industry Daily,* May 3, 1994.

*Redemption Digest and Securities Industry Daily,* May 4, 1994.

*Redemption Digest and Securities Industry Daily,* May 5, 1994.

*Redemption Digest and Securities Industry Daily,* May 6, 1994.

*Redemption Digest and Securities Industry Daily,* May 9, 1994.

*Redemption Digest and Securities Industry Daily,* May 10, 1994.

*Redemption Digest and Securities Industry Daily,* May 11, 1994.

*Redemption Digest and Securities Industry Daily,* May 12, 1994.

*Redemption Digest and Securities Industry Daily,* May 13, 1994.

*Redemption Digest and Securities Industry Daily,* May 16, 1994.

*Redemption Digest and Securities Industry Daily,* May 19, 1994.

*Redemption Digest and Securities Industry Daily,* May 20, 1994.

*Redemption Digest and Securities Industry Daily,* May 23, 1994.
*Redemption Digest and Securities Industry Daily,* May 24, 1994.
*Redemption Digest and Securities Industry Daily,* May 25, 1994.
*Redemption Digest and Securities Industry Daily,* May 26, 1994.
*Redemption Digest and Securities Industry Daily,* May 27, 1994.
*Redemption Digest and Securities Industry Daily,* May 31, 1994.
*Redemption Digest and Securities Industry Daily,* June 6, 1994.
*Redemption Digest and Securities Industry Daily,* June 24, 1994.
*Report of the Bachmann Task Force on Clearance and Settlement Reform in U.S. Securities Markets,* submitted to the Chairman of the U.S. Securities and Exchange Commission, May 1992.
*The SEC Today,* October 29, 1991.
*Shareholder Communications Corporation Survey,* March 18, 1993.
*SmartMoney,* May 1994.
Speech by Arthur Levitt, Chairman of the Securities and Exchange Commission, given before the Consumer Federation of America, March 10, 1994.
*Structuring and Administering a Dividend Reinvestment Plan,* prepared by the American Society of Corporate Secretaries, Inc., 1993.
*Trends,* March–April 1992.
*The Wall Street Journal,* July 15, 1991.
*The Wall Street Journal,* April 27, 1992.
*The Wall Street Journal,* September 30, 1992.
*The Wall Street Journal,* December 29, 1992.
*The Wall Street Journal,* March 3, 1993.
*The Wall Street Journal,* May 5, 1993.
*The Wall Street Journal,* May 12, 1994.
*The Wall Street Journal,* June 7, 1994.
*A White Paper for the Individual Investor: A Four-Part Report Concerning the Individual Investor,* prepared by the National Association of Investors Corporation, 1994.

## Chapter 6

Company quarterly and annual reports.
*Value Line Investment Survey.*
Standard & Poor's research reports.

# Index

## About the Author

Charles B. Carlson draws on a wealth of experience in direct investment programs, and actually coined the term "no-load stock." He's the respected editor of *DRIP Investor* and *No-Load Stock Insider* and market strategist of *Dow Theory Forecasts*, one of the nation's oldest and most widely read investment newsletters. Author of the best-selling *Buying Stocks Without a Broker, Free Lunch on Wall Street*, and the first edition of *No-Load Stocks*, he is a frequent guest on radio and television and is widely quoted in *The New York Times, The Wall Street Journal, Business Week, Money*, and *Kiplinger's*.

# *Your Monthly Guide To Buying Stocks Without A Broker*

*DRIP Investor* covers all aspects of no-load stocks and dividend reinvestment plans (DRIPs) — how to buy stocks without a broker, how to buy stocks at a discount, and how to buy blue-chips on the "installment plan" for as little as $10 a month.

This authoritative monthly service is written by Charles Carlson, CFA, author of *No-Load Stocks, Free Lunch on Wall Street, The 60 Second Investor*, the best-selling *Buying Stocks Without A Broker* and market strategist for the highly respected *Dow Theory Forecasts*. As a reader of *No-Load Stocks*, you may receive the Charter Rate of only $59 for a full year — a 25% savings. Money-back guarantee. You may cancel any time for a pro rata refund.

With your subscription you will receive a *DRIP Investor* custom 3-ring storage binder plus your FREE 32-page DRIP Starter Kit, a step-by-step blueprint to success in no-load stocks and DRIPs.

To take advantage of this generous offer, fill out the coupon below and mail today.

DETACH HERE

## DRIP *Investor* Charter Rate Offer

❏ YES, start my subscription to *DRIP Investor* immediately at the Charter Rate of $59 for one year, a $20 savings. I may cancel any time for a pro rata refund.

**Payment Method**
❏ Check or money order
❏ Please charge my   ❏ VISA   ❏ MC   ❏ American Express

| Name | (Please Print) |
| --- | --- |

Credit Card Number

| Address |
| --- |

Expiration Date

| City | State | Zip |
| --- | --- | --- |

Signature

NLS

**DRIP *Investor*** • 7412 Calumet Ave., Ste. 200 • Hammond, IN 46324-2692

*Not valid until accepted by DRIP Investor, Hammond, Indiana*